Critical Psychoanalytic Social Work

This international and interdisciplinary collection argues for the use of clinical-based practices and research in social work, bringing together critical psychoanalytic ideas into social work practice to help tackle contemporary issues.

With a Foreword written by Stephen Webb, this book brings together specialists from the main areas of research and clinical practices in social work, ranging from psychoanalysis, sociology, clinical psychology, ethnopsychiatry and philosophy. Arguing for a movement away from evidence-based practice, chapters discuss the need for psychoanalytic thought in contemporary social work knowledge, how this can be integrated in social work practice and training, the challenges faced by training and practicing social workers and the ethical issues relating to clinical-based practice. Filled with case studies throughout, these diverse and rich contributions will make social workers think deeply about advocacy, ethics and the systemic changes needed in the field.

This book will be invaluable reading to training and practicing clinical social workers and mental health professionals interested in social intervention. It will also be interesting to psychoanalysts as well as those studying sociology, clinical psychology and philosophy.

Sébastien Ponnou is a Psychoanalyst, Doctor in Psychoanalysis (Paris 8) and lecturer in education sciences at the University of Rouen Normandie (IUT d'Evreux – Social Careers Department, Interdisciplinary Center for Education and Training Research in Normandy – CIRNEF, EA 7454). His work focuses on clinical and psychoanalytic studies, mental health issues, clinical practices and the training of social workers.

Christophe Niewiadomski is a Professor of Education at the University of Lille, a member of the CIREL laboratory (Lille Inter-university Center for Research in Education) and a founding member of RISC (International Network of Clinical Sociology) and CIRBE (International College of Biographical Research in Education). His work aims to lay the foundations for a narrative and educational clinic in the human and social sciences by examining the specificity of biographical research in the fields of adult education, socio-educational environment and health.

Critical Psychoanalytic Social Work

Research and Case Studies for Clinical Practice

EDITED BY SÉBASTIEN PONNOU AND CHRISTOPHE NIEWIADOMSKI

With contributions by:

Mireille Cifali
Pascal Fugier
Vincent de Gaulejac
Florence Giust-Desprairies
Philippe Lyet
Marie Rose Moro and Rahmet Radjack
Jean-Bernard Paturet
Bertrand Ravon
Guy de Villers

Foreword to the English Edition by Stephen Webb
Foreword to the French Edition by Michel Chauvière

Translated from French by Chad Langford and Judith Van Heerswynghels

Routledge
Taylor & Francis Group

NEW YORK AND LONDON

Cover image: Cover Illustration Arturo Martini, Ragazzo (1930), GAM Torino;
Photography: D. Delaval, 2018.

First published 2023
by Routledge
605 Third Avenue, New York, NY 10158

and by Routledge
4 Park Square, Milton Park, Abingdon, Oxon, OX14 4RN

Routledge is an imprint of the Taylor & Francis Group, an informa business

ISBN: 9781032283470 (hbk)
ISBN: 9781032283463 (pbk)
ISBN: 9781003296416 (ebk)

DOI: 10.4324/9781003296416

Typeset in Dante and Avenir
by codeMantra

To Sandra, Judith, Nathanaël and Noah, who are an inexhaustible source of joy and inspiration.

Contents

Foreword to the English edition

Stephen Webb

This is a landmark publication which may signal a turning point in social work scholarship. One might go as far as to say that the book is illustrative of the disruptive potential of traveling theories, associated with the power afforded to the deterritorialization of thought, as a vital component in the circulation of French scholarship, not only within a British context, but traveling far more widely across the Global North and South. Indeed, under the editorial direction of Ponnou and Niewiadomski it would be no exaggeration to say that *Critical Psychoanalytic Social Work* has opened a new path in the modern history of social work. This is a path that circumvents older, and more stale and familiar preoccupations, especially in Anglophone social work. Indeed, with the publication of this book we might be witnessing only a fragment from a particularly important enterprise in its formative stage of development. That is, the renewed value of critical psychoanalysis for social work. Other works should undoubtedly follow. Part of the excitement of writing this Foreword for the collective volume is that I am aware of no other in-depth account in social work that brings the two words 'critical' and 'psychoanalytical' together with such a range of suggestiveness. Indeed, this collection of essays marks the first time that psychoanalytic and critical theory is acknowledged as a distinct orientation within social work research and theory in general in such a prominent way. As a result, it also registers the emergence and the gradual establishment of a whole hybrid terrain of theorization in between psycho-analysis, social work and critical theory. The usage of the words 'critical' and 'psychoanalytic' as related to social work betrays a multiplicity of concurrent meanings. Their origins go back to various historical phases in the often-broken lineage of ideas. As far as I can tell, the compounding of these two important concepts as 'critical psychoanalysis' was first coined by Michael Guilfoyle in an essay published in 2007 in the journal *Theory & Psychology*. A further text which resonates well with the aspirations of this book is the edited collection by Yannis Stavrakakis et al., *Routledge Handbook of Psychoanalytic Political Theory*, published in 2019. It is worth noting that Guilfoyle went to great lengths to emphasize that the critical psychoanalyst needs to recognize his or her immersion in power dynamics: to engage in deliberate reflection on his or her position within them, both inside and outside of the clinic and consulting room. Indeed, he emphasized that a critical psychoanalysis cannot be generated from outside of power. Rather, its critical functions must be related to the nature of its participation in a 'field of force relations' (Foucault, 2013). If power is intrinsic to human interaction, then it shapes social realities rather than distorts them, and we have no choice but to engage with it. It makes little sense to speak of being emancipated from power. Indeed, Foucault has directly addressed the power effects of psychoanalysis as a discourse of subjectivity. That these claims sit so comfortably alongside the main remit of critical social work goes without saying (Gray & Webb, 2013; Webb, 2019). Indeed, I write this Foreword, not as someone highly skeptical and critical of evidence-based social work, as originally asked, but as committed to the over-all international project of critical social work. This is particularly important because, as Parker (1997) noted, this critical and progressive potential of psychoanalysis is not developed in all psychoanalytic schools, some even finding, in psychoanalysis, support for particularly conservative political positions. Indeed, I would argue that publication of *Critical Psychoanalytic Social Work* is a paradigmatic event in that it serves not as a benign, nostalgic reminder of how-things-used-to-be, in say, the heyday of the 1960s American psychoanalytic tradition of social casework, but as a stark reminder of the importance of progressive, vanguardist cultural advances, which allows the transnational and the intellectually challenging to find new political footings in social work as it limps along in the contemporary moment of the COVID-19 pandemic.

There is a rich intellectual legacy to the sort of scholarly project pursued in *Critical Psychoanalytic Social Work*. A most obvious and important contribution is Sherry Turkle's classic *Psychoanalytic Politics* published in 1978. She provided a nuanced and suggestive historical account of the social and political attitudes of French culture as it assimilated psychoanalysis in a post May 1968 climate, with special emphasis on existentialism and Marxism. Like this book,

Turkle emphasized the importance of Jacques Lacan to the world of French psychoanalytic culture. Indeed, she argues that

> May 1968 marked and gave momentum to a profound though not immediately visible kind of change: the dramatic reversal of the relationship between psychoanalysis and French society and culture. In the course of the 1960s, the French attitude toward psychoanalysis swung from denigration and resistance to infatuation in one of the most dramatic social reversals of an intellectual position in modem history.
>
> (1978, p. 4)

Turkle's work was hugely important in bringing a deeper understanding of French psychoanalysis to the anti-psychiatry movement in the United States and Europe. However, the importance of Lacan's work has been massively overlooked in Anglo-American social work. Around this time André Green also became internationally well known for his writings on the 'dead mother', 'the narcissism of death' and 'the negative'. Particularly important in the reception of elements of Lacan's work are Luce Irigaray and Julia Kristeva, who pick up Lacan's problematic of sexual difference and grapple with it in different ways. British feminist social work has been far more willing to engage with the works of Irigaray and Kristeva than Lacan himself. Indeed, *Critical Psychoanalytic Social Work* provides an important corrective to the preoccupations with the triumvirate of Winnicott, Bowlby and Klein who have tended to dominate scholarship in the journal *Psychoanalytic Social Work*. Interestingly, there is not a single European, apart from Marion Bower, on the editorial board of this now – the only journal in social work dedicated to psychoanalytic approaches in the field. In contrast the Association for the Psychoanalysis of Culture and Society, with its challenging annual conferences has a much more vibrant journal, *Psychoanalysis, Culture and Society*, with worldwide appeal. In elaborating Turkle's arguments, the necessity of linking psychoanalysis to politics is made plain by Frosh (1999), who says:

> At least two possibilities emerge at this point: there are two distinct strands to the 'politics of psychoanalysis' … The first of these concerns the politics inherent in psychoanalytic theories, the implications of psychoanalytic ideas and assumptions for notions of selfhood and society, and for programmes of personal and social change. The second strand of the 'politics of psychoanalysis' concerns the application of psychoanalysis to wider political questions.
>
> (Frosh, 1999, pp. 12–13)

But what sort of politics? In 2013, I wrote the introduction to *The New Politics of Social Work* and emphasized the importance of the concept of biopolitics. The turn to biopolitical analysis in social work will be strengthened not only by the publication of this collective volume but with an engagement with a revitalized psychoanalytic approach. COVID-19 has amply demonstrated we are faced with a new politics of life – a biopolitics of life (sustaining and 'improving' life) and death (selectively letting die). Over the past two decades the Foucauldian problematic of biopolitics has become an increasingly influential research orientation in the social sciences, applied in a variety of disciplines to analyze the transformations in the rationalities of power over life in diverse spatio-temporal contexts. Totalitarianism is an example of the most extreme form of biopolitics, whereby bare life as the object of sovereign power is no longer concealed under the veneer of the positive forms of good life but is starkly revealed as such in the camps and institutional sites of fascism. Agamben marks out the historical significance of this biopolitical logic of power 'Only because politics in our age has been entirely transformed into biopolitics was it possible for politics to be constituted as totalitarian politics to a degree hitherto unknown' (Agamben, 1998, p. 120). I concur with Agamben that modern politics has been completely transformed into biopolitical regimes of power. At the time of writing, virus-inspired reflections on biopower, biosecurity and biopolitics are everywhere. It is in this context of crisis and emergency, and within this set of foundational ideas from Foucault – and onwards through the writings of Agamben, Esposito, Negri and Prozorov – that I suggest that biopolitics now has a guaranteed status as the primary framework of analysis for critical social work. Furthermore, we can concentrate our efforts in theorizing power from the double vantage point of biopolitical and psychoanalytic theory. Social work has lagged behind its counterparts in other fields of social and political science in embracing biopolitics. Of course, this is not to exclude other perspectives and paradigms, but while there are inevitably shortcomings with biopolitical theory, it can be strengthened by the sort of critical psychoanalysis so richly observed in this volume.

What this collection of essays demonstrates admirably is that psychoanalytic social work is not primarily located in the clinic, the home visit or the case recording, and neither does it merely concern the 'individual' or ego, but rather that in a critical vein it engages with processes and mechanisms constructing a 'subject' which is overdetermined by inter-sectional entanglements (gender, race, coloniality and sexuality) which open a route to a genuine socio-political and psychosocial engagement. While taking a political stance in social work necessarily involves a close historical examination of the role of socio-economic structure as well as the constitutive relations of domination, it also crucially involves formulating an ontology of the political subject. Psychoanalysis must self-reflectively engage with the role it plays in shaping the ontology of the subject, and this necessarily involves a politics. The Anglophone reception of the French scholarship of *Critical Psychoanalytic Social Work* will have important political implications as a pole of resistance to the false political neutrality and the safe technicalities of evidence, risk assessment and casework management in social work. This is not to overlook the limitations of psychoanalytic scholarship more broadly. For instance, it has very little to say about poverty or the poor; in spite of references to the poverty of dreams, poverty of affect, poverty of intellect, there is in reality very little engagement with 'real' poverty. This reminds one of a *Le Monde* article entitled, 'The Death Drive, Cruelty, and Psychoanalysis', in which Jacques Derrida, although not a psychoanalyst, criticized psychoanalysis for the inhibitions and resistances that have prevented it from having a wider sphere of influence:

> Psychoanalysis, according to me, has not yet undertaken, and thus not yet succeeded in thinking, penetrating, and changing the axioms of ethics, law, and politics, particularly in these seismic places where the phantasm of sovereignty quakes and where the most traumatic geopolitical events are produced.
>
> (cited in Quinney, 2004)

The insensitivity to wider environmental and humanitarian concerns in the cosy enclaves of the couch can become quite crazy. An even more stark example is given by Bateman and Holmes who studied the case of the treatment of a young woman who is politically active around the destruction of rainforests across Central and South America. The reporters of the case describe how the psychoanalyst interprets her concerns as a defensive acting out of an internal conflict. The analyst notes that the client's mother died recently, and that the client cut herself and attempted suicide. According to Bateman and Holmes:

> the analyst acknowledged her environmental concerns but stated that he believed her preoccupation with them in the session was an avoidance of her sense of personal devastation following the loss of her mother, which made her feel like cutting herself down and killing herself.
>
> (Bateman & Holmes, 1995, p. 169)

They go on to say that what is significant, however, is that the interpretation does not in any way support the client's face-value concerns. Instead, it suggests that she has misunderstood her interest in the rainforests: the unconscious conceals her true experience. The phrase 'cutting herself down' rhetorically strengthens the association between the client's self-harm and her interest in the environment (ibid., p. 170).

I am not for a moment suggesting that such bizarre interpretations are given in this impressive volume, but merely offering a few words of caution. On the contrary, it's my belief that *Critical Psychoanalytic Social Work* can in fact contribute to the creation of a new genre of psychoanalytic scholarship in social work that combines autobiography, theory, clinical case studies and literature. There is no doubt that these critical reflections on psychoanalysis for social work will encourage not only future intellectual production in general and set a research agenda but will also contribute to altering self-perception within social work in the French and Anglophone world. Whether or not social work follows the call of *Critical Psychoanalytic Social Work* to take up psychoanalytic theory, social workers of all stripes have good reason to consider the arguments of this book, and the excellent case study examples, in the pursuit of the ongoing work of political engagement and rich empirical analyses. I personally found it to be a breath of fresh air in the current climate of social work scholarship.

References

Agamben, G. (1998). *Homo sacer: Sovereign power and bare life*. Stanford, CA: Stanford University Press.

Bateman, A., & Holmes, J. (1995). *Introduction to psychoanalysis: Contemporary theory and practice*. New York: Routledge.

Derrida, J. (2000). 'La pulsion de mort, cruauté et psychanalyse'. *Le Monde*, 10 July, p. 11.

Foucault, M. (2013). *History of madness*. New York: Routledge.

Foucault, M. (1990). *The history of sexuality* (Vol. 1). London: Penguin. (Original work published 1976.)

Frosh, S. (1999). *The politics of psychoanalysis*. 2nd ed. Houndmills: Macmillan.

Guilfoyle, M. (2007). Grounding a critical psychoanalysis in frameworks of power. *Theory & Psychology*, 17(4), 563–585.

Gray, M., & Webb, S. A. (2013). *The new politics of social work*. London: Palgrave Macmillan.

Parker, I. (1997). Discourse analysis and psychoanalysis. *British Journal of Social Psychology*, 36, 479–495.

Stavrakakis, Y. (ed.). (2019). *Routledge handbook of psychoanalytic political theory*. London: Routledge.

Turkle, S. (1978) *Psychoanalytic Politics: Freud's French Revolution*. New York: Basic Books.

Quinney, A. (2004). Psychoanalysis is on the couch: France celebrates Freud in 2000. *French Cultural Studies*, 15(2), 114–126.

Webb, S. A. (2019) *Routledge handbook of critical social work*. London: Routledge.

Foreword to the French edition

Michel Chauvière

I would like to take the opportunity in this Foreword to acknowledge the rich variety of clinical experiences and data gathered and presented in this collective volume. The various contributions provide a stimulating perspective for all clinical-based social work, an approach which is diametrically opposed to the evidence-based practice that has significantly risen in recent years. At a time when the economic paradigm continues to be dominant and spread, and when a possible 'war on the clinic' is ready to be waged, I shall attempt to address how things currently stand with regard to this clinic and how it can be viewed as a means of support in the social and medico-social sector. My perspective will not be that of a clinician, but of a non-clinical sociologist, although naturally clinical sociology is duly represented in this volume. I situate myself outside of this practice; nevertheless, I have long been an attentive observer of its development over the past decades.

The field which over time has generally come to be referred to as 'social work' is a polysemous concept. This is not only due to the diversity of its types of public, institutions and practices. It is also a heterogeneous, fragile assemblage of different means of support, 'support' here being defined as an 'objective condition which makes it possible to participate in the experience of a subject', according to a formulation used by Robert Castel (Castel &

Haroche, 2001). In this sense, I would unhesitatingly say that the clinic is one of these means. Professionals are forced to constantly juggle between different, sometimes incompatible resources in their daily work, and obviously, this does not make their job any easier. Similarly, all our research efforts in this field are difficult, given that the object of research often escapes any attempt at disciplinary delimitation.

To approach the clinic in this way, it must obviously be considered an ordinary social object, albeit a complex one with different variables: the social workers themselves (whom I will not mention here), users (for lack of a better term), a recent history with a culminating point and a possible decline in sight (which only time will tell), struggles for justification/legitimation/adaptation, a lexicon of the variations on the theme 'clinic' (clinicians, 'my clinic', clinical revolution, clinical approaches, clinical acts, clinical support and clinical ethics, but also social clinic, medical clinic, institutional clinic, subject-oriented clinic, clinic in training and even judicial clinic) and, to top it all off, a strong culture of independence and resistance – resistance to good practices, whatever their origin, and a refusal to be subjugated to the notion of quantifiable outcomes, let alone results.

To approach the political economy of this clinic, I have chosen a synchronic path and have formulated the following hypothesis, in the form of a side step: however independent it may be, this clinic, at once ethical and practical, salaried and liberal, is on its own insufficient and therefore must not remain too isolated. Consequently, it is inseparable from other more or less competing approaches to the understanding of the social and human spheres, with which it constantly interferes, especially in the social sector.

Taking a substantialist perspective, I have thus undertaken to reason from an ideal type with four main, interdependent pillars which constitute a kind of 'square of intelligences' that can be used to better understand the social sphere as it actually is: this concerns the clinic, of course, but also forms of law, institutions and knowledge. Each pillar here can be considered a form of militant and/or salaried 'social work', in other words, as an 'action system' associated with a 'truth system' on social life. Although distinct, these four pillars together form a system, with internal balances and imbalances varying from one period to another and from one professional culture to another (Chauvière, 2011). It is each pillar individually as much as the whole that today's unbridled micromanagement seems to me to attack.

Concerning the clinic. Drawing on the work of certain clinicians involved in the field of social work, I will posit that a clinic in a daily, institutional situation based on specific circumstances has at least three main characteristics.

The first characteristic is ethical individualization. This is opposed to market individualization, where customers are too often objectified and interchangeable. In other words, it focuses on that which is singular, subjective and sensitive, that is, the ethical concern one has for each individual as a subject in the ordinary goings-on of his life. The aim is to help provide temporary structure to something which first and foremost makes sense to the subject (with his participation, if possible). This must be done before any attempt to obtain communicable and quantifiable results is undertaken. However, because it is the individual as a unique being (that is, the subject) that matters, it is a construction that is always in the making and necessarily fragile. It requires substantial scaffolding within the discipline, as well as a number of external resources. It also implies accepting an inevitable degree of uncertainty.

The second characteristic is the personal experience of a true encounter with others who are suffering, in difficulty or in need of help, sometimes silently. Although this intersubjective exchange is accomplished between two human beings – in principle equal in rights and dignity – it remains asymmetrical in terms of positions, roles, salaries and affects. This means that it is not only psychological, but also fully social and even economic. In addition, it largely involves the mediation of verbal and bodily language, usually at a low frequency so as not to damage trust. This results in a low level of traceability and consequently in the intrinsic difficulty of using standardized assessments.

The third and final characteristic is that clinical involvement is inseparable from a personal and shared analytical commitment. It combines observation, understanding, the confrontation of ideas, criticism and the production of new knowledge. Such practices are not intended to regulate or evaluate administrative and financial action or acts. First of all, these practices are clearly useful in clarifying the human situation in question and in attempting to influence the political and social environment. But they also constitute an important precaution: the encounter with another person, the generous use of speech addressed to that other person, and in return the word from that other person addressed to the practitioner – in short, the phenomena of transference and counter-transference – all create very specific difficulties. These practices are therefore also intended to compensate for the risks of self-exposure in the encounter – hence the supervision and analysis of practices and other modalities, all of which take time.

Concerning rights. We are living in a constitutional state under the rule of law (Chevallier, 2003), the law being considered in its formal dimension, according to the hierarchy of norms, but also in its substance, to better guarantee the legal security of actions and fundamental freedoms. In a constitutional state such as France, civil law and public law are not only used to settle external conflicts or disputes, as in common law, but they also have an instructional function of 'making a society'. It is therefore a major component, although always subject to reinterpretation because it remains a human tool, a far cry from the natural law of the past (Commaille, 2015).

Without the law, the conditions rendering possible and legitimate the social and medico-social actions from which we benefit would be much weaker, or even reduced to the emotions, free exchange or goodwill of the participants and, what is more, without secured allocated resources. The same can be said for labor law, another weak area, as Alain Supiot's early work clearly showed.

Today, however, despite the unavoidable reference to the rule of law, one can observe the development of increasingly instrumental and technical uses of law, particularly through what some lawyers call a 'normative densification', which often confuses law with rule, particularly with regard to multiple real-time adjustments of the management of 'human capital' and its failings (also known as 'regulation', 'governance' and so on). This is a characteristic feature of the normative productions of the last decade (especially since the French LOLF[i] in 2001). Moreover, large social businesses are now creating legal resources departments at their headquarters and recruiting specialized lawyers to optimize the benefits for the organization and to anticipate and reduce the risks involved, including even criminal risks.

But access to human and social rights (which, despite the law, is not always respected) is not the only issue at hand. There are also the equally central issues of the effectiveness of these rights, the continued progress of unconditional subjective rights, especially for the most vulnerable, and the urgent need to educate people about their rights. Otherwise, these rights will sooner or later be on a par with arbitrary philanthropy, the vagaries of charity work and the unequal consumption of services, with the risk of breaching the French social pact and its fundamental values of equality and solidarity.

Concerning institutions. In the 1970s, the term 'institution' was widely used to refer to schools, justice or health, even when their management was delegated to associations. In the 1980s, especially after decentralization in France, the term 'organization' was increasingly used (vertical organization, network organization), bringing about other issues, such as the various parties within the system, the amount of freedom to which one is entitled and questions of resources and strategy. Finally, since the neoliberal turn of the 1990s and early 21st century, the notion of enterprise, including so-called social enterprise, [ii] has progressed very quickly, extolling, admittedly, the idea of entrepreneurship, but also and above all of entrepreneurial management, be it in the public, associative or private for-profit sector. This has created an odd reversal of doctrine: public authorities are now becoming clients of social establishments. Furthermore, some of the Council of Europe's recommendations (aimed at its 47 member states) support the need for deinstitutionalization, especially in the field of disability;[iii] these recommendations have been followed by announcements of closures of medical and educational institutes and a move towards a more inclusive policy in the School for All system starting in 2022, in spite of the fact that public education is above all an institution and not a service.

Despite all these announcements, the question of the 'institution' remains no less central and unavoidable. First of all, this milestone legal structure[iv] seems to many, including myself, to be the most appropriate to the very nature of social issues. Indeed, the institution alone is truly sustainable against the harmful discontinuity of programs and calls for tender, all driven by a 'given market'.[v] The institution perpetuates past agreements, thus protecting both the rights useful to users (whom we would do better to call rights holders) and the clinical practices of social workers, but also the most cooperative practices, from a perspective that can be broadly described as 'institutional clinic' or 'judicial clinic'. The dialectic of 'the instituted and the instituting' parties[vi] is the source of a dynamic of collective life, with its high points and its moments of silence, which the social sector greatly needs on a daily basis without unnecessary interference. This is the trophic function of institutions, except perhaps in schools, which have hardly cultivated it at all – and this is where the central problem of inclusion lies. Finally, let us never forget that social issues have been constitutional since 1946 and 1958: 'France is an indivisible, democratic, secular and social Republic'. This refers to compulsory and universal social security and to everything that this system has made possible in terms of interventions and legitimacy for all social action, including at the clinical level.

Concerning knowledge. Tension has become very high between the tendency towards 'Googlization' (Cassin, 2007) (and the consumerism of non-critical knowledge via the Internet and social networks against a background of 'cognitive capitalism' enshrined in the Lisbon Treaty (2000)) and the 'social intelligence' approach of the people concerned (professionals but also users) within institutions of all kinds as the 'creative part' of their existence. Here we are poles apart from the '(so-called) intelligent enterprise'. In any working community, especially in the social sector, this relational and institutional know-how (Avet, 2010), initiated and supported by the women and men involved, constitutes a genuine critical heritage that should remain autonomous enough to hold its own vis-à-vis decision makers, financing bodies and, within certain limits, users themselves. But this knowledge is no longer sufficiently recognized or respected, let alone maintained. Training centers have often given up on this essential point, and social research is at a virtual standstill, unable as it is to find a solid foothold and paradigm within which to work (Chauvière, 2014; Alix, Autès & Marlière, 2019).

Concerning once again this ideal type, there can be no order or hierarchy in the way the four pillars are assembled. We can start from any one of them, provided we recognize the decisive role played by all the others and continue to reason in terms of organic solidarity and global intelligence. There may be activists, cause-ralliers, even professionals who demonstrate a preference for one or the other of these 'action and truth systems', sometimes knowing precious little about the other three. And yet it is crucial to bear in mind the interdependence of the four, cross-disciplinarity and the temporal dimension of the whole. This is especially true since it is precisely this type of reasoning that contemporary management condemns, preferring to deny any historicity in order to better segment actions and impose pragmatic reasoning in real time or in the very short term, a context where the clinic in action loses part of its legitimacy.

Obviously, one could reason differently, by choosing a more socio-historical path, for example. What are the foundations of clinical approaches? Might there be a French exception? The religious origins are acknowledged and mentioned in this collection, but the heritage of public service is less so. For various reasons, public service and associations, when they were still entrusted with a 'public service mission', seem to have, for a time, better protected the possibility of a space–time which was more favorable to a clinical approach to social issues. This is very likely due to their organic nature, which has made it possible to freely navigate within the spheres of freedom, responsibility and opposability dear to the Republic.

Finally, starting from the 'square of intelligences', one could still move in two other directions – trying, on the one hand, to better characterize the clinic's unique place within the square and reflecting, on the other hand, on how these different elements are related to each other and form a system.

Concerning the first direction, recognizing that the clinical approach does not seem to be cut from quite the same cloth as the other three pillars (rights, institutions and knowledge), we must attempt to qualify this small difference. Metaphorically speaking, quantum theory can provide us here with an interesting way forward. If we think in terms of space–time and of particles and waves, could we not rather call rights, institutions and knowledge **particles** and the clinic the **wave**? This means that, in space–time, these different elements, although interdependent, do not all possess the same properties.

Rights, institutions and knowledge can be regarded as more material elements or as existing resources to be understood and used in an ordinary way without excluding a certain level of uncertainty; the clinic, then, would be the observable modification of an element (a human subject, for example, but not exclusively) which comes into being and propagates itself according to other rules in another space–time – that of experience, representations, imaginations and encounters. This is a topic for further discussion elsewhere.

The second direction raises three questions: (1) Which internal and contextual forces, formal or informal, bring closer together – or, on the contrary, disassociate – these different 'intelligences in social acts' (such as continuous *versus* discontinuous public policies, values such as coordination or transdisciplinarity *versus* managerial or disciplinary order)? (2) Among these forces at work, should special attention be paid to ethical requirements (ontological and humanist references)? (3) For the person concerned by social interventions, is there not ultimately a relative equivalence between these four 'action and social truth systems'?

In the end, the clinic appears not only as an indispensable source of interventions and knowledge (often psychosocial) at the intersection of subjectivities and social issues, but also as a source of judgment and commitment in the social field. While in the past the clinic has been able to contribute, together with other stakeholders, to the development of a general doctrine of everyday, concrete social practices, the need for this overall doctrinal work has not been supported by public authorities for almost four decades now, leaving far too much room for the economic paradigm. As mentioned here, the idea of doctrine obviously goes far beyond the simple declarations of objectives or principles accompanying the obligation of internal and external evaluation imposed by the 2002-2 law, just as it cannot be content with the rights of users alone (Chauvière, 2013). The first step is to set a goal and specify how it is to be reached without putting social cohesion at risk.

For this clinical culture in the field to prosper – this clinical-based practice which this collection rightly aims to promote – we must of course recognize the importance of theoretical and political work to counterbalance the currently dominant evidence-based trend. But we must also acknowledge the crucial role played internally by collegial and interprofessional criticism of know-how, experiences and results, that is, with and by peers from different origins (rights, institutions and knowledge in particular). The very nature of the living being, as Canguilhem wrote, and the clinical complexity of social and human issues compel us to do so now more than ever.

Notes

i   The *Loi organique relative aux lois de finances* (or Organic Law on Finance Laws), 1 August 2001 brought about an algorithmic management of public affairs, requiring continuous evaluation and performance objectives.
ii Law of 31 July 2014 on the social and solidarity economy, also known as the Hamon Law.
iii One example is the Committee of Ministers' recommendation to member states of 3 February 2010.
iv On the work of Dean Hauriou at the beginning of the 20th century, see Millard, 1995. See also the recent synthesis by Lafore, 2019.
v   As stated in the European Union Services Directive of 2006; see Chauvière & Henry, 2011.
vi Resulting from alternative pedagogical and psychotherapeutic practices. See in particular Lourau, 1969. See also the work of the *Centre d'Etudes, de Recherche et de Formation Institutionnelle* (CERFI) and its journal *Recherches*.

References

Alix, J. S., Autès, M., & Marlière, É. (2020). *Le travail social en quête de légitimité*. EHESP.
Avet R. (Ed.). (2010). *Pourquoi défendre aujourd'hui la clinique dans le travail médico-social*. Nîmes: Champ social éditions, preface by Roland Gori (with Jeanne Lafont, Jean-François Coffin, Jacky Besson).
Cassin, B. (2007). *Google-moi. La deuxième mission de l'Amérique*. Paris: Albin Michel.
Castel, R., & Haroche, C. (2001). *Propriété privée, propriété sociale, propriété de soi. Entretiens sur la construction de l'individu moderne*. Paris: Fayard.
Chauvière, M. (2014). D'interminables fiançailles! Promesses et tribulations de la recherche et du travail social depuis les années 1970. In Jaeger, M. (Ed.), *Conférence de consensus. Le travail social et la recherche* (pp. 44–56). Paris: Dunod.
Chauvière, M. (2011). *L'intelligence sociale en danger. Chemins de résistance et propositions*. Paris: La Découverte, collection Cahiers libres.
Chauvière, M. (2013). La question des usagers, de l'impensé à l'agenda. In Collectif. *Penser la science administrative dans la post-modernité – Mélanges en l'honneur du Professeur Jacques Chevallier* (pp. 217–229). Paris: LGDJ, Lextenso éditions.
Chauvière, M., & Henry, J. (2011). Quel statut pour les services sociaux dans l'union européenne? Arguments pour des services sociaux non économiques d'intérêt général. *RDSS, Revue de Droit Sanitaire et Social*, 6, November–December, 1043–1058.
Chevallier, J. (2003). *L'État de droit*. Paris: Montchrestien, collection Clefs.
Commaille, J. (2015). *À quoi nous sert le droit?* Paris: Gallimard, collection Essais Folio 609.
Lafore, R. (2019). *L'individu contre le collectif. Qu'arrive-t-il à nos institutions?* Rennes: Presses de l'EHESP.
Lourau, R. (1969). *L'instituant contre l'institué*. Paris: Anthropos.
Millard, E. (1995). Hauriou et la théorie de l'institution. *Droit et Société*, 30/31, 381–412.

Introduction

Sébastien Ponnou and Christophe Niewiadomski

Social work is a polysemous sector marked by the diversity of its target groups, key players and institutions as well as the theoretical and pragmatic prisms through which it can be observed. At the international level, this diversity has traditionally been considered a great strength, a reflection of the complexity at work in social practices. Since the early 1980s to the 1990s, however, it has also been perceived as reflecting uncertainty: insisting on a supposed lack of scientific approaches in the field of social intervention, several academic and institutional players have supported evidence-based practice (EBP) in social work. The objective of EBP is to collect research data with an eye to guiding social workers' practices and increasing their effectiveness (Guilgun, 2005; McNeece & Thyer, 2004; Proctor, 2002; Sheldon, 2001). Widely represented in the international literature – particularly in English-speaking countries – EBP-type approaches have recently been the subject of intense controversy. Several authors have argued that there is a risk of standardizing practices in social work and thereby reducing them to a series of protocols (Webb, 2001; Reynolds, 2008; Couturier & Carrier, 2003). In a landmark paper, Webb elaborates a detailed critique of the methodological and ideological foundations of EBP approaches borrowed from biomedical sciences and supported by economic and managerial logics. Webb's in-depth study denounces the weakness

DOI: 10.4324/9781003296416-1

of neo-positivist approaches to relational practices and suggests recommendations for improving the evidence-based model. He also argues for the relevance of epistemological, empirical and clinical approaches in the field of social intervention.

Many studies have pursued the investigations conducted by Webb, but none of these criticisms has led to the development of alternative approaches or perspectives to the EBP model which can respond both to the uncertainty related to helping relationships of various types and to the contemporary scientific issues related to social intervention. Based on a well-argued critique of evidence-based models and their deleterious effects in the field of social intervention, the aim of this volume is to build an alternative design that can address the complexity and the ethical issues of relational practices at the core of social workers' activities. This perspective leads us to support the need for a **Clinical-Based Practice in Social Work** as a way to subvert attempts to standardize and objectivize care, education and support practices. This paradigm must serve as an operator or logical connector favoring intervention, training and research devices capable of dealing with all that is unbearable or not yet experienced, great suffering and small advances – the wanderings and the important discoveries that emerge through the encounters with others and with what they say.

Evidence-based practice in social work: the future of an illusion

The limitations of EBP approaches have already been discussed in detail in Gray, Plath and Webb (2009). Here we add some additional remarks:

1. The first concerns the very principle of evidence. Far from effective in the human sciences in general, evidence is particularly ill-equipped to lend itself to the field of social intervention. The administration of evidence requires particular epistemological and discursive conditions that we find difficult to address in the context of social work, where the issues cannot be reduced to demonstrative logics. Social intervention is not a homogeneous disciplinary field, meaning that a given situation or phenomenon can be the subject of a multitude of potentially valid and non-exclusive hypotheses. It is all the more important to exercise caution here: the objects of study specific to the social sciences concern human beings, whose complexity and uniqueness are often undermined by sophisticated methods and protocols.

2. A second pitfall lies in the methodological considerations specific to EBP approaches. They are classified according to degree of robustness and reliability according to recognized, pre-established scientific criteria: (a) systematic reviews and meta-analyses; (b) randomized control trials; (c) quasi-experimental studies; (d) case and cohort studies; (e) pre-experimental group studies; (f) surveys; and (g) qualitative studies (McNeece & Thyer, 2004). The criterion of scientificity and the strength of conviction of the evidence thus depend on the method used. While this proposal seems to make sense – a meta-analysis being *a priori* more reliable than a case study – it nevertheless poses major difficulties that are rarely addressed. The first concerns the use of methods in the human and social sciences, which depends first and foremost on the object of study, the field, the problem, the hypotheses and the means of the research. If one aims to establish the effectiveness of the method before conducting the research, one runs the risk of missing the complexity of the object of study and proceeding to a one-sided, simplistic reading of reality. Thus, some fields or hypotheses can only be studied through qualitative methods. The second difficulty related to this methodological referencing concerns precisely the lack of consideration of EBP approaches for qualitative methods. From our point of view, such methods make up the bulk of research in the human and social sciences: these include clinical studies, ethno/anthropological field observations, interviews, action research and participants' observations. All of these methods are capable of transcribing the complexity of social phenomena and professional practices. A third and even more fundamental difficulty is that EBP methods in social work view the method as a fundamental precept, as an end in itself and no longer as a means of research. Among other things, this bias implies that the results of a meta-analysis carry a higher degree of truth than the account of a clinical situation. Such a view seems to us misleading and damaging, misleading namely because it is not certain that evidence and methodological robustness necessarily convince professionals as one might expect (Lyotard, 1975). Moreover, to the extent that the EBP discourse is based on a principle – a value system – it contributes to the regression of science to a system of beliefs and unravels the logical connections from which Descartes, in his *Meditations*, lays the foundations of modern science by separating it from its references to truth (Descartes, 2014; Lacan, 1966). Science is about the production of knowledge. It is based not on unalterable laws but on plausible theories which, since they are formulated by humans, are highly likely to miss the reality of the object to which they are supposed to respond (Popper, 2005). Scientific

discourse, based on partial and provisional data, constantly produces the questions and knowledge that arise during the research process. Scientific logic makes it possible to demonstrate one thing and its opposite, by which it systematically misses the dimension of truth – the principle of refutability. Science therefore remains an uncertain system, affected by inconsistency (Le Gaufey, 2014). Truth, on the contrary, belongs to the register of the performative, of the utterance – it escapes any argumentative or demonstrative logic. In other words, it is impossible to speak of 'scientific truth' or to consider that the results of research make it possible to produce 'true results' concerning a given (social) phenomenon. We are confronted with the inconsistency of science vs. the incompleteness of truth, whose heterogeneous logics are irreconcilable. Insofar as they claim to rely on research results to answer for the truth of a given social problem, EBP approaches thus constantly run the risk of falling into scientism.

3. A third type of difficulty is related to the specific obstacles to the financing, production and dissemination of scientific research. There is now an abundant literature on the biases associated with short-circuit research funding based on initial studies that are often contradicted by subsequent studies. This type of pitfall affects the dissemination of research in both scientific journals and the mainstream media: the initial studies receive much more media coverage than subsequent studies in spite of the fact that the latter are the object of greater consensus in the meta-analyses (Dumas-Mallet et al., 2017b). Another bias is related to the manipulation and interpretation of research data. Indeed, most scientific production is now validated by statistical tests. However, the measurement scales used to affirm or invalidate a hypothesis have evolved considerably over the years, so that a result that would not have previously given rise to further development can now be considered significant. This evolution is not necessarily due to the refinement of measurement tools but to the reduction in the criteria of relevance or validity of the research (Dumas-Mallet et al., 2017a). These statistical tests, furthermore, are tools to guide research results and conclusions. However, these tools can be manipulated, even when it comes to complex procedures or tests. Some of these manipulations constitute proven attempts at fraud: falsification of data (p-hacking), ending data collection when the test becomes statistically significant, obvious discrepancies or even aberrations between the observations and conclusions of the study, and incorrect descriptions of the results and embellishments (or 'spin'). These biases are relatively common, especially in the field of research dedicated to mental and psychosocial

disorders. They are the subject of a detailed scientific literature (Gonon, Dumas-Mallet & Ponnou, 2019). Other, less serious types of distortions are also frequent: here, the aim is not strictly speaking to distort the results of research but to consider them from the angle that seems most favorable to the researcher. For example, sequencing a longitudinal study over a two-year, four-year or six-year period can significantly change the results of the study. A similar situation arises when a sample is distributed according to age groups. These biases are common and affect all scientific production. Another difficulty concerns the recurrence of conflicts of interest in the funding and dissemination of research. Thus, prevalence studies, studies dedicated to certain therapeutic approaches (particularly drugs) and studies concerning the etiology of certain diseases, disabilities or psychosocial disorders regularly suffer from conflicts of interest such that they completely invalidate the results of the research (Ponnou, Haliday & Gonon, 2019; Gonon, Dumas-Mallet & Ponnou, 2019). All these elements therefore call for a certain caution with regard to the insights provided by science on contemporary issues of social intervention.

4. A fourth type of limitation concerns the link between the registers of evidence and method and the evaluation of the effectiveness of social intervention, which itself proves to be subject to economic stakes that accentuate the difficulties of interpreting scientific discourse. In this respect, EBP does not emerge as a paradigm whose vocation is to question the models or practices at work in the field of social intervention, but rather as an undertaking to rationalize therapeutic, social, educational and relational practices in order to reduce their financial impact. The use of science, here and elsewhere, could be seen as a management and cost reduction tool, through the evaluation of the effectiveness of the action. According to this logic, EBP places a strong emphasis on standardized therapeutic or educational approaches that are effective in the short term, such as cognitive and behavioral therapies or drug treatment of mental disorders, thus neglecting the work related to meaning, speech, subjective dynamics or social and environmental factors involved in social action issues.

5. In the face of these criticisms, proponents of evidence-based approaches have developed a set of arguments centered on the ethical nature of their initiative: since the paradigm is based on evidence, itself supported by the method, the function of research ethics is to ensure the validity of the process. It is certainly desirable to develop procedures and ethics committees for human-centered intervention research. These provisions, sometimes accompanied by regulatory recommendations (see the *loi Jardé* in

France – www.legifrance.fr), make it possible to guarantee the integrity of human subjects and data collected while at the same time questioning in a timely manner the means of research used with regard to the expected objectives. There is no doubt that evidence-based approaches respond to these ethical issues in a satisfactory way; accordingly, supporters of EBP claim a form of equivalence in the ethical treatment of research-based practices and applications, regardless of the potential gaps between research and field-related issues. This level of sophistication of the relationship to ethics raises two main observations. The first concerns an ambiguous use of the notion of ethics, which is based on a procedural version that tends to tarnish its foundations (Badiou, 1993). The second concerns the overlap of research ethics and the ethics of social intervention. Indeed, advocates of evidence-based practice argue for a research ethics whereas it is essentially a question of creating an ethics for social practices or even of building a practice from an ethics and not from a technique (method). This is a fundamental distinction. Indeed, social intervention is first and foremost a practice, guided by an ethics, from which it is possible to produce research; it is not a field of research from which one then infers a practice.

6. A recurrent difficulty of EBP models concerns the possibilities of applying the paradigm in actual practice. There are five main issues related to this obstacle. First, the transition from basic to applied research always poses epistemological and technical difficulties, particularly in experimental studies requiring special conditions that cannot be reproduced in practice. Second, the results of the research, whatever the methods used, regularly recommend measures which are difficult to apply as they stand and which would require specific regulatory or support measures whose use does not depend solely on the will of social workers. Third, research results are sometimes difficult to interpret or even contradictory when the practice requires intervention of the 'here and now' type. Fourth, the conditions of practice of the educational, health and social professions rarely allow for a thorough analysis of the scientific literature on a given issue, pragmatically speaking. While the countries that have relied on the EBP model have developed institutional networks, centers and training tools to facilitate these processes, the number, variety and complexity of the issues raised for each social worker during their working day make this type of process utopian if not obsolete. Finally, the perspective of applying research results to professional issues involves a risk of uniformization and standardization of practices where social work requires ingenuity and critical thinking, reflection and debate, boldness

and creativity. It transforms social workers into experienced performers and, in so doing, destroys what is the essence of their expertise, their ethics and their vocation: the relationship between patient and practitioner. Social workers are first and foremost professionals of the 'encounter', of the relationship with the other, whatever the disability, the social difficulties, the symptoms and the obstacles. As craftspeople working at the edges and the margins to ensure that their subjects remain at the center, social workers tirelessly seek that creative formula which might reconcile the individual with the collective, and they do so without being able to rely on the certainty of typical solutions. Through clinical-based practices in social work, it is thus a question of focusing on the subjectivity and inventiveness of professionals in context with an eye to rethinking the contemporary challenges of social intervention.

Social work and clinical practices: is this a French exception?

There is currently no implementation of the EBP model in France. Admittedly, the French social intervention sector has been under unprecedented economic, evaluative and technocratic pressure since the early 2000s, but this pressure is not yet embodied in the form of reification or standardization of practices. Similarly, EBP approaches are not yet widely included in social workers' training frameworks, which focus primarily on relational practices, mediation practices, institutional dynamics, critical theories and traditional disciplinary input from the human and social sciences. To our knowledge, there exist in France no institutions or training centers dedicated to EBP approaches, and it could even be said that the notion is totally absent from the culture and perceptions of French social workers, most of whom are unaware of its existence. It should also be noted that France is conspicuously absent from the publication prepared by Gray, Plath and Webb (2009) on the modalities of implementing EBP approaches at the international level.

Conversely, recent investigations have revealed the recurrence of references to clinical approaches in the field of social intervention (Ponnou, 2016). These clinical approaches permeate the practices, institutional dynamics and training of social workers to such an extent that it is now common for professionals, when designating their practice and the interventions they perform on a daily basis, to refer to their 'clinic'. Far from being reduced to a research method, these clinical approaches are part of the professional discourse and play an important role in the identity of the key players in this sector.

From our point of view, the difficulties in implementing EBP-type concepts and the success of clinical approaches in France stem from two main factors. The first relates to the contemporary history of social work in France (Chauvière, 2007, 2009), which revolves around a universal social protection system, the principles of distribution and solidarity. Ultimately, these give little influence or relevance to the concepts of evidence or effectiveness. It was only in the 1990s–2000s that these notions emerged under the auspices of liberal governments, while economic difficulties revealed the chronic financing deficit of the Social Security system. The second factor concerns the legacy of the French theories developed during the 1960s and 1970s and which still retain an extremely strong foothold in the field of social work and in the human and social sciences. Canguilhem, Foucault, Lacan, Bourdieu and a few others each reflected in their own manner on the question of 'the clinic' and its implementation in their respective fields and disciplines. These theoretical developments have given rise to multiple applications and intense debates in the fields of care, education and social work: psychoanalytical institutions, institutional psychotherapy and pedagogy are no doubt the most noteworthy examples. These approaches have been widely disseminated in the field of social intervention and in the training of social workers. They have helped to spread a psychosocial understanding of disability, mental disorders or maladjustments and have thus strongly counterbalanced the influence of the biomedical and standardized approaches on which EBP methods are based. Finally, they have participated in the construction of a maieutic conception of social intervention (Maisonneuve, 1990), whose vocation is not to fill the immensity of supposed gaps but to allow everyone to seize their creative opportunity in an uncertain world.

The challenge of the clinic

The goal of this volume thus consists in starting from the impasses at work via EBP approaches and more or less advanced attempts to standardize social practices, and to propose an alternative paradigm based on clinical practices and research in social work.

The concept of 'clinic' – etymologically, the collection of the signs of disease at the patient's bedside – suffers from a plurality of possible meanings that is rare in social work and by extension in the human and social sciences. Developed in medicine starting in antiquity, the clinical approach extended to all disciplines of the human sciences in the second half of the 20th century. It refers jointly or separately to a diagnostic method, a therapy or a pedagogy, as well as a set of research methodologies. Recognized as a specific field in psychology, sociology, anthropology, or educational sciences (Blanchard-Laville, 1999; Blanchard-Laville & al., 2005; Canguilhem, 1966; Cifali et al., 2005; De Gaulejac et al., 2013; Foucault, 1963; Jaeger, 2014; Niewiadomski, 2012; Ponnou, 2016; Revaut d'Allones & al., 1989; Rocheix, 2010), it now has a polysemous reading based on the theoretical, practical, methodological prisms or fields of research to which it applies. Indeed, within the main disciplines of the human and social sciences, there is a specific field dedicated to the clinic. Within each field, and even more so within each discipline, there may be relatively different or even antagonistic meanings of the clinic. Medicine (particularly psychiatry) and psychology are perhaps the most eloquent examples of this conceptual fragmentation: the term 'clinic' here is used indiscriminately to refer to studies based on biological or social data. It is also used in the same way in reference to statistical surveys conducted on large random samples, or to describe the speech-based work undertaken in the intimacy of the therapist's office and based on the uniqueness both of the encounter itself and the relationship between the practitioner and the patient. These differences are generally structured around heterogeneous theoretical prisms – biological medicine and psychoanalysis, for example.

This cross-disciplinarity and diversity of references to clinical approaches in the different fields of social intervention seem to us to be relevant driving forces which can be used to support an approach which highlights the theories and practices of meaning and of relationships to others which are specific to the care, education and social professions. This reference to the clinic is rooted in the tradition inherited from Canguilhem, who in *Le normal et le pathologique* (1966) reconsidered the clinical tradition in the light of technological progress and scientific revolutions based on statistics. Canguilhem worked to dissociate standard and average in order to support the need for the clinic in the medical field and, by extension, the human and social sciences (1942, pp. 50, 61, 96–99). Indeed, the very nature of a living organism excludes any possibility of statistical calculation of a norm for it – of a standardized measurement for humans – since both statistics and scientific methods make it possible to obtain accurate but fundamentally false results.

The use of averages makes the essentially oscillatory and rhythmic nature of functional biological phenomena disappear. For example, if we look for the true number of heart beats by the average of measurements taken several times in the same day on a given individual 'we will have precisely a false number'. Hence this rule:

> in physiology, one must never give average descriptions of experiments because the true relationships of phenomena disappear in this average;

> when dealing with complex and variable experiments, one must study
> their various circumstances and then view the most perfect experiment
> as typical, but which will always represent a true fact.
>
> (Canguilhem, 1942, p. 96)

Canguilhem affirms 'the logical independence of the concepts of norm and
average and, consequently, the definitive impossibility of giving, in the form
of an objectively calculated average, the equivalent of the anatomical or physiological norm' (1942, p. 99). From this he concludes that, in medicine as in
the humanities, science makes it possible to obtain accurate but false results.
The clinic, however, favors subjective, specific approaches which are more
essentially focused on the truth or on the actual situation experienced by the
subject. Faced with these antagonistic poles, the question is whether, for each
situation, it is preferable for social intervention practitioners to have the exact
results of scientific research or whether, on the contrary, it is up to professionals to base their judgment and practice on the complex and variable elements
that emerge in the clinic in the singular intertwining of the subject and the
social context. In no way does this exclude the practitioner's interest in scientific production.

The need for the clinic arises from this alternative and from the subject's
ability to feel 'more than normal', in other words, to be 'able to follow new
standards of life' (Canguilhem, 1942, p. 133, 153). These essential considerations, which seem to be ignored by the defenders of EBP approaches,
resonate very strongly with regard to contemporary issues of care, education and social intervention practices and lead us to support the transition
from an **evidence-based approach** to a model of **clinical-based practice** in
social work. The aim of this collection is to bring together and link the various components of research and clinical practices in the human and social
sciences and to discuss their effects and challenges in the field of social intervention. The hope is that these contributions will make it possible to capture
the theoretical, practical, ethical and methodological points of reference of
a clinical-based practice in social work as an alternative to neo-positivist and
liberal conceptions of the helping relationship.

Towards clinical-based practices in social work

In this perspective, the first part of this collection highlights the need for the
clinic in the contemporary body of discourses and knowledge. **Philippe Lyet**,
in a chapter entitled 'When evidence-based practices come up against social

and scientific uncertainty', addresses the limits of rationalized and standardized approaches in a context of advanced modernity and argues in favor of relativity and the hybridization of knowledge. He thus develops participatory and collaborative research models capable of reporting on the clinical issues and perspectives at work in the field of social intervention. **Vincent de Gaulejac**, in a chapter entitled 'Social work as the test of public management', expounds on the paradoxes of managerial conceptions of social practices and their harmful effects on professionals and organizations. Faced with the injunctions of profitability and performance of paradox-generating systems in the care, education and social professions, he highlights the importance of developing collective spaces for reflection as close as possible to the experiences of the key players and based on the principles of clinical sociology in order to enable subjects having formed collectives to co-construct the meaning of their intervention and their involvement in the institution. Finally, **Bertrand Ravon**, in a chapter entitled 'Uses and reconfigurations of the clinic in the field of social intervention: a sociological perspective', takes on the genesis of clinical intervention in sociology to support its relevance in working with subjects and the sensitive, contextualized study of the unique suffering of a group or an individual. Based on an inventory of *clinical sociology* and *sociology of the clinic*, he proposes a model of interventional sociology called the *sociological clinic*, bringing together an ethnographic analysis of ordinary social intervention practices and the activity clinic, one of the challenges of which is to reconnect with a social critique accessible to social workers themselves.

The second part of this volume is intended to make the scope and challenges of the clinic resonate with the practices of social workers. In this context, based on a set of theoretical and clinical studies conducted in the human and social sciences, **Christophe Niewiadomski** develops 'The contribution of the clinic narrative in supporting professional practice'. Tracing back the contemporary issues of social intervention and, in counterpoint, of a technocratic and managerial approach to support practices, he promotes an ethical intention of the intersubjective relationship which is mindful of the mediation of the narrative as a place for self-reflection and as a possible vehicle for training via the setting into motion of the subject. In 'The clinic, psychoanalysis and social work: practice and training', **Sébastien Ponnou** builds upon the impasses of biomedical and psychosocial approaches to hyperactivity/ADHD to support the need for a Lacanian psychoanalytic clinic in the care and education practices of suffering people. He explores the issues of practice and training by discussing the handling of transference in social practices and clinical practice training programs in the professionalization of social workers.

Marie Rose Moro and **Rahmet Radjack** testify to the theoretical and methodological foundations of ethnopsychiatry and the transcultural approach in the care of people of foreign origin in France. They develop the conditions of their practice and the interest of specific mechanisms addressed to migrants and their families, bringing together cultural levers, multi-person practice and the subject-oriented clinic. It is a practice without standards, but not without principles, where otherness resonates.

The third chapter is devoted to the challenges of professionalization and training in clinical practices in the field of social intervention. **Pascal Fugier** speaks of the demonstrable effects of a participatory and clinical research initiative conducted with social workers concerning the evolution of their function and the prevention of young people's involvement in drug trafficking. In a chapter entitled 'The circulation and emergence of knowledge and practices between youth professionals: the central issue of collaborative clinical research', he demonstrates the dynamics according to which the participatory nature of the project contributes to the defense and recognition of the core profession of social workers – the relationship of help and support – and advocates for a clinic of change that contributes to the emergence of reflective practitioners and organizations. In a chapter dedicated to 'Building oneself as a professional', **Florence Giust-Desprairies** reports on a psychosocial clinical intervention carried out with social workers in crisis. Starting from the factors that weaken the identity of social workers, the author focuses her attention on the subjective and intersubjective processes that contribute to the construction of the self at work in a context of transformation or even mutation of care and support organizations for people in difficulty. **Mireille Cifali**, in a chapter entitled 'Clinical ethics applied to training', supports the use of clinical mechanisms in the training and practices of social workers. She highlights the ethical necessity of subjectivity on the part of professionals in the relationship professions, an essential condition for welcoming others and a prerequisite for any possibility of social inclusion. From this she deduces the importance of clinical practice training systems in training institutions and medico-social institutions.

The fourth and final part of this collection brings together two chapters more particularly informed by the ethical issues related to clinical-based practice in social work. In a chapter entitled 'Psychoanalytical dissent', **Guy de Villers** provides an uncompromising critique of the evidence-based medicine model. He points out its intrinsic biases and limitations, particularly in practices aimed at people with mental disorders, and highlights the foundations and ethics of psychoanalysis oriented by Freud and Lacan in the support of suffering people. In a chapter entitled 'Accompaniment in social work: a path of co-wandering', **Jean-Bernard Paturet** embarks on a conceptual and metaphorical itinerary. Interweaving notions of wandering, accompaniment, distance and vulnerability, he argues for the ethical significance of clinical practices based on speech mediation in the professions of education and social intervention.

Throughout the pages, this volume thus invites the reader to discover the diversity and richness of clinical practices and research in the field of social work and, by extension, in care and education practices. Of logical, practical and ethical necessity, these clinical-based practices in social work establish themselves as an epistemological paradigm which is bound to meet the challenges posed by contemporary issues in social intervention.

References

Badiou, A. (1993). *L'éthique: essai sur la conscience du mal*. Paris: Hatier.

Blanchard-Laville, C., Chaussecourte, P., Hatchuel, F., & Pechberty, B. (2005). Recherches cliniques d'orientation psychanalytique dans le champ de l'éducation et de la formation. *Revue Française de Pédagogie*, *151*, 111–162.

Blanchard-Laville, C. (1999). L'approche clinique d'inspiration psychanalytique: enjeux théoriques et méthodologiques. *Revue française de pédagogie*, *127*, 9–22.

Canguilhem, G. (1966). *Le normal et le pathologique*. Paris: PUF.

Chauvière, M. (2009). *Enfance inadaptée: l'héritage de Vichy. Suivi de l'efficace des années quarante*. Paris: L'Harmattan.

Chauvière, M. (2007). *Trop de gestion tue le social*. Paris: La Découverte.

Cifali, M., Giust-Desprairies, F. et al. (2006). *De la clinique. Un engagement pour la formation et la recherche*. Paris: De Boeck.

Couturier, Y., & Carrier, S. (2003). Pratiques fondées sur les données probantes en travail social: un débat émergent. *Nouvelles Pratiques Sociales*, *16*(2), 68–79.

De Gaulejac, V., Giust-Desprairies, F., Massa, A. et al. (2013). *La recherche clinique en sciences sociales*. Toulouse: Érès.

Descartes, R. (2014). *Méditations métaphysiques*. Paris: Flammarion.

Dumas-Mallet, E., Button, K. S., Boraud, T., Gonon, F., & Munafò, M. R. (2017a). Low statistical power in biomedical science: a review of three human research domains. *Royal Society Open Science*, *4*(2), 160254.

Dumas-Mallet, E., Smith, A., Boraud, T., & Gonon, F. (2017b). Poor replication validity of biomedical association studies reported by newspapers. *PloS one*, *12*(2), e0172650.

Foucault, M. (1963). *Naissance de la clinique*. Paris: PUF.

Gilgun, J. F. (2005). The four cornerstones of evidence-based practice in social work. *Research on Social Work Practice*, *15*(1), 52–61.

Gonon, F., Dumas-Mallet, E., & Ponnou, S. (2019). Médiatisation des observations scientifiques concernant les troubles mentaux: revue des biais, distorsions et omissions. *Les Cahiers du journalisme*, *2*(3), 45–64.

Gray, M., Plath, D., & Webb, S. (2009). *Evidence-based social work: a critical stance*. London: Routledge.

Jaeger, M. (Ed.) (2014). *Le travail social et la recherche: conférence de consensus*. Paris: Dunod.

Lacan, J. (1966). *Ecrits*. Paris: Seuil.

Le Gaufey, G. (2014). *L'incomplétude du symbolique: de René Descartes à Jacques Lacan*. Paris: Epel Editions.

Lyotard, J-F. (1975). De l'apathie théorique. *Critique*, *31*(333), 254–265.

Maisonneuve, J. (1990). Réflexions autour du changement et de l'intervention psychosociologique. *Théories du Changement Social Intentionnel. Participation, Expertise et Contraintes*, *5*, 81.

McNeece, C. A., & Thyer, B. A. (2004). Evidence-based practice and social work. *Journal of evidence-based social work*, *1*(1), 7–25.

Niewiadomski, C. (2012). *Recherche biographique et clinique narrative: entendre et écouter le sujet contemporain*. Toulouse: Érès.

Ponnou, S. (2016). *Le travail social à l'épreuve de la clinique psychanalytique*. Paris: L'Harmattan.

Ponnou, S., Haliday, H., & Gonon, F. (2020). Where to find accurate information on attention-deficit hyperactivity disorder? A study of scientific distortions among French websites, newspapers, and television programs. *Health*, *24*(6), 684–700.

Popper, K. (2005). *The logic of scientific discovery*. New York: Routledge.

Proctor, E-K. (2002). Social work, school violence, mental health, and drug abuse: a call for evidence-based practices. *Social Work Research*, *26*(2), 67–69.

Revault d'Allonnes, C., Assouly-Piquet, C., Slama, F. B., Blanchet, A., & Douville, O. (1989). *La démarche clinique en sciences humaines: documents, méthodes, problèmes*. Paris: Dunod.

Reynolds, S. (2008). *Evidence-based practice: a critical appraisal*. Hoboken, NJ: John Wiley & Sons.

Rocheix, J-Y. (2010). Approches cliniques et recherche en éducation. Questions théoriques et considérations sociales. *Recherches et formations*, *65*, 111–122.

Sheldon, B. (2001). The validity of evidence-based practice in social work: a reply to Stephen Webb. *The British Journal of Social Work*, *31*(5), 801–809.

Webb, S-A. (2001). Some considerations on the validity of evidence-based practice in social work. *British Journal of Social Work*, *31*(1), 57–79.

Part I

Clinical practices and research in an uncertain world

When evidence-based practices come up against social and scientific uncertainty

1

Philippe Lyet

Introduction

The ambition of evidence-based practices is to understand and prescribe action based on the results of scientific research. However, such a project remains a challenge for researchers or social workers alike, for whom such action takes place in a situation of great uncertainty. Professional practice is faced with a double challenge: one must (1) construct it by finding compromises between different logics of action and (2) be able to look ahead whereas future possibilities only become clear as the action progresses. Moreover, asserting that one has conclusive evidence seems a presumptuous claim in those cases where the results of scientific research generate more debate and disagreement than consensus. In this period of 'technical democracy' (Callon, Lascoumes & Barthes, 2001), scientific disciplines with incompatible paradigms and rationales offer interpretations and understandings that are in competition with each other.

What is particularly disconcerting when one considers the point of view I will defend in this chapter is that the idea of an evidence-based practice has, in some of its realizations, been constructed with the pretense of standardizing

DOI: 10.4324/9781003296416-3

the practice by basing it on scientific work. This should not surprise us since the world of science is marked by a strong trend:

> Legitimization by academic and scientific institutions has become for at least half a century the primary means of justification for any discourse of knowledge or understanding. This legitimization is produced by the bodies responsible for justifying and administering 'good' knowledge (the system of expertise and validation of science and research), which today form a vast standardized production system. A very powerful normative 'discourse' is at work, which tends to favor standardized methodologies.
>
> (Ruano-Borbalan, 2014, p. 25)

Nevertheless, such a claim to base practices on tangible results is surprising: it ignores the most recent debates on science and the nature of those scientific results which appear more debatable than tangible, as well as the relation between science and action. The definition of this relation is itself the subject of much debate. The first part of this chapter will expand on these elements.

Acting and understanding what happens subsequently is no longer self-evident in an 'uncertain world' (Callon & al., 2001), which is also a pluralistic world with heterogeneous logics of action (Lyet, 2017). Taking action means combining these approaches in each situation, that is, building a social transaction and inventing in each case a specific provisional compromise (Remy, 1998). These elements will be developed in the second part.

Various interpretations are in competition, and the knowledge that can be mobilized by researchers and players 'on the ground' is relative. Understanding any phenomenon implies entering into its complexity (Morin, 2005) and comparing points of view (Darré, 1999) and knowledge, as I do in what I call multi-referential joint research (Lyet, 2017). These processes, which are characteristic of the state of advanced modernity we live in, question the evolution of the science–society 'contract' (Barré, 2015).

The illusion of evidence and partial, provisional knowledge

The development of evidence-based – that is, scientifically validated – prescriptions and practices is more diversified than it may seem at first glance. But this can take extreme forms, as in the case of a social work service in a Quebec institution where interviews conducted by social workers with beneficiaries must nowadays be conducted scrupulously following a guide based on research. The managers of the organization point to the scientific origin of this guide as proof of its superiority over the usual practices of social workers.

Such an approach to the relationship between science and social workers is part of a paradigm that Jean-Louis Le Moigne (2012) has called positivist. This positivist conception of science abandons all common sense under the pretense of the autonomy guaranteed to it by the scientific institution. Dominique Pestre speaks of 'the all-too-famous metaphor of science as revelatory' and about 'this reassuring image: reality is there but ignored, and science tells the truth about it' (Pestre, 2013, pp. 65–66).

Doubts about the ability of the sciences to prescribe action

In recent decades, the positivist stance has been challenged by many, reaching the heart of the scientific institutions. An ever-increasing number of scientists are now expressing diffuse but persistent doubts, for political reasons, about their role and the usefulness of science to society. On the basis of the work of science historians, they also question the uncertainty produced by scientific advances and 'the highly provisional nature of scientific truths' (Béguin & Cerf, 2009, pp. 3–4).

Michel Callon, Pierre Lascoumes and Yannick Barthes (2001) show that scientists and experts can become conditioned by their own objectives. They are therefore not 'objective' and are interested only in the issues they debate among themselves without taking into account the totality and complexity of the problems of the people involved. They argue that social workers, through the surveys they sometimes conduct, challenge the analyses and conclusions of experts, and that a finer and more complex understanding can arise from the discussion or conflict of interpretations between scientists and social workers. The ensuing partnership – neither completely chosen, nor totally imposed – is one where knowledge and action are simultaneously built.

The three criticisms of classical science

Three main criticisms can be leveled at this positivist approach to science, which promotes the idea that the knowledge produced by scientists is more valid (more convincing) than that produced by those conducting social work.

First of all is the criticism of the principle of truth. Science consists in proposing explanations that select a series of facts chosen as relevant to analyze reality. And yet herein lies the problem: depending on the disciplines – and, within a given discipline, on different schools of thought and individual scientists – the relevant facts are not always exactly the same and the problems are different. Each individual, from his own point of view, selects what he deems relevant and neglects aspects of reality that, to others, will seem important (Darré, 1999).

The philosopher of science Dominique Pestre shows that choosing certain aspects of reality always goes hand in hand with excluding others – all forms of knowledge have as a corollary a form of ignorance:

> There is no production of knowledge without the production of concomitant and organically linked ignorance, since producing human knowledge consists first of all in addressing one's problem from a certain point of view, in stating something at the expense of something else. Positive knowledge and blind spots are produced in the same movement; they are generated in and by the same acts. The production of statements about things is simultaneously a production of relevance and inadequacy. There is no production of new knowledge without mental and conceptual reorganization – and therefore without the production of new blind spots and omissions, the two primary forms of ignorance.
>
> (Pestre, 2013, pp. 67–68)

Science thus builds a society that socializes its members and, like any other discipline, reconstructs reality in terms of what is relevant for scientists, sometimes neglecting what is relevant for the social workers concerned. The dynamics of the disciplines can therefore be seen as confining. The same questions are sometimes raised and recast. Researchers make advances on some issues but neglect many others that may be just as relevant. Science thus develops according to a dynamic that sometimes seems to produce more compliance than renewal.

We agree with the second criticism of positivism, that of reductionism:

> Faced with complexity [...] the scientific approach advocates a reduction, retaining only a limited set of variables. [...] The hyper-specialization of knowledge, within increasingly narrow spaces of knowledge, produces its own uncertainties outside this space. Excesses then emerge, aspects of reality are omitted or not taken into account.
>
> (Callon, Lascoumes & Barthe, 2001, p. 4)

The third criticism concerns the neutralization of the specificity of actual phenomena: indeed, science 'pursues a universalist claim and sets itself the task of producing knowledge with a wide range in space and time; [it] tries to neutralize as much as possible the unique aspects of the object studied' (Béguin & Cerf, 2009, p. 7). Faced with these difficulties, the desire to produce knowledge adapted to specificities 'raises the question of a link between concepts that proceed by abstraction [...] and their implementation in situations that remain unique' (Béguin & Cerf, 2009, p. 7).

What is at stake here is the principle of 'rise in generality' which is often claimed to be the process that could distinguish scientific knowledge from that of social workers. What is meant by generality if it is not an abstraction that is assumed to be the same for all those who construct it according to the same rules, principles and processes? However, any abstraction is always the result of the subjectivity or intersubjectivity in which scientists position themselves, and therefore of a singularity whose products can only be singular themselves. When scientists claim to extrapolate generalizations, they theorize analyses from the results of surveys or experiments that come from choices they have made; others could have decided on different indicators or asked other questions based on concepts and theories that make sense to them and reflect their subjectivity or, at the very least, the intersubjectivity of their community. They thus bring together biased and incomplete data with theoretical and conceptual references that are just as biased and incomplete – in other words, singular data. A rise in generality is never more than an idealization (in the sense of philosophical idealism) of a given singularity.

Having put forth these criticisms, it is vital to point out that it is not a question here of rejecting what the scientific approach brings to society. Science builds diverse paradigms; from these, it develops complex explanatory systems based on empirical investigations. All of this is discussed in communities of peers who have been socialized in the same paradigms. The scientific approach thus appears as a regular attempt to question and renew an understanding of the world, that is, a point of view, by refusing to be satisfied with what has been more or less established previously.

The construction of a scientific approach therefore always refers to the experience of a society that encourages discussion, confronts disagreement and attempts to build knowledge. Epistemological work shows that this knowledge is always partial and provisional, and philosophy and sociology of science demonstrate that it is the product of human collectives that also reveal bias. This situation undermines the simple idea that conclusive evidence exists. It is the point of view that produces the data – another angle of approach will result in other data and will interpret them differently. There is less evidence than there are questions.

Unexpected action

There is yet another reason leading us to criticize evidence-based practice: a number of recent studies suggest that action consists in arbitrating between different logics that are incompatible (or only slightly compatible) and, consequently, in favoring, temporarily at least, one point of view over another. Indeed, in the face of the multiple challenges of a given action, there is no *one best way* as claimed by the labor sciences in the first half of the 20th century, but only several options, all of which have advantages and disadvantages, as Crozier and Friedberg (1977) had already shown. Following the debates initiated by these two authors, Jean-Daniel Reynaud (1988) argued that a prescription is always an attempt to control the action of the executors, and that professionals in the field develop their autonomy on the basis of principles of action that compete and challenge the terms of that prescription. It follows that the complex interplay of those involved produces a combination of elements that is always partly unpredictable and constantly reconstructs reality. 'Walker, there is no path; the path is invented by walking', according to the words of the poet Antonio Machado.

Such an approach implies breaking with the Platonic heritage and rediscovering the *métis*, a conception of knowledge that was delegitimized for two millennia. Gérard Mendel showed that classical Greek philosophers, first and foremost Plato, ranked knowledge in a hierarchy. For them, there was no possible science of the contingent (Mendel, 1998, p. 308). On the contrary, they valued the contemplative knowledge of accuracy in the face of the uncertain knowledge of the *métis* conceived of as the 'domain of the future, the multiple, the unstable, the unlimited, of biased, fluctuating opinion' (Détienne & Vernant, 1998, cited by Mendel, 1998, p. 306).

For Jean-Claude Ruano-Borbalan, this explains that

> the question of the legitimacy of knowledge is not only linked to its elaboration and validation procedures. It is also subject to reference to an implicit Western hierarchy that is rooted in the very long history of knowledge, going back to Neo-Platonism, which recognized a difference between noble knowledge, belonging to the 'sky of ideas' and others kinds, less noble, which relate to the transformation of matter, engineering, action, etc.
>
> (Ruano-Borbalan, 2014, p. 26)

For Mendel, it is

> the act itself as an entity that carries risk, as it represents a new and original state of reality, an original creation, a 'new reality' made not of the simple addition of the subject and reality, but of their interactivity, which will leave neither of the two components intact.
>
> (Mendel, 1998, p. 36)

The thought of the act is a 'thought of doing', what Mendel calls practical intelligence. Referring to Marcel Détienne and Jean-Pierre Vernant in *Les ruses de l'intelligence*, Mendel points out that the *métis* concerns 'a type of intelligence engaged in practice, confronted with obstacles that must be overcome by cunning to obtain success in the most diverse fields of action' (1998, p. 302). For these authors, 'the colorfulness, the sparkle of the *métis* mark its relationship with the multiple, divided, undulating world in which they are plunged to exercise their action' (1998, p. 304).

We can therefore legitimately express doubts about the ambition to build social work on the basis of evidence. Indeed, the ability of the sciences to prescribe action is increasingly challenged by the very dynamics of the construction of knowledge. This construction is always part of a point of view that makes it possible to elucidate certain aspects of problems but is also unable to perceive others. It is also due to the dynamics of action which is discovered as it is being built, *a fortiori* in the hybrid society where every act is presented as an un-anticipatable singularity.

The uncertainties of the hybrid society

How can we understand the un-anticipatable nature of individual acts in a hybrid society and, more specifically, in the sector of social work? The argument I am developing is that, in each situation, social workers construct their problem by compromising between the requirements of the different logics that coexist in institutions and by 'cobbling together' (Lévi-Strauss, 2008) a unique hybridization of these logics.

Conflicting logics of social work

In recent years, several authors have formulated the hypothesis that social workers operate in reference to plural logics of which they are the bearers.

In social psychology, work on descriptive and prescriptive social representations (Jodelet, 1989) testifies to this diversity of attempts to account for this phenomenon (Amblard, Bernoux, Herreros & Livian, 2005). The same can be said for the so-called dispositional paradigm – the renewal of habitus theories by Bernard Lahire (1998), for example – or for the concept of logics of action in new organizational sociologies.

Yves Bonny has no doubt made the most successful attempt to think of the coexistence of various logics of action in 'plural institutions' that result in 'divergent positions with regard to a given purpose and the target audience of the institution, whether concurrently or successively' (2012, p. 16). He proposes to consider these logics of action and their coexistence in two ways: 'either as a space of possibilities in which all institutional agents circulate to varying degrees, depending on the contexts, situations and interactive dynamics [...] or in terms of divergences, oppositions, conflicts and relationships of domination between categories of players involved' (Bonny, 2012, p. 16). For institutional players, these conflicting logics constitute a test, at the risk of 'fragmentation, disintegration, incoherence, overt contradiction and loss of legitimacy' (Bonny, 2012, p. 18). It is then a question of looking at 'the forms of compromise developed between contradictory orientations' as well as 'the way in which players actually do this in the course of actions and interactions in real situations in order to take charge of the constitutive plurality of the institution and deal with the tensions it generates' (Bonny, 2012, p. 19).

This theory, which covers all public institutions, is in line with that which Michel Autès (1999) proposes for social work, which he believes is both fraught with and built by paradoxes. For Autès, 'what dominates [...] is the situation made up of crossroads, hesitations, overlapping forms, new ways of sharing taking shape: a set of evolutions that does not exclude the return of forms already covered, but which are never totally absent from the scene of the present' (Autès, 1999, p. 280). Colette Bec shows how assistance 'constantly seeks to achieve a balance between divergent and even contradictory interests and demands' and is part of a form of 'constantly renewed compromise' (Bec, 1998, p. 189). While Robert Castel (1981) shows how a new psychological and relational culture has renewed the traditional coercive intervention of the State, Yvette Molina (2015) highlights new orientations promoted by major evaluation reports, commissioned by the supervisory authorities between 1990 and 2000 in the form of new intervention methods (in particular, a more collective and territorial approach).

Transposed to social work, this theory is backed up by several studies that show that this professional sector has been gradually oriented by the juxtaposition of differentiated logics that have emerged over time. These have generated paradoxes (Autès, 1999) whose origin lies in diverse but converging phenomena: the accumulation of diverse institutions and professions (Molina, 2015), and more recently of mechanisms (Ion & Ravon, 2005) and partnerships that are uncertain, and the progressive sedimentation of plural references and orientations, either by the arrival of new players carrying exogenous logic or by the importation of new references in this sector of action. An example of this is the implementation of the New Public Management apparatus (Bellot, Bresson & Jeté, 2013).

Acting implies hesitating and compromising

In the field of social work, as in any other sector, the players therefore find themselves confronted with multiple, sometimes incompatible, points of reference. Not all identifiable logics of action are supported uniformly by all players, as this situation is one of the elements that will make it possible to differentiate the players in a given area of action. But each participant acts with reference to heterogeneous orientations, referring alternately to one or the other or producing intersubjective deliberations to combine these requirements and compromise between competing points of reference.

Belgian sociologist Jean Remy (1998) calls this process a social transaction. This concept, born from a new reading of Georg Simmel's work and the implicit methodology he applies, aims to reflect the fact that social workers, when they act, are led to compromise between different options and thus build a provisional social world situated between conflict and cooperation. Maurice Blanc, in the conclusion of *Les transactions aux frontières du social*, explains that 'one of Simmel's essential contributions is to consider social life as being crossed and structured by pairs of opposing forces [...], pairs of tensions that keep it moving and whose combination is fundamentally unpredictable' (Blanc, 1998, pp. 221–223). Jean Remy speaks of 'the tensions between unavoidable but partially incompatible requirements' (1998, p. 21). As a result, 'the mode of coexistence between these tensions is unstable [...]; social agents are in situations whose structure is open to several reactions' (Rémy, 1998, p. 21).

Jean Remy illustrates this theorization with the example of security contracts in Belgium:

> [This system requires us to] confront two partially opposing necessities: the need to curb the process of social exclusion and to address the feeling of insecurity [...]. The two logics – exclusion and insecurity – have

a different origin and imply partly divergent modes of intervention. One of the two may be a priority. When exclusion prevails, social workers tend to promote an assessment based on the categories of fair and unfair. This assessment is somewhat falsified if security prevails and pacification becomes of so-called 'general' interest. The social usefulness resulting from the defense of a collective good such as security can suffer some injustices. Thus, begging can be eliminated in certain places of frequent passage without taking into account the effects on the persons concerned. Collective protection may even go so far as desiring to live in socially controlled spaces even if it results in a rejection of other social categories. The two objectives, justice concerning the individual person and collective protection, only partially overlap. They are based on two different definitions of the victim. The power relationship will be expressed in daily life through the priority given to one or the other. [...] The paths that will be invented are many.

(Rémy, 1998, pp. 22–26)

*

However one approaches it, social work is always characterized by plurality and heterogeneity. This makes this field a highly complex space. This complexity lies, among other things, in the fact that recently emerging logics do not erase previous ones. These older logics continue to be supported by some, including professional social workers or training centers, which sometimes partly resist recent developments while implementing them in their own way. As part of their professional socialization, social workers encounter the different logics and support them to a greater or lesser degree. Also, the different forms of logic follow one another, coexist, accumulate or overlap and create a multi-referenced space of action that generates a certain unease:

> Social intervention professionals [...] sometimes experience severe tensions related to their position as intermediaries of social issues. The theme of uneasiness is prevalent in these professional worlds, as well as the observation that their role has become more complex and vaguer, depending on the heterogeneous expectations and needs of the people with whom they work (such as clients, beneficiaries, users, taxpayers, patients, pupils, claimants and litigants), reformist redefinitions of the aims and modalities of their missions, 'new paradigms' (including networking, risk management, contracting, evaluation and good governance practices) in vogue at the crossroads of social intervention.

(Van Campenhoudt, Fransen & Cantelli, 2009, p. 48)

Claude De Jonckheere thus speaks of social intervention as a 'tufted object', in the manner of Bruno Latour:

> It is tufted because of its undefinable form and because it is a compound of diverse and multiple elements, such as concepts, beliefs, values, experiences, norms and diverse prescriptions. [...] Therefore, to be interested in the intervention is to be interested in the social forces that affect it. We cannot take intervention as an object of knowledge without describing all the recommendations and the ideas that surround it, but also the interstices creating cracks in this apparent monolith, the effect being that social issues do not only determine the intervention, but leave indeterminate spaces in which unexpected actions can interfere.
>
> (De Jonckheere, 2013, pp. 35–36)

For sociologist Jean Foucart, such a situation requires not solid and obvious knowledge but, rather, fuzzy thinking:

> Fuzzy thinking is a complex thought adapted to the loss of the idea of society. The current system is a fluid system, one in which the unexpected and the unpredictable appear to predominate. It appears to be the most appropriate or least bad method to act on a reality that has become more changing and unpredictable than ever, where nothing can be settled in advance or even definitively. In other words, uncertainty of not only future but also present time is the key word for the use of fuzzy thinking.
>
> (Foucart, 2011, p. 13)

Conclusion

The analyses developed in this chapter have spread beyond the field of scientific research and have been taken up by many social workers. As Michel Callon, Pierre Lascoume and Yannick Barthes have already shown, such an evolution results in border shifts and competition for expertise. It characterizes what Rémi Barré calls a transformation of the previous science–society contract:

> Each historical period is characterized by a relatively stable arrangement that combines the nature and modes of functioning of the research and innovation system on the one hand and the political and social order

[…] on the other. This 'contract' consists of commitments and expectations, explicit or otherwise, between the players in both spheres.

(Barré, 2017, p. 46)

On this point, we are experiencing a transition from the post-war science–society contract to a new, emerging contract. The first was characterized by 'a linear conception of innovation, where science remains neutral, rises above all values and precedes any innovation' (p. 47). The so-called deficit model assumes that any critical questioning by ordinary people reflects their lack of knowledge and irrationality.

Rémi Barré agrees with Michel Callon, Pierre Lascoumes and Yannick Barthes, who argue that scientific knowledge is limited and that research is a matter of political choice. He speaks of technical democracy, affirming that 'the emergence of solutions that are both technically better and socially more robust will come from a systematic confrontation of the options put forward by different players, with diverse experiences, knowledge and representations' (p. 49). However, Barré notes that the emergence of a technical democracy and of complex and conflicting social and political dynamics in the field of research and innovation is a difficult one.

The development of evidence-based practice is an indication of the transition Barré is referring to. I prefer to think of this as a hybrid situation wherein an expert model and a democratic model of knowledge building coexist. The conclusive evidence model is at one end of the spectrum. The practices of connecting a scientific approach with the construction of the reflective practice of a professional group are at the other end.

The research practice I have developed, collaborating with some and debating with others, consists both in building an understanding of some methodologically constructed 'traces' of the problems (Dewey, 2010) faced by players and in organizing opportunities for the discussion (Habermas, 1992) of interpretations of researchers and other professionals who ultimately become co-researchers. In its own way, it is part of so-called intervention research (Marcel, 2016) in the sense that the professional researcher 'comes between' (Monceau, 2016) occasional researchers. It has an undeniable clinical dimension in the sense that professional researchers engage in a working relationship with the people involved in order to understand what is at stake in the singular nature of intersubjectivities.

What this type of practice loses in terms of standardization of methods and reference to theoretical disciplinary systems, it certainly gains in other ways. It destabilizes the 'totality' of co-researchers and discovers the 'infinity' (Levinas, 1990) of strangeness from the point of view of their partners.

It accompanies an action in progress that reveals unexpected events that no amount of evidence, as conclusive as it may be, can anticipate entirely.

References

Amblard, H., Bernoux, P., Herreros, G., & Livian Y-F. (2005). *Les nouvelles approches sociologiques des organisations*. Paris: Seuil.

Autès, M. (1999). *Les Paradoxes du travail social*. Paris: Dunod.

Barré, R. (2015). Le contrat science-société: dynamiques politiques et sociales d'une refondation. Le cas de l'expertise scientifique. In Lesourne, J. (Ed.), *La recherche et l'innovation en France: FutuRIS 2014–2015* (pp. 287–322). Paris: Odile Jacob.

Barré, R. (2017). Pour une mise en politique de la recherche participative. Quelques propositions programmatiques. In Tremblaye, D-G. & Gillet, A. (Eds.), *Les recherches partenariales et collaboratives* (pp. 45–60). Rennes/Montréal: PUR/PUQ.

Bec, C. (1998). *L'Assistance en démocratie*. Paris: Belin.

Béguin, P., & Cerf, M. (2009). Introduction. In Béguin, P. & Cerf, M. (Eds.), *Dynamique des savoirs, dynamique des changements*. Toulouse: Octares.

Bellot, C., Bresson, M., & Jetté, C. (Eds.) (2013). *Le travail social et la nouvelle gestion publique*. Quebec: Presses Universitaires du Québec.

Blanc, M. (1998). La transaction, un processus de production et d'apprentissage du 'vivre ensemble'. In Freynet, M-F., Blanc, M., & Pineau, G. (Eds.), *Les transactions aux frontières du social*. Lyon: Chronique sociale.

Bonny, Y. (2012). Les institutions publiques au prisme de la pluralité. In Bonny, Y. & Demailly, L. (Eds.), *L'institution plurielle*. Villeneuve d'Ascq: Presses Universitaires du Septentrion.

Callon, M., Lascoumes, P., & Barthe, Y. (2001). *Agir dans un monde incertain. Essai sur la démocratie technique*. Paris: Seuil.

Castel, R. (1981). *La gestion des risques, De l'antipsychiatrie à l'après-psychanalyse*. Paris: Editions de Minuit.

Crozier, M., & Friedberg, E. (1977). *L'acteur et le système*. Paris: Seuil.

Darré, J-P. (1999). *La production de connaissances pour l'action. Arguments contre le racisme de l'intelligence*. Paris: Maison des Sciences de l'Homme.

De Jonckheere, C. (2013). Constitution du travail social en tant que discipline. Problèmes épistémologiques et politiques. In Affuts (Eds.), *Quels modèles de recherche scientifique en travail social?* Rennes: Presses de l'EHESP.

Dewey, J. (2010). *Le public et ses problèmes*. Paris: Gallimard.

Foucart, J. (2011). Réseaux fluides et pratiques sociales: vers un nouveau paradigme. Une méthodologie floue: la recherche participative. *Pensée plurielle*, *3*(28), 11–23.

Habermas, J. (1992). *De l'éthique de la discussion*. Paris: Flammarion.

Ion, J., & Ravon, B. (2005). Institutions et dispositifs. In Ion, J. (Ed.), *Le travail social en débat(s)*. Paris: La découverte.

Jodelet, D. (1989). Représentations sociales, un domaine en expansion. In Jodelet, D. (Ed.), *Les représentations sociales*. Paris: PUF.

Lahire, B. (1998). *L'Homme pluriel. Les ressorts de l'action*. Paris: Nathan.

Le Moigne, J-L. (2012). *Les épistémologies constructivistes*. Que sais-je? Paris: PUF.

Levinas, E. (1990). *Totalité et infini*. Paris: Le Livre de Poche.

Lévi-Strauss, C. (2008). La pensée sauvage. In *Œuvres*. Paris: La Pléiade.

Lyet, P. (2017). *Recherches conjointes multiréférentielles et hybridation dans le secteur du travail éducatif et social. Contribution à la 'reconstruction' épistémologique et méthodologique en sciences humaines et sociales*. French accreditation to supervise research (HDR), educational sciences, Université de Cergy-Pontoise.

Marcel, J-F. (Ed.). (2016). *La recherche-intervention par les sciences de l'éducation*. Dijon: Educagri éditions.

Mendel, G. (1998). *L'acte est une aventure, du sujet métaphysique au sujet de l'acte pouvoir*. Paris: La Découverte.

Molina, Y. (2015). Les travailleurs sociaux des groupes professionnels en transformation. Thesis in sociology, Ecole des Hautes Etudes en Sciences Sociales (EHESS), thesis director Grelon A. www.cmh.ens.fr/Yvette-Molina.

Monceau, G. (2016). Transformations sociales et recherche-intervention. In Marcel, J.-F. (Ed.), *La recherche-intervention par les sciences de l'éducation*. Dijon: Educagri éditions.

Morin, E. (2005). *Introduction à la pensée complexe*. Paris: Seuil.

Pestre, D. (2013). *A contre-science. Politiques et savoirs des sociétés contemporaines*. Paris: Seuil.

Remy, J. (1998). La transaction sociale: forme de sociabilité et posture méthodologique. In Freynet, M-F., Blanc, M., & Pineau, G. (Eds.), *Les transactions aux frontières du social*. Lyon: Chronique sociale.

Reynaud, J-D. (1988). Régulation de contrôle et régulation autonome dans les organisations. *Revue Française de sociologie*, *XXIX*(1), 5–18.

Ruano-Borbalan, J-C. (2014). Les voies de la construction des savoirs légitimes. In Jaeger, M. (Ed.), *Conférence de consensus. Le travail social et la recherche*. Paris: Dunod.

Van Campenhoudt, L., Franssen, A., & Cantelli, F. (2009). La méthode d'analyse en groupe. *SociologieS* [online], Théories et recherches. http://sociologies.revues.org.

Social work as the test of public management

2

Vincent de Gaulejac

Introduction

The introduction of managerial ideology into the management of social institutions raises a number of questions. New Public Management (NPM)[1] produces intense psychological pressure on social workers. Many sociologists, particularly among clinicians, have analyzed this phenomenon, which developed first in private companies and then in the public sector, and which now appears in the non-market sector such as hospitals, administrations, local authorities and educational or social institutions. In this context, the issue of mental health in the workplace is becoming a major issue. The relentless complaints about suffering, the increase in depressive symptoms, the generalized feeling of harassment, hyperactivity, burnout and the upsurge of suicides in the workplace are all signs of a deep sense of malaise. The causes of this phenomenon are multiple. In this chapter, we wish to focus on the processes that transform social services into paradox-generating organizations.[2] We have analyzed the emergence of the managerial revolution in multinational companies since the 1970s, at IBM in *L'emprise de l'organisation*, and elsewhere in *Le coût de l'excellence*. This 'revolution' was then exported to the management of

DOI: 10.4324/9781003296416-4

public institutions and states under the pretext of modernization. It serves as a model for NPM, which now manages all areas of social action.

The massive and hasty introduction of the paradigms and principles of NPM confronts social workers with a management system that, under the guise of efficiency and accountability, forces them to make paradoxical demands constantly. A clinical situation addressed in the context of a research group illustrates the processes that lead to the implementation of a paradox-generating organization and the consequences for the agents, some of whom then develop defensive reactions, whereas others seek individual and collective working-off mechanisms.

Paradox as a system of control

Psychologists at the Palo Alto school, following the work of Bateson (1977), have shown how a paradoxical communication system contributes to 'losing one's mind' (Wazlawick, Helmick-Beavin & Jackson, 1972). The double bind consists in setting up a process of subordination/domination based on paradoxical injunctions. One often cited example concerns the relationship between a mother and her child. The mother gives her son a green tie and a red tie for his birthday. The boy, who is very happy to receive a gift and very proud that his mother is happy to see him growing up, goes to his room, puts on the green tie and goes back to see his mother. 'Why are you wearing the green one? Don't you like the red one?' she says to him. The boy is a bit confused and goes back to his room. He puts on the red one and goes back to show his mother. 'Why are you wearing the red one? Don't you like the green one?' The child is no longer sure what to do. He goes back to his room and puts on both ties, one on top of the other. His mother looks at him with a sorry look and says, 'You're going to drive me crazy'. So whatever he does, the child is caught in the wrong. 'The double bind generates unsolvable sequences of actual experiences' (Wilden, 1983). The mother draws him into a ridiculous situation and then blames *him* for it. The child is trapped in a communication system in which he is bound to be inadequate, unsatisfactory and powerless; on top of it all, *he* is held responsible for this state of affairs. A mechanism of control is at work here. The double objective and emotional dependence in which the child finds himself is maintained and reinforced by a psychological dependence. Such a system locks individuals into a state of permanent submission. In companies and public institutions, the dependence is of a different kind. It is linked to the subordination introduced by the contract of employment, but also to psychological mobilization, in particular for agents who commit themselves and adhere to the values of public service.

The situation of double bind arises when several people are engaged in an intense relationship of great psychological or material value to them in such a way that they cannot or do not desire to free themselves from it. It is character-ized by a communication system in which messages are issued in the form of contradictory injunctions to which a third constraint is added that makes any escape impossible. Forced to respond to two perfectly incompatible requests (since one must disobey in order to obey), the subject is defeated while bear-ing the responsibility for his inability to respond satisfactorily to the requests made of him. He then finds himself in a hopeless, untenable situation, unable to choose between mandatory, antagonistic requirements. Whatever he does, he can be caught out, and this destroys from the inside any possibility to react and to escape from the control of his hierarchy.

Dependencies of this kind are at work in many organizations. It is not only a question of using psychological leverage within an affective relationship, but also an organizational system of control that uses paradox as a management tool, leading all agents to accept, collectively, operating procedures that they individually disapprove of. Basing our discussion on a situation experienced in an institution in charge of the reintegration of people in need, we will deci-pher the implementation of a paradox-generating system.

A situation of organizational paradox

The scene takes place in a social service responsible for helping people in sit-uations of exclusion.[3] Three people are gathered around a table. The depart-ment head has summoned Chantal and Jacqueline, who have just completed a training course in computing. Chantal is not worried. Not only did she appre-ciate the training, but she would also like to pursue it further. She wants to enroll for a second module to improve her skills. Jacqueline has more difficul-ties: 'It's hard for me', she says. 'I have trouble understanding what the point is. I'll be retiring in two years. As a telephone receptionist, I don't really see what all of this is for'. The department head's response is uncompromising. 'I'm surprised at your attitude', she says. 'I thought you had the skills to fol-low this course. You must learn how to use a computer and stay up to date. The telephone is an outdated tool; you now have to master email and the Internet. Everyone in the department must adapt to change. You must remain employable!'

Faced with the resistance (her 'unwillingness to ...') on the part of Jacqueline who 'won't even make an effort', the department head goes to see the director of the institution. The director is no less relentless. Jacqueline must fall into line. Making an exception is out of the question – it would not be fair to the others. Employees are paid by the State; it would not be fair to taxpayers if these employees did not produce rational, efficient, high-quality service. 'We all have to work the same way. We are being asked to cut costs. It is my policy to be fair to everyone.' Faced with such insistence, Jacqueline replies timidly 'I'll try'. This leads to the director's scathing answer: 'I'm not asking you to try but to succeed', then adding 'You were unemployed when you were hired, you were given a chance. Don't waste it'.

Jacqueline has been working in the department as a telephone receptionist for six years. Her evaluations are good. She is appreciated by everyone. Her only fault is having trouble with computers. Despite training and the help of her colleagues, 'it's just too hard'. It does not help that, as a receptionist, she does not see the point of this new tool. The management registers her for a second training course. The day before the course, she calls to inform her supervisor that she is ill. Two months later she will be put on long-term sick leave and wait for retirement.

Jacqueline's director believes that he has given Jacqueline a chance. He no longer feels obliged to keep her since she does not adapt to the NPM model. 'This is not a C.A.T.', [4] he concludes. Jacqueline feels harassed. She does not understand the management's determination to train her for something that makes no sense to her. She has been doing her job very well and has never received a negative comment. She does not understand why she should have to use a computer when it is so easy to answer the phone and see people directly when you have something to say to them. The department head notices that Jacqueline is in a state of depression, that she can no longer sleep at night. She knows that, with two years to go before retirement, she only has one way out – taking sick leave, which is not particularly difficult since she is indeed depressed.

A loop of sorts has henceforth been established. It combines two processes, one social, the other psychological. On the one hand is an 'objective' exclusion process that leads the institution to dismiss an employee seen as unfit for modernization. On the other hand is a process of 'subjective' invalidation which leads to the employee herself being held responsible for this exclusion, as she does not want to seize the opportunity to evolve. She has shown herself to be 'unwilling' to take training courses to facilitate her progression. She is resistant to management-defined guidelines to 'improve the services provided to users'. Her own difficulties and incompetence are a burden to her colleagues. She does not master the new communication tools considered essential to 'the smooth running of the service'. Her psychological fragility and repeated absences disrupt the distribution of tasks, forcing other employees to replace her. Modernization is necessary to improve the quality of service and to respond to a request from the board of administration to ensure that the grants received by the institution are used properly. It would therefore be inappropriate for the collective effort not to be shared by all. Jacqueline must not become a burden to others. It is the responsibility of each person to meet the equitable objectives defined by management.

The 'human' factor has struck again

Jacqueline is clearly unsuited to the changes in our world. Change is natural, it is a factor of progress, it is necessary. Questioning is the expression of a 'resistance to change', which modernizing managers explain is the fate of all those who are resistant to progress. In other words, it is Jacqueline's behavior that is the problem. *She* is responsible for the problems in the department. Such an explanation avoids questioning these developments and the management methods that go along with them.

Two elements surfaced during the discussion that followed the research role-play workshop, called an 'organidrama'. No one dared to question the guiding 'line', as if everyone felt powerless to discuss the merits of NPM, a symbol of progress and modernization. Yet many of the participants felt confronted with situations similar to Jacqueline's. It is as though they subjectively identified with Jacqueline and her situation while at the same time resigning themselves to the objective conditions that had brought the situation about – as though the capacities of collective resistance had become blunted. At the individual level, people protect themselves by either adapting or marginalizing themselves. When people put themselves on the sidelines, it becomes difficult for them to denounce the institutional violence that has led them to make this choice in the first place. Indeed, they are doubly stigmatized: first, for not being able to adapt to change; second, for not being able, or not knowing how, to resist exclusion.

The exclusion of the 'weakest link' is experienced as the inevitable consequence of an inescapable evolution. The group then analyses the paradox that consists, for a social institution, in generating the kind of exclusion that it is supposed to combat. In the end, Jacqueline's status will change from employee *at* a social service to user *of* a social service. If she were not two years from retirement, she would probably be offered training to change professional direction or would resign herself to having become unemployable. When Jacqueline falls ill, she 'escapes' all this. She will not become dependent on social assistance because she will now be assigned to the medical field of health. The human cost is likely to be disastrous. The economic cost to the community is also very high – probably higher than the salary she was paid when she was feeling well. For the institution, the symbolic cost is minimized by management, who see it as only a minor consequence of an indisputable, undeniable logic of adaptation. Yet this symbolic cost is high for Jacqueline's colleagues, who are more or less complicit in this 'innocent' violence. How can they continue to give meaning to the social work that the institution asks them to accomplish when they see that the institution's management style results in the exclusion of its most vulnerable members? No one will speak of the damage caused by Jacqueline's eviction. Guilt and shame accompany the fear that the same threat can affect any one of them. After all, Jacqueline was doing her job well. She was appreciated by the hierarchy and well-liked by her colleagues.

Producing exclusion to improve productivity

This story illustrates the processes at play in the current changes in the professional sphere. In the private sector, these processes seem linked, naturally enough, to the logic of profit. The pressure of financial profitability has never been so strong as today, and this has led to an increased demand for productivity. However, this context does not prevent workers from working in the company, sometimes even with pleasure as long as they understand and accept the rules of the game. When profitability is considered a basic given necessary for the survival of the company, it is not surprising to expect improvement in productivity, adaptation to the company's requirements and flexibility to meet the demands of a constantly changing market. Whatever one's 'political' opinions towards capitalism, whether one agrees with or criticizes this system, the rules of the game are clear. It is about producing, often at the lowest cost possible, a perfectly identified good or service. Productivity is measured by 'improving' rates of production or increasing the quality of the service provided. Workers in this context know perfectly well when they are doing 'good work', and they also know how to resist constraints and negotiate with the powers that be when said powers are too demanding or ill-intentioned.

In the example above, this sense of purpose is jeopardized. This is a 'social service', whose mission is to promote the reintegration of people experiencing difficulty. Insofar as it puts its own agents into a process of social disintegration, there is a major contradiction between the aims of the organization and the means used to implement them. We have shown in *La lutte des places* that exclusion is caused mainly by a combination of economic, social and symbolic processes that mutually support each other, leading individuals into a spiral of deteriorating family and social ties (Gaulejac, Blondel & Taboada-Leonetti, 2016). It is paradoxical, to say the least, that institutions responsible for accompanying these people, for combating 'disaffiliation' (Castel, 2014, create exclusion themselves. How can such a paradox come to be without provoking radical opposition from people who, most often, have chosen to be social workers because they do not accept the idea that part of the population is being left behind by social 'progress'?

The new managerial newspeak trivializes and legitimizes seemingly irresistible functional logics. 'We have to make this work', says the director, bound by the requirements of his hierarchy, who are expecting results. Functionality imposes its law on other considerations, be they social or existential, to the point of challenging institutional purposes. In the end, organization takes precedence over the institution. The operative is no longer a means of action but its purpose. Instrumental rationality is king. The agent exists in order to *make it work*. The 'it' here refers not to the Freudian conception of the unconscious but to an organizational requirement – an illustration of the ideology of human resources which considers the human being as a means of organizational development when the organization should be at the service of its institutional missions, in this case promoting social inclusion.

Managerial ideology considers the individual a resource rather than a subject. The individual is thus instrumentalized in the service of financial, operational and technical objectives that result in his losing sight of the meaning of his acts, or even the meaning of his existence. Within this person, a split then develops between *the resource-individual*, who agrees to submit to the requirements of his employer and the *subject-individual*, who resists instrumentalization. In the face of changing management practices, resignation and adaptation are subjectively easier to accept insofar as they enable one to avoid a permanent struggle against the system and promote a minimum of recognition in a job that ensures one's livelihood.

Resistance to the subject, resistance of the subject

Jacqueline, however, has decided to resist. Unlike her colleague Chantal, she is really not interested in praise for being a dynamic, motivated, adaptable employee. She does not want to pretend and does not want to give more than her daily tasks require of her. She feels she is doing her job properly. To her mind, it is not the company's place to demand an additional psychological and mental investment. To be a *subject* is to resist what does not make sense to you. To be a *subject* is to exist without complying with injunctions, training and transfers that are imposed without one's seeing a logical reason behind them. Both for her and for her colleagues, the rationality put forward by management is perfectly illogical. Jacqueline might have been able to accept her superiors' request had there been no obvious gap between the instruction given to her (pursuing training in computer skills) and her daily activity (answering the phone, promoting communication between the inside and the outside and establishing good professional relationships). The instruction to follow a course is built on an abstract vision of change ('it is necessary to modernize') whereas meaning is built on a concrete experience of the activity. Functional logic is no longer operative when it stems from an idealized conception of orders that are no longer based on actual work. Ordinarily, the requirement of operationality is perfectly understandable by any agent, but it is no longer acceptable when it is perceived as irrational.

In paradox-generating organizations, managerial discourse based on objectivist, functional and utilitarian paradigms leads to a kind of 'managerial newspeak' that makes senseless, dysfunctional, useless demands (Vandevelde-Rougale, 2017). And yet these demands are supported by the management, the executives and even certain agents in the name of modernity, progress and technical rationality. Such support is based on a dominant representation that progress has a cost, that resistance to change is a 'natural' reflex that must be overcome. Jacqueline can be seen here as representing the archetype of the past, of the refusal to adapt, of the forms of resistance that must be broken because they hinder necessary innovations. The question is no longer whether a given change is appropriate or timely, but how to remove those who prevent it from being implemented. The problem is not whether mastery of the computer is essential to perform the task. It is Jacqueline's resistance that becomes problematic, her obvious unwillingness, especially since everyone around her has done their utmost to support her in the face of change.

In short, the 'real' problem for the institution's managers stems from Jacqueline's claim to be a subject at work who, in order to exist, needs to give meaning to what she is asked to do. 'You have to follow suit,' demands the boss. Power imposes norms, instructions and various forms of discipline to make bodies productive and minds docile (Foucault, 1975). If the subject resists, he must be eliminated. In order to exist and survive, Jacqueline will ultimately fall ill. Caught in the contradiction of submitting or resigning, adapting or being excluded, being recognized as an agent or being cancelled as a subject, it is in illness that she finds a way out. This allows her to attend to her depression, a consequence of the pressure she has been suffering from for several months, and to acquire an intermediate social status between that of an employee and that of a pensioner (Carreteiro, 1993). She can thus continue to exist as a subject, objectively and subjectively.

Objectively, she has a status that allows her to preserve the 'supports' needed to have a social existence (rights, income, an institutional place and social recognition). She can thus avoid the risk of being pigeonholed as a person whose identity is defined negatively (that is, without employment, income, status or professional activity). She can thereby escape the spiral of social disintegration. Subjectively, she develops a symptom, depression, which – paradoxically – gives her a sense of relief: she can escape from the pressure to follow a course, the inability to adapt, the guilt for not doing so and the shame of her incompetence. Having so forcefully been told that the problem comes from her, she will accept the accusation through depression: 'Something's the matter with *me*'. By internalizing the negative image of herself she is confronted with, she gives herself the means to get out of the tension created by having to conform to a normative ideal that she cannot and will not satisfy (Dujarier, 2006). In this way, she avoids the double process of instrumentalization (with respect to the organization) and stigmatization (with respect to her colleagues).

We can interpret Jacqueline's illness as a defeat on the part of the subject, who identifies with the aggressor by adopting the attacks against her. Depression corresponds to a feeling of depreciation of the Self in the face of the demands of its ideal: the interiorization of the feeling of being worthless, incompetent, incapable. But taking sick leave is also a way out of this paradox. By accepting that something is the matter with *her*, that the problem lies within her, Jacqueline gives herself the means to solve it: all she has to do is take care of herself. She takes responsibility for herself and escapes from a paradoxical system experienced as destructive. She comes out of it alive. What we observe here is a resistance on the part of the subject: she regains control by accepting her existence. The alternative is cruel. To exist in the company, she must agree to submit to requirements that the moral conscience disapproves of. To exist as a subject, she runs the risk of being excluded.

So, is this fiction or reality? Jacqueline's story is the expression of a 'social imaginary' (Castoriadis, 1975) in which managerial discourse legitimizes a form of domination based on paradox. Institutions produce the very exclusion they are supposed to fight against. This reversal of values is invisible, the violence it induces is 'innocent', those who implement it are perfectly legitimate and those who are subjected to it end up feeling guilty.

Everyone tries to 'do their job' in a context where some are prevented from doing it as they see fit, others are excluded when they thought they were working well and yet others seek to 'modernize' their approach, thinking they are improving things. In this implicit system, everyone does their best, but the best for some leads others – some of them, at least – to elimination. It is not easy to identify exactly who is responsible for the harm done. No one person is really to blame; rather, everyone contributes to producing this system. Although the causes may be abstract, the effects are tangible. This explains the widespread feeling of harassment, the difficulty in targeting the causes of the malaise experienced, the impression of powerlessness in the face of this process: a dull, diffuse, vague violence, the perpetrators of which are impossible to identify because each of them more or less realizes that he is participating in it while defending himself against it. This permanent reversal of the causes, which the people themselves bear upon their shoulders, is one of the reasons why it is difficult to fight against this type of violence. Everyone feels inhibited and unable to react, and this in turn reinforces guilt, internalization and powerlessness. Without understanding the systemic and organizational causes of the process, the employee may very well think 'The problem here is *me*'.

Ways out

How can we extricate ourselves from these entangled paradoxes? The supporters of the Palo Alto School have shown that the way out of a paradoxical communication system is through metacommunication. By communicating about the system, by dismantling its mechanisms and by analyzing why it is paradoxical, the subject can escape from it. In the example of the red tie and the green tie cited in the introduction, it is vital that the child be able to tell his mother that he is not trying to drive her mad, but rather that he does not know how to respond to her requests because she constantly puts him before an unresolvable situation. In most cases, the child is not able to carry out this analysis, except as part of therapy. In an organization, the processes at work are similar, but the context is different. It is the organization itself that is paradoxical. It is therefore not enough to disassemble the logics of communication. It is necessary to analyze how paradoxical systems are set up and how individuals contribute to implementing and reproducing them if we are to facilitate individual and collective working-off processes and to unpack their inner workings, first intellectually and then in practice.

This system of control circles in on itself to such an extent that the defensive reactions we put into place to protect ourselves against it actually help to reinforce it. It is a system that could easily make one feel paranoid. The feeling of persecution comes from the constant to-and-froing between these organizational logics and the psychological processes that we mobilize to deal with them. This is indeed one of the characteristics of a paradoxical system: it is made up of mutually incompatible injunctions which one absolutely must obey without there ever being a way to reconcile them. Nevertheless, the violence brought about by the system and the risk of mental health issues force us to find a way out and lead us to fiercely resist the system lest we fall into depression.

A distinction must be made here between defensive reactions and working-off mechanisms. Defensive reactions refer to the conscious and unconscious mechanisms implemented by the subject to cope with violence and live with the paradoxical system. These include, for example, denial, withdrawal into oneself, identification with the aggressor and passive acceptance of instrumentalization. The most common involves a kind of split. The subject apparently agrees to respond to the organization's injunctions to fit into the mold and to adhere to the system. Part of the subject is ready to identify with the system; another part, hidden, resists and refuses to be caught. The subject then experiences a split between two parts of his personality. In extreme cases, the break can lead to a genuine case of split personality. The feeling of schizophrenia commonly evoked in paradoxical organizations expresses this inner tension between two components of the psyche, one that puts itself at the service of the system, the other that resists it; one that allows itself to be instrumentalized, the other that tries to preserve the psychological integrity of the subject. These processes are largely unconscious. It must be understood that active and conscious resistance has a very high psychological cost, that it mobilizes energy at all times and that is particularly difficult in a context where the pressure to produce is high. The essential characteristic of defensive reactions is that they facilitate living both with and within the organization to the point of feeding into its paradoxical components while at the same time promoting the desire to escape them. These mechanisms of control and voluntary servitude via which the subject seems to participate in his own subjection have often been analyzed, starting with La Boétie (Enriquez, 2007).

Working-off mechanisms refer to the processes by which the subject moves away from the paradoxical system, either by escaping, by transforming it from within or by seeking to destroy it. In Jacqueline's case, the dominant one is the escape route. She will not enter into a process that she feels will put her at odds with herself. She cannot identify with the requirements of modernization which she feels are not designed to improve her fate and whose rational nature she contests. Once she realizes that the hierarchy will not change their positions, she allows herself to 'fall ill' so that she can get out of the system. A defensive reaction and a working-off mechanism are intertwined in her behavior. The pressure on her contributes to her actually getting sick and, at the same time, she takes the lead in escaping depression. She moves into a state of transitional illness while she awaits her retirement. Some find it easier than others to implement escape strategies based on objective conditions that make it possible to leave without giving up their income, their material and social security and on the subjective conditions that allow them to leave in good health or at the very least to experience their departure less in terms of failure than in terms of liberation.

The most difficult question concerns the possibilities of transforming paradoxical systems from within. This is the challenge facing researchers, social workers, labor unions, human resources departments and, above all, those actually caught in such paradoxical systems. These systems jeopardize both the mental health of those involved and social cohesion. Concerned exclusively with the struggle for positions, people forget the collective interest and the importance of the investment needed to build a shared, common world.

Therein lies the need to build collective spaces for reflection and action in order to move to the level of metacommunication – that is, communicating about the system – and to take apart its paradoxical effects. Reflection here can turn into the power to act (Roche, 2016). Understanding organizational contradictions and the conflicts they generate helps to free oneself from a context that renders some powerless and others ill, provided that this analysis can be adopted by those struggling with these paradoxes. It is therefore necessary to multiply these forums of analysis within organizations themselves. Monitoring groups, analysis groups and regulation groups can promote this collective vision, as long as those who lead them promote the transition from the exploration of experienced conflicts to the analysis of paradoxes. Such groups must be given the theoretical and methodological tools so that they might better understand the links between actual experience and the institutional level. This is a prodigious project for psychosociologists and clinical sociologists alike.

Conclusion

The management methods introduced today in the world of social work lead to the production of paradoxical injunctions that create a system. Taking the perspective of clinical sociology (Gaulejac, Hanique & Roche, 2008), we took as our point of departure a situation close to the experiences of those involved and presented a case that illustrates the gradual transformation of an organization under the pressure of managerial logic aimed at improving productivity. These pressures lead management and supervisors to actually produce exclusion in spite of the fact that its purpose, as an institution, is precisely to combat exclusion. From the moment the individual is considered a resource at the service of the organization, his ability to become a subject is neutralized. The managerial system, dominated by an instrumental rationality, objectivizes the individual, reduces thought to criteria of scientific proof and submits behavior to utilitarian concerns. How can we resist this destructive ideology? Some learn to live with it, others try to invent ways to move away from these paradoxical systems, still others attempt to escape, hoping to find spaces that escape managerial ideology and the cult of high performance.

As researchers and as professionals, we must reflect upon the conditions under which working-off mechanisms are possible. You cannot heal an organization, even one that makes those who work there ill. We may not be able to help these people to escape from it, but at the very least we can intervene with respect to what makes them ill. The clinical approach makes it possible to build collective reflective spaces for all those who no longer know what direction to take. This, for example, is what is proposed in the monitoring and research groups that we lead on different themes such as 'The subject's relation to work', 'Violence of success, violence of failure', 'Envy and struggle for positions' and 'The subject's response to conflict'.

To escape these paradoxes, a significant number of our contemporaries have decided to step outside the traditional framework. They join the cohort of 'dark heroes of historicity', of all those for whom forging links is better than 'good' practice, of all those who invent in the ordinary aspects of daily life other ways of existing together, of all those who refuse to sacrifice their lives to the illusions of high-performance culture.

Notes

1   Within the context of this chapter, we do not have the space to discuss the characteristics of this new 'governance'. The reader is referred to De Gaulejac, 2009, 2015; Perrot & DuPasquier, 2005; Chauvière, 2007.
2   This notion is presented in De Gaulejac & Hanique, 2018.
3   The example comes from an involvement and research group on the theme 'work on the subject, the subject at work'. The group consisted of 15 people: social workers, trainers, heads of institutions in the medico-social, educational and professional integration sectors. Participants were invited to replicate conflicts experienced in their institution following a specific methodology, called *organidrame*.
4   In France, a C.A.T. (*centre d'aide au travail*) is a Work assistance center. These centers, now called ESAT (*Etablissement et Service d'Aide par le Travail*, or Establishment and Assistance Center Through Work) are medical and social establishments for protected work reserved for people with disabilities with an eye to facilitating their social and professional integration.

References

Bateson, G. (1977). *Vers une écologie de l'esprit*. Paris: Seuil.

Carreteiro, T. C. (1993). *Exclusion sociale et construction de l'identité: les exclus en milieux 'défavorisés' au Brésil et en France*. Paris: Éditions L'Harmattan.

Castel, R. (2014). *Les métamorphoses de la question sociale: une chronique du salariat*. Paris: Fayard.

Castoriadis, C. (1975). *L'institution imaginaire de la société*. Paris: Seuil.

Chauvière, M. (2007). *Trop de gestion tue le social*. Paris: La Découverte.

Enriquez, E. (2007). *Clinique du pouvoir*. Toulouse: Érès.

Foucault, M. (1975). *Surveiller et punir*. Paris: Gallimard.

Gaulejac, V. de, Blondel, F., & Taboada-Leonetti, I. (2016). *La lutte des places*. Paris: Desclée de Brouwer.

Gaulejac, V. de (2009). *La société malade de la gestion*. Paris: Points.

Gaulejac, V. de, Hanique, F., & Roche, P. (2008). *La sociologie clinique, enjeux théoriques et méthodologiques*. Toulouse: Érès.

Gaulejac, V. de (2015). *Travail, les raisons de la colère*. Paris: Points.

Gaulejac, V., & Hanique, F. (2018). *Le capitalisme paradoxant, un système qui rend fou*. Paris: Points.

Harlé, A. (2010). *Le coût et le goût du pouvoir: le désenchantement politique face à l'épreuve managériale*. Paris: Dalloz.

Dujarier, M. A. (2006). *L'idéal au travail*. Paris: PUF.

Perrot, M. D., & DuPasquier, J. N. (2005). *Ordre et désordres de l'esprit gestionnaire*. Lausanne: Éditions Réalités Sociales.

Roche, P. (2016). *La puissance d'agir au travail*. Toulouse: Érès.

Vandevelde-Rougale, A. (2017). *La novlangue managériale*. Toulouse: Érès.

Wazlawick, P., Helmick-Beavin, J., & Jackson, D. (1972). *Une logique de communication*. Paris: Seuil.

Wilden, A. (1983). *Système et structure: essais sur la communication et l'échange*. Montréal : Boréal Express.

Uses and reconfigurations of the clinic in the field of social intervention
A sociological perspective

3

Bertrand Ravon

Introduction

Based on a double reading with sociological, historical and pragmatic perspectives, this chapter aims to give an account of some of the uses and reconfigurations of the clinic in the broad field of social intervention. The focus will be on the user/beneficiary (the helping relationship clinic), on the vulnerability of his social environment (the social clinic) and the professional challenges of the social workers who accompany the user (the activity clinic).

We will argue for a certain de-psychologization of the clinic in the field of social intervention, an area which is itself undergoing profound change. We will make the following two observations: the field of social work is now extending far beyond strictly psychological interventions; and there is increasing pressure on social services in terms of absorption capacity. These factors challenge the field's fundamental stance, which consists in addressing the negative side of the situation.

DOI: 10.4324/9781003296416-5

Sociology put to the test in the clinic

Let us begin by specifying what type of sociological viewpoint we can adopt on the clinic depending on the degree of involvement of researchers, whose skills-sets are varied: they are, in turn, historians, analysts or practitioners. Since for sociologists the clinic can be both an object of investigation and a place of practice, we will start by opposing two distinct but complementary approaches: clinical sociology and the sociology *of* the clinic.

The sociological project of making clinical psychology an object of analysis is part of the tradition begun by Norbert Elias. It links psychological processes – such as psychological self-control or the self-regulation of affects – to a specific dynamic of civilization taking place at the time of the creation of modern states (Elias, 1991). More recently, there has been research on subjectivity as an object of public policy (Cantelli & Genard, 2007), on the increase of psychological suffering (Ehrenberg, 2010) and on the existential hardships of social vulnerability (Martuccelli, 2014). This research systematically analyzes, in the era of late modernity, the generalized social requirement of individual involvement and its processes of accountability, participation, activation or empowerment.

> The contemporary individual is no more psychological today than he was yesterday. He has, however, since the advent of modernity, been beset by a series of hardships that can find, in psychology, a partial but fruitful language of analysis.
>
> (Martuccelli, 2007, p. 50)

The sociologist can also take as his object the clinic at work in given social configurations with a view to examining its practices. In this respect, Robert Castel's pioneering studies on 'psychoanalysm' (1973) and mental health (1981) paved the way for the criticism of the psychologization of social work (Bresson, 2006) in terms of analyzing spaces for listening (Fassin et al., 2004), 'self-help' (Vrancken & Macquet, 2006), clinical treatment for unemployment (Orianne, 2006) and contemporary psychiatry (Coutant, 2012; Otéro, 2015). Other studies, focused more on social work, have been conducted on the psychosocial clinic (Ravon, 2005), the clinical concern for integration (Laval, 2009) or the clinic of precarity (Pégon, 2011).

These sociologies *of* the clinic differ from each other with respect to their proximity to practicing psychologists. When the proponents of these different sociologies are unfamiliar with clinical practices and their systems of reference, and mainly guided by the all-out denunciation of social psychologization processes, they risk spinning out of control. On the contrary, when the sociology *of* the clinic is supported by a pragmatic approach that does not presuppose the meaning of clinical practices but rather interprets them on the basis of a concrete analysis of how they are implemented, it can fulfill its role of understanding generalized individuation processes without losing any of its critical vigilance (Ravon, 2005).

The clinical sociology project is also supported by the analysis of the processes of subjectivation and by the critique of the psychologization of the social sphere. However, it differs from the sociology *of* the clinic in the type of relationship it maintains with the related discipline of psychology, at least in its clinical and psychosociological approaches of psychoanalytic or psychodynamic orientation. It is attentive to the unconscious issues of the subjects (individuals or groups) in order to better explore the 'psychological dimensions of social phenomena'. It is also multidisciplinary from the onset: 'It would be more appropriate to speak of "clinical social sciences", or even "clinical sociopsychology"' (Gaulejac et al., 2012, p. 10). 'The interest in integrating the clinical approach into a sociological perspective' is thus based on the ability to question 'the different forms of the production of knowledge', to redefine the 'conceptions of objectivity and subjectivity', to use 'subjective methodologies in the production of knowledge', to analyze 'the notion of subject in the face of subjugation processes', or to question 'the position of the researcher and the social worker (Gaulejac et al. 2007, p. 24).

Thus defined as an interdisciplinary approach, clinical sociology is characterized in particular as a method of intervention (Herreros, 2009). By placing at the heart of its practices and analyses the question of transference and counter-transference, that is, the subjective involvement of the researcher, but also by importing some key concepts from clinical psychology, clinical sociology can be criticized by sociologists themselves. Some of them highlight the dependence of clinical sociology on psychologists' categories such as 'neurosis' or 'narcissism' (Martuccelli, 2007), with the risk of a shift from sociological tool of analysis to symptom (Genard, 2015). At the same time, it can be criticized for its attachment to the notion of suffering, which tends to make conflictual social relations an object of compassion (Fassin et al., 2004), where other observers, no less critical, nevertheless make it a powerful indicator of the crisis of our advanced societies (Renault, 2004).

Beyond the various approaches and the controversies they generate, sociologies interested in the clinic are the object of frequent questioning addressed to the society of individuals. How can we understand the link between the process of subjectivation and production of a subjugating society? How can we account for the individualized treatment of the social question? How can we conceive of social injunction so that it might become the actor of its own change?

*

It is at the crossroads of these two complementary approaches that we will now conduct a sociological analysis of the clinical mechanisms at work in the broad field of social intervention in order to contextualize their different uses without reducing them to a single psychologization enterprise. Whether it is addressed to the beneficiaries of social intervention or to its professionals, or is part of the deficit paradigm of social integration at work since the end of the 19th century – or in the much more recent paradigm based on a capacity-centered anthropology that incites people to act – the clinic refers to different experiences that we will assign to three categories: (1) *the helping relationship clinic*, when the focus is on the beneficiary and the relationship associated with it; (2) *the social clinic*, when the vulnerability of the social environment of the person being cared for and the underpinning psychosocial supports are at stake; and (3) *the clinic of professional challenges*, when the issue concerns the institutional, organizational or ethical difficulties that social workers encounter in their job.

The helping relationship clinic: from psycho-pedagogy to relational work

If we follow the history of social work since its foundation at the beginning of the 20th century, psychology is the main discipline of reference. Since 1968, sociology too has made a number of breakthroughs and has emerged today as a discipline of primary importance, at least in training centers. With Binet and the implementation of advanced training courses (1909), a clinical model of social intervention developed under the name of psycho-pedagogy. Placed under the psychologist's gaze and measure, the deficient child is no longer 'abnormal' but 'delayed', no longer 'incurable' but 'irregular'; in a word, he becomes perfectible (Ravon, 2000). In a way, Binet invented what would become the very heart of the profession during the years of growth and specialization of social work in the 1960s and 1970s: namely, a technique for identifying and compensating for the failings of social integration. What is at stake here is not so much the psychopathological measurement of disability as that of inequality relative to some kind of deficiency, which always measures an inferiority (Castel, 1981) or a (developmental) 'delay that can be observed so as to be able to make up for it' (Rancière, 1987, p. 198). Binet does not use the term, but the 'scientific pedagogy' he develops, in the form of psychological tests, is clinical throughout: visual descriptions of the schoolchild's body, psycho-physiological measurements and moral surveys of families combine to paint pictures of 'social and physiological poverty'. Daniel Lagache's later definition of clinical psychology, of which he is considered the founder, takes up the characteristics of Binet's psycho-pedagogical approach: 'the study of individual human conduct and its conditions (heredity, maturation, physiological and pathological conditions, life history) – in a word, the study of the total person *in situ*' (Lagache, 1949, cited by Ciconne, 1998, p. 10).

At the end of the 1960s, psychologists in social and medico-social institutions added to their objective assessment of the disorders of 'unsuitable' children and adults a more subjective focus. Rogers' non-directive pedagogy, to which we owe the very notion of a helping relationship (Laval, 2000), spread rapidly and widely within the field. Guided by an 'attitude of unconditional positive consideration' favorable to 'self-esteem' or 'raising oneself up' towards the person being cared for (Rogers, 1967, p. 248), the psychologist can then develop a subject-based clinic. The question of listening becomes central. This is shown by the success among social workers, especially specialized educators, of the work *Summerhill* by psychoanalyst A. S. Neill (1971). Against the model of 'instruction' producing 'shaped, conditioned, disciplined, repressed' children, and against a social system that manipulates individuals so much that they forfeit their 'free consent', the aim was to promote the conditions for their self-determination.

The function of clinical listening has taken various forms and has been recognized as a central competence of social workers (Chauvière, 1999); with a few exceptions, they orient their intervention based on interviews diagnosing the gaps and difficulties that need to be addressed. The extended use of this 'interventionist psychology' is no longer reserved for psychologists. It corresponds to a considerable transformation of social work at a time when, without a strong institutional program, without a real possibility of integration and without a precise educational future, social workers can only resort to their capacity to listen to those they are trying to help (Ion, 1998). With the exponential development of social support practices, the *relationship with the other* becomes an essential reference point for social policies, and the helping relationship gives way to 'how to help relationships' (Laval & Ravon, 2005). It is therefore no longer a question of working *on* others, but of 'working *with* others' (Astier, 2007).

Didier Fassin has proposed a critical reading of what he calls a 'policy of listening', which he characterizes as a 'socialization of psychology': 'a process by which the notions of psychology can become the commonplace of social action, regardless of the agents that implement it: psychologists kept away from the know-how of their profession or social workers now more sensitive to the psychological approach of their public than to their sociological reading' (Fassin, 2007, pp. 67–68). Fassin sees in this reconfiguration of the helping relationship a change in perspective of the intervention, humanitarian rather than social, led by moral sentiments rather than a principle of social justice (Fassin et al., 2004), one where the professional is inhabited by an 'ethos of compassion' (Fassin, 2007), and where, despite the effort to render the helping relationship more symmetrical, it remains fundamentally unequal.[1]

To summarize, we have witnessed a general transformation in the clinical framework of the beneficiaries of social work: initially identified as *individuals* whose delays or shortcomings must be objectified in order to better integrate them, and then as *subjects* to be listened to with an eye to emancipation, users now tend to be recognized as *people* with relational skills that must be associated with the production of the intervention itself (Ion, Laval & Ravon, 2007). This reconfiguration corresponds to a transformation of the clinic's places of practice: the Binet-style school–laboratory and its psycho-pedagogical experiments; the psycho-pedagogical consulting rooms of the psychologist and their rather closed space to promote the 'face-to-face bond'; and, today, practices of moving beyond the walls of specialized institutions and private practices. Indeed, new ambulatory practices have emerged since the 1990s: these include creating reception and listening areas, implementing mobile teams and making direct contact with people in the street. Listening is first and foremost about moving towards and meeting people (Ravon et al., 2000). The user now tends to be defined no longer on the basis of his status as a beneficiary, but rather on the basis of what is at stake for him at the very moment of the intervention. It is therefore advisable to go to people to establish, in a given situation, what resources and means might be available to enable the social worker to define, with the user, the appropriate action (Ravon & Vidal-Naquet, 2016).

Social clinic: psychological suffering, social vulnerability and psychosocial support

The 'psychosocial clinic' (Furtos, 1999, 2000, 2005) provides a good example of this reconfiguration of social intervention. One of its main characteristics is that it addresses problems in the very places where they are expressed, that is, in areas of vulnerability where social precariousness manifests itself through severely deteriorated social living conditions (precariousness, substandard housing, life in the streets), through socially marginalizing situations (severed ties resulting from unemployment, divorce, the death of a loved one, exile), or by 'environmental defects' (violence or neglect within the family, occupational stress, urban and school segregation). This approach – initially called 'the clinic of salvaging' – emerged at the borders of social work and mental health at the end of the 1990s in a context strongly marked by the first projects to combat exclusion. It focuses on psychological damage (narcissistic fragility, self-deprecation or psychological collapse) resulting from negative socialization processes (Furtos & Laval, 1997). Based on Robert Castel's socio-logical analyses of disaffiliation (Castel, 1995), the psychosocial clinic focuses on psychological suffering but from a non-pathologizing perspective: this clinic does not construct 'psychological suffering' through a list of symptoms reflecting the psychological processes of the internalization of suffering, but rather from the relationship that is woven (or not) between the protagonists involved in the situation of help (Ravon, 2008).

Clinicians using this approach are thus characterized by their ability to travel to shelters, daytime reception centers, local centers, work welfare bene-fits request centers (French RSA) and so on.[2] They are invited to actively 'hang out' in these places (Jourdan, 2005). Most of the time, they do not have an office, no name on a door and no predefined work schedules (Demetriades, 2002). It is a matter of reaching out to people in difficulty without waiting for them to come forward, thereby allowing them to solicit help as and when they wish via a system of 'free consent' (Furtos, Lahlou & Laval, 1999). Those intervening are obliged to be there in person, on location – a place that is neither a traditional space for consultation nor an institutional establishment, but that place where the initial meeting itself occurred. These professionals do not establish a fixed position so as to explicitly maintain themselves in an intermediate, interstitial position (Lovell, 1996; Demailly, 2006). This serves to guarantee an optimal listening environment precisely because it is not structured by the institution; rather, it is defined by the uncertain, unprepared nature of the meeting (Roussillon, 1987; Fustier, 2000).

Unlike the psycho-pedagogue, who, constrained by the duration and rel-atively clear purpose of his mission, must implement educational strategies, and unlike the clinical psychologist, constrained by the temporality of the biographical narrative of the subject whose story he is listening to, the psy-chosocial worker here has only a tactical means of action that depends on the circumstances and is therefore inseparable from the situation in which it is used (Soulet, 2003). Such a position is particularly obvious when professionals, according to the situation, 'de-specialize' their behaviors. For example, psy-chologists accustomed to intervening on an outpatient basis routinely conduct the first interviews in such a way as to distance themselves from connotations associated with being a 'shrink' – without such distancing, no dialogue can take place. This is especially the case with users who, in a social assistance situation, identify interviews with therapeutic care and refuse to participate since they do not consider their request to be related to a need for care (Furtos, 2005).

The medical or therapeutic status is thereby neutralized, making it possible for users to formulate certain 'non-requests', be they requests that are impossible to make or cross-requests, when a user intentionally makes a request for care to a social professional and vice versa. There is no de-professionalization occurring here. On the contrary, de-specialization practices can be understood as an additional professional skill that opens up the helping relationship by creating a 'benevolent environment' (Vidal-Naquet, 2005), outside of which no negotiation is possible.

Thus characterized, the psychosocial clinic deviates doubly from the frame of reference of clinical psychology inherited from psycho-pedagogy. First, the psychosocial approach is not so much a clinic for the subject in need as it is a clinic for social deterioration. With the models of social solidarity that emerged at the end of the 19th century, the right to assistance was conceived in the form of compensation and reparation. Aid was mainly conceived of in terms of redistributing rights to individuals who had been identified in terms of deficiencies, but with the promise of a place in an integrated world. The diagnosis of inferiority was therefore made in a progressivist manner, with educability as the guiding principle. The psychosocial clinic poses the problem in a significantly different way by referring to a 'malaise' linked to rocky social pathways rather than to initial inadequacies, disabilities or maladjustments that would conveniently explain the situation. First, the psychosocial clinic views negative social experiences expressed by the subject as they relate to social causalities. Therefore, it can no longer be the target of the usual criticisms made in terms of psychologization, insofar as it does not attribute the social dimension to the responsibility of those individuals who are most concerned. Second, the goal is more to support and care for vulnerable people than to heal or educate them (Hermant, 2004). Helping means reducing and managing the risks to which everyone is exposed, albeit in significantly different ways depending on the case. In a specific, localized context of social deterioration, the subject of help is immediately identified in terms of his autonomy, with his resources and his points of attachment and anchors. The challenge here is to support his capacities to manage his vulnerability in concrete ways. The solidarity model based on educability, where the inferiority of an individual is measured in terms of his possible progression, has given way to a new form of solidarity, where the diagnosis of vulnerability encourages supportive actions and perspectives for prevention or risk reduction. In this sense, protecting the vulnerable person also means promoting the activation of his role as an 'actor of his own change' (Ehrenberg, 2010).

Activation (Vrancken & Macquet, 2006), rehabilitation (Franck & Charrier, 2018), recovery (*Rhizome*, 2017), empowerment (Bacqué & Biewener, 2013): the challenge of strengthening the capacity to act now extends across the entire field of social intervention. Clinical practice is thus reconfigured in two ways. On the one hand, psychological suffering 'is now a reason to act on social problems and no longer just a reason to cure psychopathology. This change in the status of psychological suffering transforms this suffering into a distress signal, which then becomes a lever of action' (Ehrenberg, 2010, p. 302). The social question manifests itself as an existential problem in that it makes it impossible for the person to meet the social requirement of self-realization in a world that is cruelly lacking in means of supports that allow autonomy (Soulet, 2005, 2007). The real focus of the clinic is therefore not so much the person's psychological antecedents as the consequences of the various processes of social deterioration. On the other hand – and contrary to traditional clinical approaches focused on the identification of deficiencies – the psychosocial clinic is oriented towards the search for unknown or untapped means of support, resources and capacities. In this respect, the psychosocial clinic can be considered a form of high-end social intervention that consists in supporting people who are actors of their own change and whose precarious, broken or diminished lives can nonetheless bring about new capacities to act.

If we consider clinical activity as an 'attractor of negativity' (Pinel, 1996), we must therefore recognize its reconfiguration around a change of perspective, as though in neglecting the study of individual dysfunctions linked to the symptoms of the psyche, it was reorganized based on the analysis of societal deregulations attributable to neoliberalism. From this perspective, the psychosocial clinic is becoming politicized:

> In recent decades, other forms of social suffering have spread, ones which in a way do not possess any precursors in the history of capitalist societies; they are much less accessible to empirical observation because they manifest themselves in the psychological domain, so that we have only clinical indicators to understand them.
>
> (Honneth, 2006, p. 322)

In doing so, the clinic makes it possible to document the criticism of institutions based on the 'feeling of injustice of those who are subjected to the social order' (Renault, 2004, p. 24).

The clinic of professional challenges: from expertise to deliberation

The initiation of an intervention in a psychosocial clinic often stems from a concern on the part of social workers who will call upon the psychologists in their professional environment. This clinic is thus initially conceived as a 'second-line clinic', which addresses users' problems based on the uneasiness of the social workers. According to Jean Furtos, the 'effect of psychological suffering' leads these workers 'to a degree of professional malaise and indeterminacy that requires self-reflection'. In the path opened by the Strohl-Lazarus report (1995), where the question of psychological suffering of social origin is elaborated on the basis of alerts formulated by the social workers, he adds that 'the uneasiness of social workers is part of the psychosocial clinic; it is almost the condition for it' (Furtos, 2005, p. 12).

Social workers' sense of malaise therefore derives from the feeling of inability to cope with situations when they can no longer give meaning to their work, or when they can no longer learn from their experiences. Historically, this malaise has been problematized in two different ways (Ravon, 2014).

This malaise was first defined in the 1970s on the part of health professionals involved in user/provider relationships in terms of professional burnout syndrome resulting from excessive relational demands related to the difficulty in coping with patients' suffering and the inability to respond effectively. The sheer exhaustion of emotional capacities is well known in the field of social work, especially among workers engaged in helping relationships that are endless, pointless, devoid of progression and therefore have no discernable horizon. A great many clinical systems for analyzing professional practice or supervision have thus come into existence over the past 40 years, with the general idea of offering a space for professional reflection combined with the emotional regulation of practices (Ravon, 2009).

Additionally, since the 1990s this malaise has been understood based on certain damaging effects on the daily practice of the profession, resulting from the profound transformations of working conditions. These include rationalization, segmentation and flexibility of work, precariousness of professional status, an obsessive search for cost reduction, an increase in the amount and intensity of work, the proliferation of standard evaluations of an activity that is systematically regarded as the reflection of an individual. To these two problems (the helping relationship and working conditions), we can add a third, related to the individualization of care and the specific nature of each action – this implies seeking consent on the part of the user. In this case, the social worker does not know *a priori* what needs to be done; he is therefore constantly confronted with indeterminacies, especially ethical ones, which are never settled once and for all (Ravon & Vidal-Naquet, 2014).

> Because of the structural uncertainty that governs the concrete activity of social workers and the immense role that their inner selves play

in shaping it, they can never know if they are doing the right thing. Moreover, they know that, whatever they do, they cannot do justice to the paradoxes they face in the exercise of their work. [...] Required to adjust to the constraints of the situation, i.e. the constraints of the users' experience, social workers must build their own position in inter-action with the user and agree not to control the framework of their intervention. They are confronted with a continuous problem of *pro-fessional self-design of* their intervention in situations to make it socially meaningful and effective.

(Soulet, 2016)

These different professional challenges concerning the helping relationship, the working conditions – especially organizational conditions – and on-the-spot decision-making mobilize a different work clinic each time.

Generally speaking, it is clinical psychologists who lead the groups ana-lyzing the practice of helping relationships, with quite varied analytical tra-ditions, although the so-called 'Balint group' model is a strong reference in this area.[3] In any case, practice analysis groups provide social workers with an opportunity to present what can no longer be repressed (Henri-Menassé, 2009). Through collective development work, the elements that are not repressed are 'projected' into the group and, in the best of cases, 'deposited' or, better yet, 'recycled': specialists refer to 'metabolization' (Roussillon, 1987; Fustier, 1999).

With regard to the deterioration of working conditions, another clinical tradition, listed under the terms 'work analysis' or 'activity clinic', initially anchored in the industrial field, has become widespread in the past 25 years, and more particularly around the theme of suffering at work (Dejours, 1998). In the tradition of work ergonomics and psychopathology, this 'method for action' is based in particular on the ability of analysis to restore conflict in work collectives in order to revive the profession in its new contexts of realiza-tion (Clot, 2014). Distinct from practice analysis in that it is directed towards business transformation (Clot, 2007), this clinic is still marginal in the field of social and medico-social work.

This clinic can also be rivaled by the 'institutional regulations' that clinical psychologists are increasingly proposing in order to address organizational issues from the perspective of their negativity and from the institution that implements them. This approach, which is reminiscent of the so-called 'insti-tutional analysis trend', [4] 'leads to not seeing any difference in level between professional practice and the institution in which it is carried out' (Monceau, 2008). The analysis is therefore not reduced to a discussion between practitioners or their practices, but rather is the subject of a deliberation extended to the other actors of the institution, from technical and administrative agents to managers (Gaillard, 2017).

Finally, reflection on and analysis of one's practices are unlikely to resolve a situation and to find new ground when addressing the ethical challenges related to uncertainties about the norms of good. Another clinic, which we will call the 'meaning of activity clinic' (Ravon & Vidal-Naquet, 2014), could be implemented to deal with action:

> Not as the result of intention or the application of rules and standards, but as defining its objectives in its own right. [...] The 'meaning of activity clinic' could then have as its perspective to decide no longer on the notion of what is good in order to build new norms but, more modestly and in a dialogical way, on what is acceptable.
>
> (Ravon & Vidal-Naquet, 2014)

In this sense, the purpose of reflecting on action is not so much to arm the professional a little better as a subject of his practice as to help him to seek and find new directions in his work environment, ones which will enable him at least to maintain the possible action and at best to identify new approaches with an eye to acting differently.[5]

This inventory of the different social work clinics indicates a strong extension of professional self-reflection. It is of course impossible to detail all these analytical practices here. Beyond the disciplinary opposition between the psychological or sociological valence of the clinic, two conceptions of self-reflection can be distinguished.

On the one hand – and the Balint group is a perfect example of this – the 'reflective practitioner' model (Schön, 1994) developed in the early 1980s is based on the idea that the experience of action is the best place to learn professional intelligence. Knowledge, built up before the action and then reflected upon afterwards, is 'mentalized' by the professional, who, by the accumulation of experiences, solidifies his skills and professional action. On the other hand, to this 'mentalist' conception of knowledge which reinforces the dimension of expertise and control by the professional of his activity (Mezzena, 2014), we will oppose a measured conception of self-reflection based on trial-and-error and deliberation (Champy, 2009); the meaning of intervention here is defined as the action progresses, situation after situation, according to the unforeseeable factors linked to encounters with users.

> Thus, the request for reflective assistance does not lie in the search for a solution [...] but in the maintenance of a reflective space that makes it

possible to continue to hold the possibility of a new outcome. In other words, the reflective exercise allows the action to continue, despite everything. Deliberation among peers does not return in the aftermath of problematic situations about what should have been done; it "rewrites" the action after the fact by extending it. By sharing the challenge of action, collective deliberation not only extends its understanding. It also transforms practice into experience, revealing both its limits and its new potential.

(Ravon, 2016)

Whatever their specificities, these different work clinics have today become essential vectors of institutional regulation. They are essentially the only places of deliberation where social work can be thought of collectively on the basis of its actions and in an environment saturated with organizational constraints that take precedence over the job of helping – what the psychologists call the 'primary task' (Gaillard, 2017). However, such regulation can only be effective if the clinical analysis of practice, activity, institution or work can convert the identification of *symptoms* into critical *indicators* that can support the collective debate on the meaning of what we do, here and now. In other words, the generalization of clinical analyses, which have often developed only among specialists themselves, is decisive – be this critical clinic specialized, adaptive or subversive (Périlleux, 2015).

Conclusion

Although in no way an exhaustive inventory of clinical devices in the field of social intervention, the reasoned survey proposed in this chapter invites us to be very cautious about the lessons to be drawn, given the very plurality of objects and approaches to the clinic. That said, the extension of the clinic into social intervention shows above all the proliferation of situations of 'psychological suffering' linked to experiences of social vulnerability, and in particular those in which people are led to take responsibility for it. The social injunction to become the agent of one's change is a challenge for clinicians, accustomed as they are to looking at the negative side of the situation. They must henceforth 'believe in' and 'hope for' the 'strengths of the individual person'. At the same time, suffering at work has spread among professionals, who have become powerless in the face of often hopeless situations, caught between the singular demands of users and standardized organizational constraints. Through its regulatory capacities, the clinic is also faced with the tricky challenge of having to ensure public debate on the meaning of social work.

Thus defined, the clinic, at least in the field of social intervention, cannot be reduced to a tool for producing evidence. Nor can it be reduced to the objectification of situations of vulnerability and of suffering on the part of professionals. Its ability to include individual cases in a collection of already-made observations has opened up to a new age of knowledge, one where we can 'finally discuss the individual in scientific terms' (Foucault, 1963). However, it has not yet led, as it has in the medical field, to nosographies. This is in spite of the fact that tools for assessing the risks of vulnerable populations seem – for the time being unsuccessfully – increasingly required by financing bodies. In other words, the inventory of the clinic in action in the field of social intervention shows above all relational situations of encounter and group situations of self-reflection. These are situations where the key material is the experience of vulnerability, whether professional or related to the users' life contexts.

It therefore seems that the major contribution of the clinic in the field of social intervention is that it embraces the experience of life in all its vulnerability. Canguilhem pointed this out in his famous 1943 essay: 'We believe that there is nothing in science which did not first appear in consciousness, and [...] that it is the patient's point of view that is basically the true one' (Canguilhem, 1966, p. 53). By insisting 'on the fact that the patient is a conscious subject striving to express what makes him feel his experience by stating his illness through the experienced lesson that binds him to the doctor' (Canguilhem, 1966, p. 53), Canguilhem opposes the clinical posture to the positivist orientations that, since Claude Bernard, objectify this experience and make it a laboratory subject. What this means is that 'life makes itself known, and recognized, only through the errors of life which, in all living things, reveal their unfinished constituent parts' (Macherey, 1990, pp. 286–287).[6]

Taking into account the point of view of the suffering subject in a clinical situation, whether a user or a professional, and recognizing him in all his capacities to experience situations as he sees fit, is what could ultimately define the clinic in and of social intervention.

Notes

1   Indeed, if the relationship is framed by the consideration of the other as a fellow human being, it cannot be the subject of reciprocity, compassion being by definition asymmetrical (Fassin, 2010).
2   These places refer to different types of institutions for people who are marginalized, excluded, looking for work or receiving minimum social benefits.
3   The Balint Group, founded in England in the 1950s, is a professional support system initially intended for general practitioners. These 'research-training' groups are not

designed to become a therapeutic place for participants, but a place for transforming their professional skills through a better psychological understanding of themselves and the relational situation in which they are involved (Balint & Balint, 2013).

4   'Institutional analysis', at the crossroads of the critical sociology of organizations and psychoanalysis, immediately posits analysis as an act of intervention (Lourau, 1970). It is historically the result of the 'institutional psychotherapy' movement initiated by François Tosquelles and then developed by Jean Oury. Institutional psychotherapy refers to a particular moment of transformation in psychiatric care practices in the early 1950s, based on the 'pathological' nature of the institution, which needs to be taken charge of and cured in order to rebuild the relational network surrounding the patient (Tosquelles, 1995).

5   This clinic is still experimental. Following the tradition begun by Balint on the one hand and by institutional analysts on the other, it is based on the analysis of practice, but without making it a psychological question (individual or group) because it is above all interested in the sociological contextualisation of action. This is why we call it a sociological clinic (Ravon, 2012). At the same time, it borrows the dialogical approach of the controversy surrounding professional acts from the activity clinic, but without conducting an analysis of the work itself, in order to focus instead on the acceptability or unacceptability of the activity based on the analysis of problematic situations (Ravon, 2016).

6   I thank Numa Murard for bringing this text by Pierre Macherey to my attention.

References

Astier, I. (2007). *Les nouvelles règles du social*. Paris: PUF.

Bacqué, M-H. & Biewener, C. (2013). *L'empowerment, une pratique émancipatrice*. Paris: La Découverte.

Balint, M., & Balint, E. (2013). *Psychotherapeutic techniques in medicine*. New York: Routledge.

Binet, A. (1909). Les signes physiques de l'intelligence chez les enfants. *L'année psychologique*, *16*(1), 1–30.

Bresson, M. (Ed.) (2006). *La psychologisation de l'intervention sociale: mythes et réalités*. Paris: L'Harmattan.

Canguilhem, G. (1966). *Le Normal et le pathologique*. Paris: PUF.

Cantelli, F., & Genard, J-L. (Eds). (2007). *Action publique et subjectivité*. Paris: DGLJ.

Castel, R. (1973). *Le psychanalysme*. Paris: Flammarion, 1981.

Castel, R. (1981). La gestion des risques De l'anti-psychiatrie à l'après-psychanalyse. Paris, Minuit, 1984.

Castel, R. (1995). *Les métamorphoses de la question sociale. Une chronique du salariat*. Paris: Fayard.

Champy, F. (2009). *La sociologie des professions*. Paris: PUF.

Chauvière, M. (1999). La sphère clinique du travail social. *Lien social*, 500. www.lien-social. com/-500-#ancre-sommaire

Ciccone, A. (1998). *L'observation clinique*. Paris: Dunod.

Clot, Y. (2007). De l'analyse des pratiques au développement des métiers. *Éducation et didactique*, *1*(1), 83–93.

Clot, Y. (2014). Clinique de l'activité. In Zawieja, P. & Guarnieri, F. (Eds.). *Dictionnaire des risques psychosociaux* (pp. 97–101). Paris: Le Seuil.

Coutant, I. (2012). *Troubles en psychiatrie.* Paris: La Dispute.

Dejours, C. (1998). *La souffrance en France.* Paris: Le Seuil.

Demailly, L. (2006). Dispositifs institutionnels, dispositifs interstitiels en santé mentale. In Laval, C. & Ravon, B. (Eds.), *Réinventer l'institution. Rhizome, 25,* December, 40–44.

Demetriades, C. (2002). Psychologue en mission locale: une mise en perspective des cadres proposés. *Le journal des psychologues, 201,* October, dossier 'L'insertion des jeunes. Rôle des psychologues en missions locales', 43–48.

Ehrenberg, A. (2010). *La société du malaise.* Paris: Odile Jacob.

Elias, N. (1991) [1949]. *La civilisation des mœurs.* trans. 1973. Paris: Calmann-Lévy.

Fassin, D. et al. (2004). *Des maux indicibles. Sociologie des lieux d'écoute.* Paris: La Découverte.

Fassin, D. (2007). Un ethos compassionnel. In Soulet, M-H. (Ed.), *La souffrance sociale nouveau malaise dans la civilisation* (pp. 51–72). Fribourg, Switzerland: Academic Press Fribourg.

Fassin, D. (2010). *La raison humanitaire. Une histoire morale du temps présent.* Paris: Gallimard/Seuil.

Foucault M. (1963). *Naissance de la clinique.* Paris: PUF.

Franck, N., & Charrier, P. (2018). *Traité de réhabilitation psychosociale.* Paris: Elsevier Masson.

Furtos, J. (1999). Filiation et objet social, désaffiliation et perte des objets sociaux, réaffiliation?. *Actes du séminaire. Pertinence d'une clinique de la désaffiliation?.* Lyon: ORSPERE.

Furtos, J. (2000). Epistémologie de la clinique psychosociale (la scène sociale et la place des psy). *Pratiques en santé mentale, 1,* pp. 23–32.

Furtos, J. (2005). Souffrir sans disparaître. In Furtos, J. & Laval, C. (Eds.), *La santé mentale en actes – de la clinique au politique.* Toulouse: Érès.

Furtos, J., Lahlou, J., & Laval, C. (1999). *Points de vue et rôles des acteurs de la clinique psychosociale.* Rapport de recherche pour la FNARS et la DDASS du Rhône. Lyon: ORSPERE.

Furtos, J., Laval, C., et al. (Eds.) (1997). *Souffrance psychique, contexte social et exclusion.* Actes du colloque ORSPERE/école Rockfeller. Lyon: ORSPERE.

Fustier, P. (1999). *Le Travail d'équipe en institution, Clinique de l'institution médico-sociale et psychiatrique.* Paris: Dunod.

Fustier, P. (2000). *Le Lien d'accompagnement. Entre don et contrat salarial.* Paris: Dunod.

Gaillard, G. (2017). Intervenir en institution: préserver de la groupalité et restaurer de l'intermédiaire. *Revue de psychothérapie psychanalytique de groupe, 68*(1), 89–100.

Gaulejac, V. Hanique, F., & Roche, P. (Eds.) (2007). *La sociologie clinique Enjeux théoriques et méthodologiques.* Toulouse: Érès.

Gaulejac, V. Hanique, F., & Roche, P. (2012). Avant-propos à l'édition de poche. In *La sociologie clinique Enjeux théoriques et méthodologiques.* Toulouse: Érès. 1st ed. 2007.

Genard, J-L. (2015). Sociologie critique, sociologie morale. In Frère, B. (Ed.), *Le tournant de la théorie critique* (pp. 37–66). Paris: Desclée de Brouwer.

Henri-Menassé, C. (2009). *Analyse de la pratique en institution.* Toulouse: Érès.

Hermant, H. (2004). *Clinique de l'infortune La psychothérapie à l'épreuve de la détresse sociale.* Paris: Les empêcheurs de penser en rond.

Herreros, G. (2009). *Pour une sociologie d'intervention.* Toulouse: Érès.

Honneth, A. (2006). *La société du mépris.* Paris: La Découverte.

Ion, J. (1998). *Le travail social au singulier.* Paris: Dunod.

Ion, J., Laval, C., & Ravon, B. (2007). Politiques de l'individu et psychologies d'intervention: transformation des cadres d'action dans le travail social. In Cantelli, F. & Genard, J-L. (Eds.), *Action publique et subjectivité* (pp. 157–168). Paris: DGLJ.

Jourdan, M. (2005) Accoler/racoler: le psy qui traîne. In Joubert, M. & Louzoun, C. (Eds.), *Répondre à la souffrance sociale*. Toulouse: Érès.

Lagache, D. (1949). Psychologie clinique et méthode clinique. In *L'évolution psychiatrique*, I, 155–178.

Laval, C., & Ravon, B. (2005). Relation d'aide ou aide à la relation? In Ion, J. (Ed.), *Le travail social en débat(s)* (pp. 235–250). Paris: La Découverte.

Laval, C. (2000). La relation d'aide à l'épreuve de la souffrance psychique et sociale. In Micoud, A. & Peroni, M. (Eds.), *Ce qui nous relie*. La Tour-d'Aigues: Editions de l'Aube.

Laval, C. (2009). *Des psychologues sur le front de l'insertion. Souci clinique et question sociale*. Toulouse: Érès.

Lourau, R. (1970). L'analyse institutionnelle. *Arguments*, 44. Paris: Minuit.

Lovell, A. (1996). Mobilités des cadres et psychiatrie 'hors les murs'. In Joseph, I. & Proust, J. (Ed.), *La folie dans la place. Raisons pratiques no. 7* (pp. 55–81). Paris: EHESS.

Macherey, P. (1990. De Canguilhem à Canguilhem en passant par Foucault. In *Georges Canguilhem, philosophe et historien des sciences, colloque 1990* (pp. 286–294). Paris: Bibliothèque du Collège international de philosophie, Albin-Michel.

Martuccelli, D. (2007). La souffrance et le modèle de l'individu psychologique. In Soulet, M-H. (Ed.), *La souffrance sociale Nouveau malaise dans la civilisation* (pp. 31–50). Fribourg (Switzerland): Academic Press Fribourg.

Martucelli, D. (2014). La vulnérabilité, un nouveau paradigme?. In Brodiez, A. von Bueltzingsloewen, I. Eyraud, B., Laval, C. & Ravon, B. (Eds.), *Vulnérabilités sociales et sanitaires. De l'histoire à la sociologie* (pp. 27–40). Rennes: PUR.

Mezzena, S. (2014). *Connaissance et professionnalité dans la pratique comme territoire à équilibrer. Enquêtes et perspective dans l'activité des éducateurs*. Doctoral thesis, Université de Genève.

Monceau, G. (2008). Entre pratique et institution. L'analyse institutionnelle des pratiques professionnelles. *La nouvelle revue de l'adaptation et de la scolarisation*, 41(1), 145–159.

Neill, A. S. (1971). *Libres enfants de Summerhill*. Paris : François Maspero.

Orianne, J-F. (2006). Le traitement clinique du chômage. In Bresson, M. (Ed.), *La psychologisation de l'intervention sociale : mythes et réalités* (pp. 131–140). Paris: L'Harmattan.

Otéro, M. (2015). *Les fous dans la cité: sociologie de la folie ordinaire contemporaine*. Montreal: Boréal.

Pégon, G. (2011). *Le traitement clinique de la précarité. Collectifs d'intervention, parcours de vulnérabilité, pratique de care. L'exemple du Carrefour Santé Mentale Précarité*. Thesis in sociology, Université Lyon 2.

Périlleux, T. (2015). Pour une critique clinique. In Frère, B. (Ed.), *Le tournant de la théorie critique* (pp. 67–92). Paris: Desclée de Brouwer.

Pinel, J-P. (1996). La déliaison pathologique des liens institutionnels. In Kaës, R. *et al.* (Eds.), *Souffrance et psychopathologie des liens institutionnels* (pp. 48–79). Paris: Dunod.

Rancière, J. (1987). *Le maître ignorant*. Paris: Fayard.

Ravon, B. (Ed.), avec Pichon, P. Franguiadakis, S., & Laval, C. (2000). *Le travail de l'engagement. Rencontre et attachements: une analyse de la solidarité en direction des 'personnes en souffrance'*. Rapport de recherche Mire/Fondation de France. Saint-Etienne: Crésal.

Ravon, B., & Vidal-Naquet, P. (2014). Epreuve de professionnalité. In Zawieja, Ph. & Guarnieri, F. (Eds.), *Dictionnaire des risques psychosociaux* (pp. 268–272). Paris: Le Seuil.

Ravon, B., & Vidal-Naquet, P. (2016). L'épreuve de professionnalité: de la dynamique d'usure à la dynamique réflexive. *SociologieS* [online], Dossiers, Relation d'aide et de soin et épreuves de professionnalité, put online 16 June 2016, consulted on 17 October 2018: http://journals.openedition.org/sociologies/5363

Ravon, B. (2000). 'L'échec scolaire'. Histoire d'un problème public, Paris: In Press Editions.

Ravon, B. (2005). Vers une clinique du lien défait? In Ion, J. et al. Travail social et 'souffrance psychique' (pp. 3–36). Paris: Dunod.

Ravon, B. (2008). Le souci du social. L'expérience publique des problèmes sociaux; vers une sociologie de la clinique. French accreditation to supervise research (HDR), Université de Lyon 2.

Ravon, B. (2009). L'extension de l'analyse de la pratique au risque de la professionnalité. Empan, 75(December), 116–121.

Ravon, B. (2012). Refaire parler le métier. Le travail d'équipe pluridisciplinaire: réflexivité, controverses, accordage. Nouvelle Revue de Psychosociologie, 14, 99–113.

Ravon, B. (2014). Usure professionnelle. In Jorro, A. (Ed.), Dictionnaire des concepts de la professionnalisation (pp. 341–344). Brussels: de Boeck Editions.

Ravon, B. (2016). Risquer la trahison. Analyse dialogique de l'activité et régulation continue: l'exemple de la reprise collective d'une intervention à domicile. SociologieS [online], Dossiers, Relation d'aide et de soin et épreuves de professionnalité, put online 16 June 2016. http://sociologies.revues.org/5560

Renault, E. (2004). L'expérience de l'injustice. Reconnaissance et clinique de l'injustice. Paris: La Découverte.

Rhizome. (2017). Apprendre le rétablissement. Bulletin national Santé mentale et précarité, no. 65–66.

Rogers, C. (1967). Le développement de la personne. Paris: Dunod.

Roussillon, R. (1987). Espaces et pratiques institutionnelles. Le débarras et l'interstice. In Kaës, R. et al. (Eds.), L'institution et les institutions, Etudes psychanalytiques. Paris: Dunod.

Schön, D. (1994). Le praticien réflexif. A la recherche du savoir caché dans l'agir professionnel. Montreal: Les Éditions Logiques.

Soulet, M-H. (2003). Faire face et s'en sortir. Vers une théorie de l'agir faible. In Châtel, V. & Soulet, M-H. (Eds.), Agir en situation de vulnérabilité (pp. 167–214). Laval (Quebec): Les presses de l'Université Laval.

Soulet, M-H. (2005). La vulnérabilité comme catégorie de l'action publique. Pensée plurielle, 10(2), 49–59.

Soulet, M-H. (2007). Vulnérabilité sociale et souffrance individuelle. In Soulet, M-H. (Ed.), La souffrance sociale Nouveau malaise dans la civilisation (pp. 9–16). Fribourg, Switzerland: Academic Press Fribourg.

Soulet, M-H. (2016). Le travail social, une activité d'auto-conception professionnelle en situation d'incertitude. SociologieS [online], Dossiers, Relation d'aide et de soin et épreuves de professionnalité, put online 16 June 2016, consulted 17 October 2018. http://journals.openedition.org/sociologies/5553

Strohl-Lazarus, R. (1995). Une souffrance que l'on ne peut plus cacher. Rapport du groupe de travail 'Ville, santé mentale, précarité et exclusion sociale', DIV/DIRMI.

Tosquelles, F. (1995). De la personne au groupe. A propos des équipes de soin. Toulouse: Érès.

Vidal-Naquet, P-A. (2005). A demi-mot : de l'écoute à la connivence. In Joubert, M. (Ed.), Villes et 'toxicomanies'. Toulouse: Érès.

Vrancken, D., & Macquet, C. (2006,). Le travail sur soi: vers une psychologisation de la société. Paris: Belin.

Part II

Clinical practices in social work

The contribution of the clinic narrative in supporting professional practice

4

Christophe Niewiadomski

Introduction

We will argue here that the knowledge and skills that social work and 'human relationships professions' must mobilize today to accomplish their tasks do not rely exclusively on prescriptive practices based on 'evidence' inspired by the biomedical and epistemological realm of the natural sciences. Instead, such knowledge and skills can benefit from a clinical, interdisciplinary and comprehensive perspective. Situated at the crossroads of the subjective and the objective, the individual and the collective, and the psychological and the social, this clinical perspective makes it possible to better understand what affects individuals who are increasingly uncertain within a society whose expectations are now affected by the 'crisis of meaning' linked to the malaise of modern life.

Based on a set of theoretical and clinical studies conducted in the human and social sciences, this contribution thus aims to explore the perspectives offered by a 'narrative clinic' and the historical and epistemological links that this clinic maintains with the psychoanalytical clinic.[1]

After analyzing the contemporary evolutions that affect the field of social intervention, we will attempt to explain how the narrative clinic, as opposed

DOI: 10.4324/9781003296416-7

to scientific knowledge, attempts to promote listening to the subject caught up in the complex set of his various connections and determinations, conscious and unconscious motives, paths and experiences. We will show how, in the support-related professions, the narrative clinic – by setting the subject in motion – adopts an ethical perspective on the intersubjective relationship and argues for the mediation of the narrative as a place of reflexivity and a possible vector for training processes.

Contemporary transformations of the social context

The weakening of the function of social integrator that work had hitherto represented in our industrialized societies and the erosion of the wage-based society (Castel, 1995) are currently triggering a considerable change in the perception of the social context as it was perceived during the second half of the 20th century. The social and political context is now highly overdetermined by the effects of a neoliberal globalized economy; the hypothesis that renewed growth can support the functioning of a welfare state that effectively responds to the exclusion and impoverishment of more and more people is inevitably disappearing (Rosanvallon, 1981). As a consequence, a significant part of the population in industrialized countries is now facing structural vulnerability linked to an 'integration deficit' that requires social support to alleviate difficulties related to self-sufficiency. Forced to settle into a situation of 'sustainable transition', where precariousness is becoming an inevitable fact of life, those who are 'excluded' and 'socially maladjusted' thus gradually swell the ranks of a 'problematic population'. Its members no longer belong exclusively to the traditional categories of disability, illness, old age or deficiencies that social workers previously had to face. Now forced to curb the increasingly frequent processes of exclusion, social intervention is changing.

Indeed, professionals in the social sector increasingly help people who are probably more concerned with work-related issues than with assistance such as it was conceived of until recently. The aim is now to support a population of 'able-bodied indigents' affected by social disaffiliation (Castel, 1995, 2009) and by the rise in precariousness (Capdevielle & Rey, 2012) who end up being excluded by the current situation (Castel, 1992). In addition, there are several founding principles of social action upon which educational agents had formerly based their training which are now being undermined:

- A first principle was based on the idea that intervention in social work and social integration depended on a balance between collective solidarity and individual responsibility. However, in a society where the welfare state is weakening and individuals are increasingly being left to their own devices, this balance is now being challenged.

- A second principle was organized around the centrality of work as the main provider of social guarantees such as insurance programs related to pensions, illness or accidents. In this perspective, educational agents intervened at the periphery of the system. However, salary-related conditions are crumbling and social insecurity is rising, while at the same time exclusion from employment is increasingly widespread. As a result, the great social integrator that work once represented is weakened since it is no longer accessible to many people.
- A third principle is also fading away: the function of social intervention no longer seems to produce social promotion and equalization of opportunities, but rather serves to fight exclusion by trying to contain it.
- A fourth and final principle is also called into question: public funding once organized the redistribution of part of the wealth to social work; it is now being replaced by mechanisms involving competing private companies. Thus, at a time when the associative sector and public services are opening up to the commercialization of social issues (Chauvière, 2007), we are also witnessing a relative decrease of intervention at the level of the State with the transfer of powers to local authorities. There are greater territorial disparities, even as the dominant discourse on social cohesion of recent decades has focused on fiscal rationalization and 'user-centeredness'. Users are placed in increasingly difficult objective situations and are encouraged more and more frequently to depend on their own efforts. They must now demonstrate their willingness to make 'efforts to integrate' in a context where integration is becoming more problematic given the increase in social inequalities.

For their part, social workers are confronted with the development of exclusion and poverty and must assimilate the transition from a social assistance model previously based on the notion of solidarity to a model of 'accountability' on the part of the user. Consequently, it is not so much the injustices of an unequal social relationship that will be questioned, but rather the personal responsibility of subjects in difficulty. Unable to provide for themselves, they will now have to demonstrate their willingness to integrate into society. The contextual dimensions of psychological suffering linked to the effects of social precariousness are thus too often ignored, leaving the subjects themselves to be blamed for their difficulties in integrating. In this way, the social and cultural overdeterminations that affect the individual are minimized, while the notion of a project at the individual level is magnified, thus blocking the process of exclusion a subject experiences. If he wants to benefit from the material assistance that motivates his request, the subject then has no alternative but to integrate the discourse of responsibility that he hears.

This manner of holding the individual responsible for his condition is not only particularly damaging; it also places social workers in an uncomfortable position. There is a dangerous trend towards the 'psychologization' of economic and social problems. On top of that, the social worker is required to become a social control agent responsible for applying standardized procedures that are designed to respond to the effects of a 'causality of fate' supposedly affecting a population experiencing long-term social disaffiliation. This process frequently leads to particularly severe suffering in social workers. Indeed, for many professionals, this instrumentalization of educational work can damp down the voices of the subjects in favor of an obligation for results that is too often disconnected from the reality of the specific situations encountered. Finally, the legislative and organizational changes weighing on the professional practice of social workers today (Chauvière, 2007) contribute to the emergence of new contexts of activity. These contexts force practitioners to rethink how they work as well as how they view their professional involvement in ways that sometimes no longer make sense (Autès, 1999). Discouragement, stress and even suffering at work (Dejours, 1998) thus appear. They are all the more detrimental as the spaces in which these professionals could potentially exchange ideas on these issues are becoming scarcer. Confronted with the magnitude of needs coupled with the lack of resources, they feel increasingly helpless in the face of the massification of the social problems they are called upon to manage.

Supporting people in socially precarious situations in the era of a biographical society

In this context of changing practices, overly technical evidence-based orientations in social work seem, from our point of view, ill-suited to the complexity of the situations faced by social workers. Social workers generally aim at implementing a support project which always involves individual subjects in a socio-historical trajectory. Each subject's trajectory is subordinated to an environment and to a time, both of which must be carefully taken into account to avoid the all too frequent pitfall of attributing the difficulties individuals encounter to them alone. However, for the social worker, several dimensions must then be coordinated: the attention that must be paid to the subject is combined with the concern to respond to administrative and regulatory injunctions that define the framework of an intervention that is supposed to be able to adjust to the objectives of standardization and adaptation as defined by society. Thus, the logics of the subject and its reference group, the logics of administrative institutions, the logics of scholarly discourse and the logics of people's pragmatic expectations, must all combine for the benefit of the support proposed.

However, the problem of guiding individuals by means of social services has become considerably more complex in recent years. Today, there is no longer one, but many social issues that affect extremely diverse populations dependent on heterogeneous living conditions. Thus, some people – for very diverse reasons such as physical or psychological disability, illness or old age – will find themselves, temporarily or permanently, unable to work and support themselves, and will solicit social service workers to alleviate problems related to self-sufficiency. Without minimizing the difficulties involved in helping these groups, it should be noted that social action professionals have long been prepared to deal with the problem of assistance and care for these poor populations, provided that sufficient resources are allocated to them. We have seen, however, that other populations, primarily from those socio-demographic categories particularly affected by the changing economic context, also make extensive use of the services provided by social intervention professionals. These users, having been 'left behind' by economic and social activity, generally do not have the resources they need to ensure the minimum level of subsistence. The weakening of the wage-based society has gradually led to the extension of the problems encountered by populations who did not have the economic, cultural and symbolic capital that would otherwise steer them clear of the consequences of long-lasting disaffiliation.

In this context, the contemporary model of 'user empowerment' on which the medico-social sector is now based can be perfectly understood as the respect for the rights and duties of beneficiaries. It is nevertheless organized around an ideal figure typical of the contemporary subject, suggesting that the subject is in a position to make informed choices in order to organize his existence in a radically changing environment. However, in many ways, the 'excluded' and 'socially disaffiliated' who today seek guidance from social workers are characterized above all by a lack of security, consideration, solid assets and stable ties. They are far removed from this ideal figure typical of a free individual with agency who is master of his destiny. Thus, for Castel:

> An increasing number of individuals have lost – or are unable to access – the benefits of 'social property': the long-term unemployed, or the young seeking employment, the ever-increasing number of people

whose professional and social trajectories have been chaotic and who go back and forth between employment and unemployment, if they are not declared 'unemployable' to begin with. They cannot be denied the status of individuals, but they are very problematically individuals, if, once again, being truly an individual means being capable of a certain social independence and control of one's conduct, which are indeed qualifications attributed to the modern individual.

(Castel, 2004, p. 128)

Moreover, the individual today constructs his identity less from institutionally assigned statuses (social class, gender, type of job held, etc.) (Dubet, 2002) than from the social injunction to become 'himself' by giving serious thought to the processes of subjectivation. Expected to conquer an identity less and less determined by what preceded him, he is also confronted with an environment that has become uncertain and changing while his social trajectory, affected by the imperatives of flexibility and mobility, require him to constantly adapt to the race for change and the need for autonomy, creativity and efficiency.

Finally, despite the prevalence of models of work organization centered on the cult of individual performance, the social practices of the contemporary individual are now closely dependent on the injunctions of a society that is increasingly attentive to the expression of the individuality of its members (Martuccelli, 2010), but also to the way in which these members justify the meaning of their conduct. This injunction to realize one's individual identity is the sign of a profound modification of the relationships between the individual and society. It is also a sign of a transformation of the perception that the individual has of himself, to such an extent that we can regard reflexivity – a process strengthened by the desire to question himself – as one of the main characteristics of advanced modernity. In this perspective, the individual is now subject to the requirements of what Christine Delory-Momberger (2009) calls the 'biographical condition'. In this sense, reflexivity is not only becoming a major issue today for social players encouraged to search within themselves for the driving forces behind their actions, the principles of their conduct and the values that can give meaning to their existence (Gaulejac, 2009), but also a request to report on this significant reflexive work to others. In the context of a biographical society (Astier & Duvoux, 2006), the individual is summoned to become 'the entrepreneur of his own existence'; he organizes his activity on the basis of both a strong dimension of individuality and a call to be autonomous with respect to institutions. These institutions, furthermore, require him to justify his conduct. They expect him to elaborate a biographical account wherein social, economic and institutional constraints are now perceived as essentially falling within the scope of individual responsibility.

While self-reporting in this new socio-historical situation can contribute powerfully to a sense of autonomy and function as a form of emancipation, or even as a form of resistance for some people (Delory-Momberger & Niewiadomski, 2009), its elaboration is strongly dependent on the structuring of the social space and its rules with respect to the individual. Pierre Bourdieu has shown that the social space is structured by objective positions which are defined in relation to each other from a set of resources that cause struggles for appropriation by social players. These resources, called 'capital', are traditionally subdivided into four categories: economic capital, social capital, symbolic capital and cultural capital. According to Bourdieu, the distribution of this capital in the social field organizes the differentiation of social classes. Bourdieu conceptualized the notion of 'class habitus' to account for the effects of the internalization of social world structures on the parties involved and showed that individuals do not 'by nature' occupy their position. Habituses, a set of dispositions to perceive, think and act, thus determine particular forms of 'being in the world' according to the particular group or social class the subject belongs to. However, the biographical skills of individuals do not escape this logic, and the 'biographical capital' they hold, although it does influence their biographical skills, will differ considerably according to the place they occupy in the social space. Indeed, in producing a self-narrative, the individual is confronted with the problem of 'legitimate speech', that is, the logic of the market for symbolic goods that crosses the social space. The weakest and least endowed with capital are confronted with a reinforcement of the social inequalities to which they are subjected, while the 'obligation to individuality' – a possible vector for freedom and autonomy for those with greater resources – is transformed here into its opposite. It condemns, for example, the poor, the excluded and the disenfranchised to consider themselves primarily responsible for their condition. Required to justify himself biographically to the institutions which he addresses in a perpetual narrative of himself, the individual weakened by his objective position is soon forced to internalize the responsibility for his condition subjectively (Niewiadomski, 2012). Thus, when a user in difficulty requests a social benefit from an institution, he is generally required to provide an account of his incapacities in order to justify the request and explain his inability to resolve the difficulties alone. The institution tends to favor the notion of responsibility and that of an 'individual project', thus enjoining the individual to find within himself the resources of his social integration and employability while ignoring the social and cultural overdeterminations that affect him.

The emphasis on the values of performance, success and quantification that now pervades the social sector as a whole thus stifles the mediation and remediation work that educators must carry out. The gradual transition from an obligation of means to an obligation of result thus confronts these educators with situations that are simply 'impossible' because they largely eliminate the recognition of the intersubjective clinical situation from which the subject could, with the help of the social worker, try to better appropriate his psychological, physical and social space. The unpredictability of educational interaction and of its heuristic potentialities is now denied in favor of a culture of urgency and effectiveness. For example, during a training session focused on the issue of tutoring, social workers expressed the difficulties they encountered in having to drastically limit the duration of measures aimed at reintegrating groups with so-called 'great difficulties':

> We are now faced with populations with whom we are being asked to co-construct a professional integration project in a limited amount of time, while the foundations enabling work of this type are not there. These people, often very destructured, need time to come to a clearer vision of the nature of their request and their project. We ourselves face major difficulties in enabling them to make choices, to regain their autonomy. As a result, our work is now limited to the painful feeling of putting a bandage on a wooden leg.

Therefore, how can we at the clinical level promote the construction of meaning that can facilitate, for both social workers and users, the subjective incorporation of objective social inequalities and their individual and collective effects? This requires a particular clinical posture that differs considerably from the application of a set of techniques that educators, with socially legitimized knowledge, are sometimes called upon to apply on the basis of supposedly convincing data. Let us now try to clarify the origins of such a clinical orientation.

From observation to listening: the legacy of psychoanalysis

The use of the term 'clinical', etymologically derived from the Greek *klinikos*, refers first of all to the practice of the doctor at the bedside, that is, to the medical clinic, which finds its historical and epistemological foundations in the anatomo-clinical and then experimental method (Foucault, 1963).

At the end of the 18th century, the development of autopsies saw the emergence of the first stages of anatomo-clinical medicine. This exceptional practice, which until then had been under the strict control of the Christian church, became more general after the French Revolution and allowed the medical community, from the direct observation of *post-mortem* lesions, to proceed by inference to a form of diagnostic reasoning aimed at understanding the workings of living organisms. The development of this 'dead body clinic' quickly made it possible to lay the foundations of nosology and medical semiology, which then continued to be perfected under the influence of Claude Bernard (1866), whose borrowings from the physico-chemical concepts of the time soon gave rise to experimental medicine. During the 20th century, the successive appearance of sulfonamides, followed by antibiotics, profoundly changed the survival rate of patients suffering from infectious diseases. Biological and histological examinations and medical imaging made it possible for clinicians to hone the rules of diagnostic inference; at the same time spectacular strides were made in the development of surgical practices, particularly in organ transplants. The result of these clinical advances is now the basis of the notion of evidence-based medicine, the scientific legitimacy of which is based on randomized clinical trials and the statistical contribution of meta-analyses from specialized literature, in order to identify those therapies most suited to a given pathology.

In the field of psychological disorders, Freud brought about a fundamental break with this clinical orientation in his work with patients suffering from hysteria. Although these patients were at the time very closely observed, and in perfect coherence with the concern for scientific objectification that underlies observation-based clinical treatment, they were hardly listened to at all. Freud met Charcot in Paris and attended sessions where Charcot's patients were put on stage to be observed by viewers on the occasion of spectacular social events. For the nascent psychiatry of the time, the individual's psyche was thus viewed through bodily manifestations. Freud, however, considered that the sometimes dramatic disorders presented by these patients, who were otherwise free of organic lesions, were in fact the result of repressed psychological conflicts expressed through these somatic symptoms. Freud's hypothesis was radical. Since the disorders observed in these patients were clearly not based on anatomical logic, the focus became centered on representation alone. Freud therefore presupposed that the symptoms exhibited were due to a lack of spoken words and that the clinical manifestations that were visible took place instead of words that remained unspoken because of repression. Freud thus broke with the practice of observing in favor of clinical listening. He considered that the prompting of the patient's subjective speech – given that the patient unknowingly possesses the meaning of his disorder – leads to an understanding of what escapes the rational observation.

However, because of the logic of the unconscious and of psychological mechanisms, access to the meaning of the symptom required the establishment of a specific experimental framework. Psychoanalysis gradually developed, with therapeutic work moving from an observation-based clinic to one of listening, one in which the aim was now to promote the emergence of what could not previously be expressed. In a clinical situation where the patient is invited to say whatever comes to mind, without omitting representations deemed inappropriate or assumed irrelevant, the analysand is no longer an object of observation subject to the inquisitive and knowing gaze of the practitioner, but rather a subject who tries to express himself through the rule of free association. Lapses and slips, disfluent language and narrative inconsistencies become clinical materials which are all the more important as they make it possible to bypass the censorship that accompanies the unconscious functioning of a subject who is trying to gradually become himself.

This paradigmatic reversal had decisive consequences on the understanding of the functioning of psychological disorders, but also profoundly influenced medical practices and the human and social sciences as a whole, laying the epistemological foundations for a 'listening-based clinic'.

The contribution of the narrative clinic in the fields of medicine and social intervention

In the health field, the evidence-based medicine model appears to be rather well suited to acute medical and surgical disorders. But the question of another clinical orientation, one centered on listening, is raised when practitioners deal with difficulties relating to chronic pathologies or disorders of the psychological sphere. Indeed, the ageing of the population and the development of chronic diseases pose the problem of long-term support for patients and, consequently, the need to take into account their lifestyles, culture and subjectivity. Furthermore, practitioners today are confronted with work-related suffering and the difficult problem of the 'broken link' clinic (Ravon, 2005), that is, more specifically in the field of mental health, and with the impact of social phenomena on psychopathological disorders (Lazarus, 1995).

Given these challenges, the evidence-based medicine model misses the mark, because it is based on the legacy of an observation-based clinic in which the patient's discourse makes sense first and foremost in relation to the practitioner's own frames of reference. For the practitioner, the patient's discourse, seen as tainted with subjectivity and limited to the knowledge of the layperson, must be relativized in order to focus instead on objectively identifying the origin of symptoms. It is this reasoning, based on rigorous observation of clinical signs, that allows the practitioner to make a diagnosis that inevitably feeds into the categories of prognosis and treatment. In response to the limits of a purely biomedical approach to health, a model of narrative medicine (Charon, 2006) is now developing in order to promote listening to the patient more attentively and to attest to the importance of the patient's experience when taking his illness into account (Dominicé & Waldvogel, 2009; Baeza & Janner Raimondi, 2018).

It should be obvious here how paradigmatic links are established between the evidence- based medicine model and the evidence-based practice in social work model. In both cases, the underlying epistemology, centered on an objectivizing and positivist approach, proceeds from the same overshadowing of a subject who has the potential capacity to state the knowledge he possesses about his own situation. The paradigm of a narrative clinic (Lani Bayle, 1999; Niewiadomski, 2012), however, refers to spaces and systems that extend beyond the realms of medicine, psychiatry or psychology. Focused on the biographical narrative, this paradigm generally derives from psychoanalytical epistemology. It encompasses a whole field of practices and research (Niewiadomski & Delory-Momberger, 2013) with an eye to developing a clinical orientation where the focus is less on care than on understanding the complexity of the interactions between the subject and a perpetually changing environment (Gaulejac, 2009)., The purpose of the narrative clinic – which belongs to the field of biographical research (Delory-Momberger, 2009) – is to study the processes of subject construction within the social space, that is, to grasp the ways in which individuals shape their own experiences, how they give meaning to the situations and events in their lives, and how they act and construct themselves in their historical, social, cultural and political environments. In this perspective, this approach focuses on individuals' experiences in social situations and the narrative reconstruction of the life history of one or more people through their oral and/or written narratives. This clinical orientation has four characteristics:

- First, this approach takes the subject's discourse on himself seriously and recognizes that attention to individuality has now become a major issue in research in the human and social sciences. It also claims that this discourse is a reliable way of understanding the complexity of the co-emerging relationships between individuals and society. The classic epistemological reservations that concern the questioning of a 'discourse of truth' through the use of biographical categories and the notion of 'biographical illusion' (Bourdieu, 1986) will be familiar to the reader. However, more than a discourse of 'truth' in the sense of the strict historical truth of reported facts, what is probably important to collect in a narrative reflects the 'truth' of a subject; in a given context, this produces a particular point of view on reality. No one will disagree that this point of view is tinged with subjectivity. Nevertheless, this subjectivity, inherent in human functioning and its categories of thought, is no less active in its practical consequences.

- Second, this approach differs significantly from the biomedical clinic, which, as we have seen, draws its epistemological foundations from the anatomical–clinical method: a particular sign points to a particular syndrome and then to a particular treatment; in the interest of efficiency, the practitioner pays relatively little attention to the patient's subjectivity (that is, to 'the body that he is'), preferring to apply therapeutic procedures supposedly adapted to the treatment of a partial object (that is, the 'body that he has'). The biomedical approach seeks to implement an observation-based clinic and the 'management' and objectification of the subject, which sometimes takes place at the cost of effacing the subject. Conversely, the narrative clinic favors a clinic that listens to a 'willing individual subject' and takes into account an individual who is clearly not reducible to observational data that can be collected.

- Third, the narrative clinic is based on a multidisciplinary theoretical framework designed to link the understanding of the subject's subjective reality with the objective reality of social facts. Indeed, when the biographical research perspective is adopted, the fields of psychoanalysis, sociology, social anthropology, ethnomethodology and psychosociology can be brought together effectively. In an attempt to break free from disciplinary barriers without ignoring them, the narrative clinic is particularly interested in the study of interactions between psychological and social processes.

- Fourth, a clinical posture aimed at being fully open to another person's discourse is not possible without professionals in the educational field working on *themselves*. Educational support presupposes that professionals can offer the user temporary help: he can thus face the challenges he is going through, understand the meaning of his unique trajectory and ultimately find his own path. However, this work requires practitioners to be doubly cautious: they must sublimate their tendency to influence the patient and avoid alienating the patient's desire to their own educational perspectives. In other words, they must work on their involvement in transference and counter-transference and endeavor to decode as precisely as possible the phenomena that affect these people. They must do so through a plural reading that can make the intersection of determining factors of diverse origins possible.

At a time when work organization models seem to be increasingly focused on entrepreneurialism, individual performance, quality evaluation, the obligation for results, user responsibility, contractualization and projects (Gaulejac, 2015), important transformations are being implemented in the social sector based on supposedly logical and pragmatic management criteria in order to define a set of instructions meant to guarantee 'best practices' (Niewiadomski & Bagros, 2003). While such practices may facilitate the highly valued processes of evaluation and of management and accounting control so common in current managerial policies, it is not at all certain that evidence-based practice in social work contributes to the effectiveness of on-the-ground social workers. A recent study conducted among professionals in the health and social field in an addiction service demonstrates the extent to which the instrumental rationality that presides over the application of such guidelines leads to largely counterproductive effects for both the professionals and users (Niewiadomski, 2017). In a summary article, we drew attention to the following situation:

> The participants in this research all testify to the growing influence of managerial logic in the daily life of their profession. This managerial logic is experienced as a logic of control in which the computerized coding of acts and quantitative evaluation procedures seem to them to lead to a genuine prescriptophrenia. Similarly, the tools and procedures for technicizing their trade lead to a gap between actual work and prescribed work. Thus, evaluation programs integrate only part of the actual work. But what is involved in support before and after hospitalization, as well as what contributes to the patient's movements of subjectification, are not covered by these tools and procedures and cannot be fully quantified. Moreover, these professionals notice a change in the time devoted to administrative and bureaucratic work, with time spent in front of their computer screens taking precedence over the time spent supporting their clients.
>
> (Niewiadomski, 2017)

Furthermore, because of the influx of new categories of individuals affected by social disaffiliation, the professional situations social workers are confronted with today are due to situations of psychological malaise rooted in specific, concrete social situations. These situations do not necessarily refer to the classical categories of psychopathology. Consequently, for social workers, the challenge is not so much to be interested in a subject that is a 'sign' of a pathology (even if it is of social origin) as to consider him a whole and a bearer of his own history. However, this approach can only be meaningful if the subject is able to give meaning to it himself in order to avoid the apparent confusion of his situation and to project himself into the future. Nevertheless, the subject – who is generally unaware of the social, familial and cultural determinations to which he is subjected – cannot carry out this work without appropriate assistance. It is therefore important to accompany this biographical detour and the related processes of subjectification in order to promote the construction of a historicity understood as the 'ability to move from the status of an object determined by history to that of a subject producing his own history' (Gaulejac, 1987). By looking back on himself and his history, by analyzing the social overdeterminations to which he has been subjected, the subject thus acquires autonomy and the possibility of giving a less negative meaning to what he is. This is the only way that a meaningful reintegration project can then be developed with the subject.

Conclusion

In contrast to evidence-based practice in social work, the clinical approach discussed here recognizes not only an individual 'user' of social services to whom standardized procedures will be proposed, but also an individual subject, in all the senses of this word. He is the 'willing subject' of the psychoanalytical clinic, but also a 'historical–social subject', a 'reflexive subject', capable of giving feedback on his experience, and finally, an 'acting subject', revealing who he is through his actions. From this perspective, the challenge is to offer him support that goes beyond the care given to an ordinary user by taking into account a given subject in a situation of temporary difficulty. The social worker will provide temporary accompaniment and support to help the user face the challenges he is going through in order to participate in understanding the meaning of the individual's trajectory as well as to help him find his own path. As opposed to prescriptive, or even evidence-based, practices, this work requires us to adopt a clinical posture focused on listening to the uniqueness of the subject and on avoiding the appropriation of his desire for our educational perspectives. Nevertheless, in the course of this approach, professionals may find themselves deeply affected by the suffering of others and by the feeling of powerlessness to deal with the difficulties encountered. The capacity for disillusionment is central and allows us to envision a professional commitment free of our personal expectations. To this end, Eugène Enriquez introduces the notion of 'the ethics of finiteness' – 'the ability of man to admit his finiteness, his mortality, his shortcomings and his flaws and to work on them in order to find his place in life with as high a level of awareness as possible' (Enriquez, 2000, p. 299).

> Recognizing his flaws allows him to accept narcissistic wounds, to submit to a process of mourning, to admit his moments of helplessness – in short, to achieve a certain degree of lucidity about himself and others. Analyzing oneself in this way encourages selflessness, a moderate love of oneself that opens up to love for others or, if this appears excessive, to interest in others.
>
> (Enriquez, 2000, p. 299)

It is therefore important to preserve the mechanisms for analyzing the practice and supervision of teams so that professionals can verbalize and reformulate their difficulties and feelings.

Under these conditions, being able to offer social service users a sufficiently empathic and secure space to express themselves with a view to developing a project based on the reappropriation of their personal history can contribute to freeing the capacities for action of a subject who has temporarily lost his reference points and sense of meaning, given his situation of material precariousness. It is to be hoped that proper educational support will enable him to regain the energy needed to make informed decisions about the direction of his own life. Such is the fundamental purpose of a narrative clinic in the field of social work.

Note

1   This contribution is a revised synthesis of previous work, the most salient elements of which can be found in the following work: Niewiadomski, C. (2012) *Recherche biographique et clinique narrative.* Toulouse, Érès.

References

Astier, I., & Duvoux, N. (2006). *La société biographique: une injonction à vivre dignement.* Paris: L'Harmattan.

Autès, M. (1999). *Les paradoxes du travail social.* Paris: Dunod.

Baeza, C., & Janner Raimondi, M. (2018). *Grandir avec la maladie. Esquisses biographiques de portraits d'adolescents malades chroniques*. Paris: Teraèdre.

Bernard, C. (1966). *Introduction à l'étude de la médecine expérimentale*. Paris: Garnier-Flammarion.

Bourdieu, P. (1986). L'illusion biographique. *Actes de la recherche en sciences sociales, 62–63*, 69–72.

Capdevielle, J., & Rey, H. (2012). *La mondialisation des inégalités*. Paris: Seuil.

Castel, R. (1992). Définir le social? In Karsz, S. (Ed.), *Déconstruire le social*. Séminaire 1. Paris: L'Harmattan.

Castel, R. (1995). *Les métamorphoses de la question sociale. Une chronique du salariat*. Paris: Gallimard.

Castel, R. (2004). La face cachée de l'individu hypermoderne: l'individu par défaut. In Aubert, N. (Ed.), *L'individu hypermoderne*. Toulouse: Érès.

Castel, R. (2009). *La montée des incertitudes. Travail, protections, statut de l'individu*. Paris: Seuil.

Charon, R. (2006). *Narrative medicine: Honoring the stories of illness*. New York: Oxford University Press.

Chauvière, M. (2007). *Trop de gestion tue le social. Essai sur une discrète chalandisation*. Paris: La Découverte.

Dejours, C. (1998). *Souffrance en France. La banalisation de l'injustice sociale*. Paris: Seuil.

Delory-Momberger, C., & Niewiadomski, C. (2009). *Vivre – Survivre. Récits de résistance*. Paris: Téraèdre.

Delory-Momberger, C. (2009). *La condition biographique. Essai sur le récit de soi dans la modernité avancée*. Paris: Téraèdre.

Dominicé, P., & Waldvogel, F. (2009). *Dialogue sur la médecine de demain*. Paris: PUF.

Dubet, F. (2002). *Le déclin de l'institution*. Paris: Seuil.

Enriquez, E. (2000). La recherche et l'intervention psychosociologiques à l'épreuve de l'éthique. In Feldman J. & Kohn, R. C. (Eds.), *L'éthique dans la pratique des sciences humaines*. Paris: L'Harmattan.

Foucault M. (1963) *Naissance de la clinique*. Paris: PUF.

Gaulejac, V. de. (1987). *La névrose de classe*. Paris: Hommes et groupes.

Gaulejac, V. de. (2009). *Qui est 'Je'? Sociologie clinique du sujet*. Paris: Seuil.

Gaulejac, V. de. (2015). *Travail, les raisons de la colère*. Paris: Seuil.

Lani Bayle, M. (1999). *L'Enfant et son histoire, vers une clinique narrative*. Toulouse: Érès.

Lazarus A. (1995). *Une souffrance qu'on ne peut plus cacher*. Inter-ministerial report.

Martuccelli, D. (2010). *La société singulariste*. Paris: Armand Colin.

Niewiadomski, C., & Bagros, P. (2003). *Penser la dimension humaine à l'hôpital*. Paris: Seli Arslan.

Niewiadomski, C. (2012). *Recherche biographique et clinique narrative*. Toulouse: Érès.

Niewiadomski C., & Delory-Momberger C. (Eds.) (2013). *Territoires contemporains de la recherche biographique*. Paris: Teraèdre.

Niewiadomski, C. (2017). Une recherche-action pour interroger l'expérience des usagers et les conditions contemporaines d'exercice des métiers du soin et du travail social en région Nord-Pas de Calais. In Niewiadomski, C., Portelance, L., & Perez-Roux, T. (Eds.), *Collaborations chercheur(s)-praticien(s): nouvelles formes, nouveaux enjeux? Revue Éducation et Socialisation, 45*. http://journals.openedition.org/edso/2627.

Ravon, B. (2005). *Vers une clinique du lien défait*. In Ion, J. (Ed.), *Travail social et souffrance psychique*. Paris: Dunod.

Rosanvallon, P. (1981). *La crise de l'État-Providence*. Paris: Seuil.

5

The clinic, psychoanalysis and social work
Issues in practice and in training

Sébastien Ponnou

Introduction

The aim of this chapter is to highlight the impasses of evidence-based approaches and to show the need for clinical psychoanalysis in the treatment of the suffering of children and their parents. Taking this perspective, I will rely on a series of research studies focusing on Attention Deficit Disorder with or without Hyperactivity (ADHD) and on work devoted to the psycho-analytical conceptions of the clinic to infer the issues of practice and training in the field of social work.[1]

*

The diagnostic criteria for Attention Deficit Disorder with or without Hyper-activity (ADHD) were first defined in the DSM-III in 1980 based on a triad of symptoms: attention deficit associated (or not) with excessive impulsivity and hyperactivity. ADHD is the most common mental disorder among school-age children. For this reason, it has been the subject of thousands of international research projects (as of January 2019, there were more than 30,000 references in Pubmed). The number of studies on hyperactivity in the past thirty years has increased from 177 between 1987 and 1989 to 2,053 in 2015, an indicator that scientific knowledge has changed considerably over that same period.

DOI: 10.4324/9781003296416-8

Initial studies in the 1990s argued for a neurological, neurodevelopmental and genetic etiology of ADHD and supported the benefits of methylphenidate (Ritalin®, Concerta®, Quasim®) in the treatment of hyperactive children. Subsequent studies and meta-analyses have largely reduced or even refuted the impact of these biological factors and the benefits of drug treatment related to the risks of academic failure, delinquency or addiction associated with ADHD.

However, the prescription rate of methylphenidate in France has been increasing at an alarming rate since the mid-1990s. In 2005, the French Ministry of the Interior recommended the early reporting of children at risk of hyperactivity as a way of preventing delinquency, supporting a controversial report by the National Institute of Health and Medical Research (INSERM) on conduct and behavioral disorders in children (2005).[2] In 2011, the only study available in France showed a prevalence rate of 3.5 to 5.6%, concluding that this pathology was under-diagnosed and under-medicated and that a genuine epidemic of ADHD was expected in the following years.

Several recent studies have questioned the causes of the gaps between international scientific consensus, perceptions on the part of the general public and the reality of care and education practices in France. These studies have highlighted massive systematic distortions in scientific research linked to scientific bias, media bias and conflicts of interest between the pharmaceutical industry, experts, specialized services and associations of parents with children diagnosed with ADHD (Bourdaa et al., 2015; Ponnou & Gonon, 2017; Ponnou, Haliday & Gonon, 2020; Gonon, Dumas-Mallet & Ponnou, 2019). These distortions and conflicts of interest are all the more serious as they shape the layman's perception of the issues, as well as health policies and demands for care and care practices. They represent a serious obstacle to the use of alternative practices like psychoanalysis or psychosocial approaches, which have proven effective in a clinical setting and constitute a specificity of French psychiatry and psychopathology. I will demonstrate the scope of this approach by presenting a specific clinical situation in an institution.

Taking as a point of departure the impasses of biomedical and psychosocial approaches to ADHD on the one hand, and the effects of psychoanalytical practices on children diagnosed as 'hyperactive' on the other, I have focused more broadly on the psychoanalytical conceptions of the clinic to discuss perspectives and challenges in terms of social practices and the training of social workers. I will present all of these approaches and results in such a way as to contribute to clinical-based practice in social work.

Limitations of biomedical and psychosocial approaches to mental disorders and the need for psychoanalysis: the case of hyperactivity/ADHD

The impasses of neurological and genetic approaches to ADHD

From a biomedical perspective, brain imaging studies published in the 1990s suggested that advances in neurobiology would soon lead to the validation of diagnostic tools (Dougherty et al., 1999). However, there is currently no known test for ADHD (Weyandt, Swentosky, & Gudmundsdottir, 2013). Ask a doctor to diagnose hyperactivity by brain imaging, and you may be disappointed. Indeed, hundreds of studies in structural and functional brain imaging have shown differences associated with ADHD, but none of these differences corresponds to brain damage. It is therefore impossible to describe ADHD as a neurological disease or disorder. Moreover, these differences are quantitatively minimal and are only statistically significant when considering groups of children. Some earlier studies also suggested that ADHD is caused by a dopamine deficiency or dysfunction of the dopamine neurotransmitters. This perspective has been rigorously tested and refuted (Gonon, 2009). We can thus conclude that the hypotheses concerning the neurological etiology of ADHD now appear scientifically weak or dated (Gonon & al., 2012).

Moreover, neurobiological studies tell us nothing about a potential cause of ADHD. The brain is a fundamentally plastic organ, and brain imaging studies are unable to determine whether the observations made are the cause or consequence of a given type of psychological development specific to subjects with hyperactivity symptoms.

In addition, earlier studies reported a strong genetic etiology for ADHD. These associations or their causal impact have been largely refuted by subsequent studies and meta-analyses. Currently, the most established and significant genetic risk factor is the association of ADHD with an allele of the gene encoding the dopamine D4 receptor (Gizer, Ficks, & Waldman, 2009). According to this meta-analysis, this risk factor is only 1.33 (Gizer et al., 2009). More specifically, this allele is present in 23% of children diagnosed with ADHD and only 17% of children in control groups (Shaw, Gornick, & al., 2007; Smith, 2010), amounting in fact to no effect at all. A recent review of more than 300 genetic studies thus concluded that 'the results from genetic studies on ADHD remain inconsistent and do not lead to any conclusions'

(Li et al., 2014). More generally, genetic studies – which are increasingly powerful and test millions of DNA variants in thousands of patients – all make the same observation: the weight of genetic risk factors in the occurrence of mental disorders (including ADHD) decreases as the quality of studies improves (Gaulger et al., 2014; Gonon, Dumas-Mallet & Ponnou, 2019).

Harmful effects of treatment with methylphenidate

Studies in the 1990s reported that treatment with psychostimulants was effective in alleviating the symptoms of ADHD. The only psychostimulant authorized in France is methylphenidate in its simple form (Ritalin®) or in delayed form (Concerta®, Ritaline-LP® and Quasym®). The beneficial and seemingly paradoxical effect of treatment finds its explanation in the fact that psychostimulants increase attention. The alleviation of hyperactive and impulsive symptoms is a consequence of an increased attention span. However, according to several American studies that have followed very large cohorts of children for years, psychostimulant treatment has no long-term benefit related to the risks of academic failure, delinquency and substance abuse associated with ADHD (Currie, Stabile & Jones, 2014; Gonon, Guilé & Cohen, 2010; Humphreys, Eng, & Lee, 2013; Loe & Feldman, 2007; Sharpe, 2014; The MTA Cooperative Group, 1999).

In addition, several studies have highlighted the harmful effects of long-term psychostimulant treatment on children's health (www.psychwatchaustralia.com/treating-adhd). Doctors and health institutes are well aware of these risks, which are documented and listed by the French National Agency for the Safety of Medicines and Health Products (or ANSM). These include sleep disorders, weight loss, potential aggravation of psychiatric pathologies and violent or suicidal acts and proven risks of cardiovascular and cerebrovascular diseases such as sudden cardiac death, acute myocardial infarction and stroke. However, according to official sources, prescriptions of methylphenidate in France increased by 167% between 2005 and 2009, and again by 44% between 2008 and 2011, that is, by more than 10% per year between 2012 and 2015 (ANSM, 2013, p. 8; ANSM, 2017). This increase is nothing less than extraordinary. However, in a 1995 interview with the newspaper *Le Monde*, the representative of the Ciba-Geigy® laboratory, authorized to market methylphenidate in France, argued that his company's approach was disinterested: '[F]or our part, [...] we are not expecting a massive increase in sales [...] This drug is not the only one for which marketing is not a source of profit' (Nau, 1995).

The trap of prevalence studies

Another difficulty concerns ADHD prevalence studies. A prevalence study makes it possible to observe the frequency of the occurrence of a health-related phenomenon in a given population: it is effectively a snapshot of the number of cases for a pathology at a given time. However, while no cases of ADHD were reported in France before the 1990s, the rate of onset of this disease suddenly became pandemic: one child per class, then one in ten. In France, the diagnosis of hyperactivity did not begin to emerge until after the introduction on the market of methylphenidate drug treatment in 1995. Since no biological marker can confirm the diagnosis of ADHD, it cannot be considered a disease, but rather a 'heuristic construct' (Frances & Widiger, 2012). However, this heuristic seems at the very least suspicious insofar as it is linked to the commercialization of the molecule known – wrongly – to cure hyperactivity. ADHD exemplifies this extraordinary reversal of classical clinical and medical logic (Canguilhem, 1966; Foucault, 1963): the question is no longer how to find a treatment likely to cure the disease or of developing a therapy that relieves a patient's suffering, but rather one of building the nosographic framework best adapted to the use of a given molecule.

Since ADHD is only described in terms of behavioral symptoms, its diagnosis is relatively subjective and varies according to culture and social representations. Accordingly, the prevalence of ADHD is 10% in the USA. However, this representation varies considerably from one state to another: in 2007, for instance, a study estimated the prevalence rate of children with ADHD at 5.6% in Nevada and 14.3% in Alabama. In the northern Italian region of Lombardy, the prevalence rate of hyperactivity was estimated at 0.5% in 2012, while in France, the only available study estimates this prevalence at between 3.5% and 5.6% (Faraone, Sergeant, Gillberg, & Biederman, 2003; Visser et al., 2010; Bonati & Reale, 2013; Lecendreux, Konofal, & Faraone, 2011). In addition to demographic and cultural differences, variations in international ADHD prevalence rates – between 0.4% and 16.6% – are determined by the methodology used, be it a clinical study, a telephone survey, a questionnaire given to parents and teachers or a drug distribution study (Polancyk et al., 2014). Unsurprisingly, studies based on telephone surveys and questionnaires present significantly higher prevalence rates than clinical studies where the practitioner and the child meet directly. Unfortunately, these clinical studies are particularly difficult to implement from a methodological point of view. This difficulty leaves the field wide open to aberrant extrapolations, which systematically point to diagnostic delays and the increased need for prescription.

Scientific bias, media bias, massive and systematic conflicts of interest

Information available in the media and in the professional literature (in the fields of medicine, psychology, education and social work) dedicated to ADHD focuses on biomedical approaches to hyperactivity, supporting the biological origin of this pathology and, consequently, the effectiveness of drug treatment. Consequently, more than 87% of the information available on television, 83% of the information published in the press and 94% of the data presented on the Internet runs counter to international scientific consensus (Ponnou, Haliday & Gonon, 2020). The same can be said for doctoral theses devoted to ADHD in France (91.3%), particularly medical theses (94.4%). High levels of distortion have also been reported in the specialized literature for teachers and social workers (Kohout-Diaz, 2013; Ponnou, Kohout-Diaz & Gonon, 2015). These distortions are extremely problematic insofar as they shape the perceptions of both the general public and professionals, guiding both care requests and care practices (Roebroeck & Ponnou, 2018). They induce a risk of over-diagnosis and over-medication of ADHD and contribute to masking the social risk factors for both hyperactivity and the relevance and effects of psychoanalytically oriented practices on so-called 'ADHD children' and their families.

I have questioned the causes of these systematic distortions and highlighted the scientific biases, media biases and massive conflicts of interest that could contribute to these gaps. I will now give some examples, first at the international level:

- Concerning examples of scientific falsifications and bias, the most obvious example concerning ADHD is perhaps the study by Dougherty and colleagues, published in 1999 in the prestigious journal *The Lancet*. The study concluded that the brain level of the dopamine transporter is 70% higher in hyperactive patients. The dopamine transporter is a membrane protein that regulates neurotransmission involving dopamine. This article was widely covered by the mainstream press because it claimed to explain the cause of ADHD and the rationale for the treatment of it, since psychostimulants inhibit this transporter. What the authors failed to mention in the 1999 article is that 4 of their 6 patients had previously received long-term treatment with a psychostimulant, information that was not published until 2005. Subsequent studies have shown that dopamine transporter levels are similar in control subjects and untreated patients with ADHD and that prolonged treatment with psychostimulants increases this rate. This has had particularly harmful consequences in terms of research, professional practices and perceptions of the general public insofar as it has greatly contributed to conveying the idea of neurological causality and supporting the use of psychostimulants in children with ADHD. Another example is the study by Barbaresi and colleagues (2007), which reports that treating children with ADHD with a psychostimulant neither improves their reading performance nor reduces their risk of early school leaving. However, on the sole basis of a class repetition rate that is slightly lower, they conclude that this treatment improves their school performance in the long term. This serious form of distortion, referred to as spin, consists of a glaring inconsistency between the observations described in the article and the conclusion drawn at the end of the article and/or in the summary. Unfortunately, this practice is widespread in the field of evidence-based research (Gonon, Dumas-Mallet & Ponnou, 2019).

- With respect to examples of media bias, the study by Dougherty and colleagues (1999) was covered by twenty-two press articles in the week following its publication. Of the 11 subsequent studies, only one was covered, and by only three press articles, none of which indicated that the original study, although covered by their publication, had been contradicted by the subsequent study. Similarly, the conclusion of the study by Barbaresi and colleagues was simply reproduced in 20 of the 21 articles in the Anglo-Saxon press that covered the study. Only the *Guardian* article correctly described all the observations and therefore criticized the conclusion drawn in the study. In reality, journalistic standards favor novelty and the spectacular and very strongly favor studies published by prestigious scientific journals. This observation can be explained by the fact that these journals produce press releases summarizing some of the articles they publish; these press releases are then the direct source of more than 80% of press articles reporting biomedical discoveries. Most press articles are very closely inspired by these press releases and uncritically repeat the biases and exaggerations found therein. Moreover, the press hardly ever informs the public when the studies it has covered are subsequently contradicted (Gonon, Dumas-Mallet & Ponnou, 2019).

More specifically, in France:

- The only study on the prevalence of ADHD in France is based on a telephone survey that concluded that this pathology was under-diagnosed and under-medicated (Lecendreux et al., 2011). This study, conducted by researchers from a specialized department of the Robert Debré Hospital in Paris, had a significant scientific impact and on the media as well.

It is systematically cited in magazines or the general press, professional literature or theses in medicine and human sciences. However, beyond its methodological weaknesses (this telephone survey was delegated to a survey institute and conducted by operators trained 'on the fly'), this study was financed by the pharmaceutical laboratory Shire®, which markets the most widely prescribed version of methylphenidate in France. It therefore seems to us that the conflict of interest is significant enough to call into question the validity of the study and the probity of the experts whose opinion was solicited.

- Similarly, the information available on the Internet refers largely to the only association of parents of children with ADHD in France (www.tdah-france.fr). Statements by the members of this association or references to the association's website are present in thirteen websites and fifteen press articles. The website and the members of the association support a biomedical approach to ADHD. However, the website mentions the payment of grants from the SHIRE® laboratory to the association: the information disseminated there is thus subject to conflicts of interest as well. In addition, in 2004, the association received the 9000-euro proximology prize awarded for its support to families of ADHD children and finance by the same pharmaceutical laboratory marketing Ritalin®.

- The experts most frequently interviewed on television, in the press and on the Internet come from the same department of the Robert Debré Hospital (as does the main author of the prevalence study mentioned above) and advocate a pharmaceutical approach in the treatment of ADHD. These experts also maintain close links with the ADHD–France website. These observations suggest that a handful of experts have significant influence in the mainstream media. Such influence can also have an impact on the practices of professionals. Social work students, for example, believe that information transmitted by the media has a significant influence on their perceptions of mental disorders (Roebroeck & Ponnou, 2018). In general, these distortions shape prevailing attitudes, care requests, professional practices and even health policies. The president of the association Hypersupers-TDAH France, for instance, although involved in recurring conflicts of interest with the pharmaceutical industry, has recently been appointed to the National Council on Autism Spectrum Disorders (ASD) and Neurodevelopmental Disorders (NDD), which ensures the shared monitoring of the deployment of the national strategy for autism 2018–22.

- Another type of conflict of interest concerns the sponsorship of public hospital services by the pharmaceutical industry. See for example:

www.u2peanantes.files.wordpress.com/2018/05/v5-maquette-tdah-3-nantes.pdf.

There are networks and mechanisms of influence which, despite all ordinary scientific considerations and despite the interests of children and their families, are a hindrance to research dedicated to ADHD in France and internationally. Even the associations supposed to represent these families contribute to this phenomenon:

> The pharmaceutical industry requires certain hospital services to conduct clinical trials and to obtain marketing authorization for their products. The results of these studies allow not only the recognition of partner hospital services but also the possibility for them to participate in conferences giving their activity increased visibility and allowing the financing of projects internal to the service. The association participates in the recruitment of families, who provide cohorts of patients for clinical trials that contribute to the co-production of scientific facts.
>
> (Jupille, 2011)

These limitations, distortions, biases and conflicts of interest all incite us to adopt a particularly cautious attitude regarding the possibilities of applying the results of biomedical research on ADHD in the field of social intervention. They relativize the strength of the evidence, and consequently, the scope of evidence-based approaches and their potential application in terms of care and education practices.

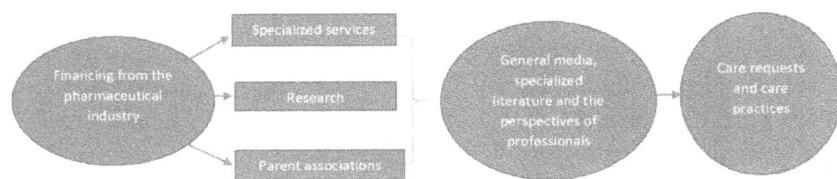

Figure 5.1 Conflicts of interest and the pharmaceutical industry's influence on care requests and practices

Interests and limits of social and environmental risk factors for hyperactivity/ADHD

Serving as a counterpoint of sorts to biomedical approaches, many social and environmental risk factors have been documented and confirmed in the international scientific literature. These include exposure to toxic levels of lead, premature birth, severe maltreatment of children, children with mentally ill parents, poor parent–child interactions, low family economic level, low parental education, children of single-parent families and children born to teenage mothers. Finally, excessive exposure to television before the age of three seems particularly harmful to the development of a child's attention span. These same risk factors have been identified in France (Needleman et al., 1979; Linnet & al., 2006; Szatmari et al., 1990; Biederman, Faraone & Monuteaux, 2002; Biederman & al, 1995; Tallmadge & Barkley, 1983; Froehlich et al., 2007; Christakis, Zimmerman, DiGiuseppe & McCarty, 2004; Harlé & Desmurget, 2012; Swing, Gentile, Anderson & Walsh, 2010; Galéra et al., 2011).

In addition, several studies have shown that the American education system contributes significantly to the increase in the diagnosis of ADHD. In one Virginia city, for example, 63% of schoolchildren who had skipped a year of school were treated with psychostimulants (LeFever, Dawson, & Morrow, 1999). In the general American population, the prevalence of ADHD varies according to month of birth, confirming that the youngest pupils in a class are at highest risk (Elder, 2010; Evans, Morrill, & Parente, 2010). A Canadian study showed that the number of boys treated with a psychostimulant is 41% higher if they were born in December than if they were born in January. For girls, this increase reaches 77% (Morrow & al., 2012). Elder (2010) shows that the hyperactive behavior of the youngest children in a class is more frequently judged pathological by their teachers than by their parents. It should be borne in mind that teachers report hyperactive children by completing the Conners (1969) rating scales.[3] We know that American teachers are encouraged by their superiors to report possible cases of ADHD to parents. Since the 1990 Act, American schools have received additional funding for each child diagnosed. This funding varies from county to county. The pharmaceutical industry provides teachers with the necessary documentation (Phillips, 2006). Finally, schools are evaluated according to the performance of their pupils; the schools are thus encouraged to increase the academic level of their pupils. One study comparing American states established a positive correlation between the binding nature of these incentives and the prevalence of ADHD (Bokhari & Schneider, 2011). Unfortunately, similar studies are lacking in France, where they would allow us to take a more critical look at contemporary hyperactivity issues and teaching practices.

The social and environmental risk factors highlighted in the international literature seem interesting to us insofar as they can be addressed by appropriate socio-educational policies and practices. Accordingly, the rate of premature births is 13% in the USA, while it is only 6% in France. Similarly, according to the WHO, the number of births per 1000 teenage girls is 42 in the USA and 10 in France (but only 4 in Holland). Unfortunately, these social factors are too often masked by the prevalence of biomedical discourse, the result being that social workers are not informed of risk factors at the core of their profession (Ponnou, Kohout-Diaz & Gonon, 2015).

However, despite their importance, these social factors do not have a predetermining effect: we should not apply them systematically as this can limit the effectiveness of care and education practices. Preventive measures are all the more complex to implement since some family situations have cumulative risk factors. In addition, the effects of these risk factors vary considerably depending on the children and their environment. For example, one Canadian study shows that the preventive measures used sometimes fail to achieve the expected results and lead to increased stigma and difficulties (Parazelli et al., 2003).

I will now argue that it is possible to start from a posture based not on scientific knowledge but rather on what each individual subject says and manifests in a clinical context. Indeed, if we take into account the words of the child and his parents and the history and experiences specific to each individual, help for greater well-being and a more highly integrated social fabric then become possible. Clinical approaches to ADHD are evident in the French-speaking literature dedicated to this pathology and have the advantage of overcoming the impasses related to diagnosis and etiology. Indeed, from this perspective, symptoms of ADHD are considered to be the way a child expresses that yet uncertain truth about himself: it is only via bodily symptoms or 'disorders' that this truth can manifest itself. These conceptions necessitate reaching out to the child, and if possible, to his parents, through speaking. It is a matter of embracing the child's symptom, of hearing him so as to accompany him as he considers, then discovers what in him is trying to express itself and to support him in his self-construction and integration into society.

The need for psychoanalysis

The impasses and limitations of biomedical and psychosocial approaches to hyperactivity supported by scientific approaches and evidence-based models reveal the need for psychoanalysis in the care of so-called hyperactive children and their families. I will now propose to show the interest of psychoanalysis through a clinical presentation within an institution.

*

Franck was nine years old when he arrived at a therapeutic institute to which he had been sent upon notification from a French departmental center for disabled persons (MDPH[4]) and at his mother's request following a deterioration of her relationship with him: she found herself at her wits' end. A diagnosis of hyperactivity had been made by a specialized unit the year before he was admitted to the institution, and he was being treated with methylphenidate, which had no visible effect on his agitation. Franck had the classic symptoms of hyperactivity, but with no signs of comorbidity or associated disorder. He was a happy child, at ease with respect to the faculty of speech, to knowledge and to the relationships he had with adults and peers. His academic performance was reasonable despite his agitation. He liked going to school and was involved in various projects and activities. Admission to the institute was granted on condition that the question of medicalized treatment remain the responsibility of the prescribing hospital service. Ordinary schooling was maintained. Franck became a boarder during the week and returned to his mother's home for weekends and school holidays.

Franck's story was marked by the sudden separation of his parents three months before he was born. His father had left home without any apparent reason after several years of life with Franck's mother and despite having acknowledged paternity at the beginning of the pregnancy. He literally disappeared without any explanation. Franck's mother then embarked on a desperate quest to find this man, who would vanish every time she located him and tried to reestablish contact with him. Franck did not know his father, nor had he ever met him.

Beyond the typical manifestations of ADHD – major at that time – an initial point of reference in working with the child was a particular symptom the mother herself had diagnosed: Franck was said to be lactose intolerant. However, she refused any medical investigation. In parallel with the standard procedures and accommodations rendered necessary by this supposed symptom, I decided to work on intolerance, with both Franck and his mother. Indeed, the difficulties at play in the mother–child relationship – which the symptom sums up perfectly – play an important role in the reasons for Franck's placement in the institution. This clinical intervention at first consisted in working with Franck on small everyday details over five years, coupled with occasional interviews with his mother. Intolerance quickly gave way to a pluralized 'intolerable', which then became dialecticized and could thus be the subject of work concerning symbolization. For Franck, this meant an intolerable form of maternal omnipotence embodied in the punishments inflicted on him by his mother (isolation, toys taken away from him) – practices that the institution identified and named: inter-diction. For the mother, the difficulties caused by her son's behavior opened the door to the intolerable abandonment that was wreaking havoc on her – that of her ex-partner, Franck's father – which served as a condensation point for a kind of untreatable *jouissance* to which she was constantly connected and of which she was the object. Franck embodied this overwhelming abandonment, of which he had become the basis, the trace and the unbearable remnant. Hyperactivity could then be interpreted as a replay of the father's flight forward as well as a means of defense that the subject used against a foreign *jouissance*, inherited, intimated by the Other and returning to the body.

The use of each one's narrative as well as open spaces through group practice had rapid effects: de-condensation of the unbearable aspects of the mother–child partnership, dissipation of the symptoms of agitation and hyperactivity associated with the extraction and displacement of *jouissance* of the Other of which Franck had taken bodily charge. Consequently, drug treatment was ceased, third-party references for both mother and child were built and the possibility of forging new forms of social relations and relationship to knowledge emerged.

★

Franck's situation seems revealing to us insofar as it specifies the Lacanian approach to hyperactivity and highlights the interest of psychoanalysis in the support and guidance of children diagnosed with ADHD and their families. In the initial situation, Franck was in the position of object of *jouissance* of his mother's fantasy. His agitation echoed 'the impossible separation of a fundamentally present Other' (Cottet, 2012; Lefort & Lefort, 1988). Hyperactivity evokes 'a clinical movement that opposes the static nature of the maternal fantasy' (Cottet, 2012, p. 82). This relatively common position[5] – which perhaps specifies the position of the hyperactive subject – finds here its point of attachment inasmuch as Franck condenses the intolerable *jouissance* of the father's abandonment of the mother. The emphasis on the transition from intolerance to intolerable involves the construction and sharing of a meaningful framework that allows the child to move from this point of identification to the object of maternal fantasy. Diametrically opposed to the reductionism and pure speculation of biological psychiatry (Gonon, 2011), speech-oriented treatment leads to lasting effects that enable the subject to seize upon his opportunity to create with respect to his relationship with the Other and with society.

Psychoanalytical conceptions of the clinic

The steps taken regarding ADHD have led to taking a closer look at the psychoanalytical conceptions of the clinic. I thus systematically analyzed the term 'clinic(al)' in the database of the École de la Cause Freudienne (ECF) and in all the corpora of Sigmund Freud, Jacques Lacan and Jacques-Alain

Miller, whose texts and seminars were collected digitally. This work consisted in interpreting this unpublished material by grouping relevant occurrences according to quantitative (frequency) and qualitative (meaning) criteria. I condensed the results obtained into four main categories: (1) clinic, transfer and psychoanalytical politics of the symptom; (2) the clinic is 'real' that is impossible to bear; (3) clinical and ethical aspects of psychoanalysis; and (4) the clinic and the teaching of psychoanalysis. I propose to present their salient features in order to infer their perspectives in terms of how to handle transference in social practices and in terms of writing the clinic and training social workers.

Clinic, transference and psychoanalytical politics of the symptom

Freud manifested little interest in the question of the clinic, and when doing do, referred it almost exclusively to the field of psychiatry. Lacan and Miller sometimes echo this theme, producing a well-argued critique of the clinic's categorical uses and highlighting the basis of a clinic inspired by psychoanalytical knowledge. From the very beginning of his teaching, Lacan argues that the description of clinical material was conditioned by the doctrine adopted by the clinician with regard to the knowledge he had at his disposal, insofar as he was also responsible for the patient's symptom: 'What I bring on the subject of the clinic is this: namely that, as analysts, we have to participate in the symptom' (Lacan, unpublished, lesson from 5 May 1965; Lacan, unpublished, lesson from 20 April 1966). Lacan argues that the symptom is structured starting from the signifiers and knowledge in the social field and makes knowledge the pivot of transference: in the process of an analytical cure, the subject assumes on the part of the Other, represented by the analyst, knowledge about his being, his suffering, his pathology or therapy, and even more essentially, knowledge about his symptom. And it is in the context of this supposed knowledge – in other words, of the place of transference – that the subject engages in analytical work. The complementation of the symptom by the analyst, via the knowledge that the subject supposes on the part of the analyst, implies that the psychoanalytical clinic becomes the knowledge of the transference that, in the course of the experience, functions as truth. From this, Lacan deduces the clinician's share of how the symptom that the subject delivers to him takes form and is treated. With Lacan, transition from the medical clinic to the psychoanalytical clinic, or even from a biological clinic to a discursive clinic, begins with a politics of the symptom tied to the transferential dimension.

This then becomes the focus of analytical work. Lacan has no problem with the reference to doctrine, that is, to pre-established conceptual material that can serve as a grid of analysis for the practitioner, insofar as: (1) he moves from the simple objectification of the patient to considering the responsibility of the analysand with regard to the symptom; (2) he considers the responsibility of the clinician in the treatment of the defined symptom as singular knowledge, already constituted and 'in waiting', which affects the subject without his knowledge; and (3) the psychoanalytical clinic specifies itself to be a transference clinic based on a *presumption* of knowledge (Ponnou, 2016).

The clinic is 'real' that is impossible to bear

The Clinical Section of the Department of Psychoanalysis of the University of Paris 8 opened in 1977. It was then that Lacan gave his clearest definition of the clinic: 'the clinic is "real" as impossible to bear' (Lacan, 1977). The psychoanalytical clinic refers to the 'real' that Lacan defines as unbearable. When it is related to 'real', the clinic escapes the power of symbolism and imagination, words and images, categories and diagnostic nomenclatures. Consequently, the form it takes depends on the equivocation introduced by the use of the verb 'to bear': insofar as it is not borne by the signifier – it is precisely that which escapes the power of words, representations and knowledge – it refers to human pain, to the unbearable. A clinic of the unspeakable, even a clinic as the name of that which bears no name. This orientation definitively displaces the psychoanalytical clinic from the impasse of categorizations and sheds new light on the individuality of the subject. References to discourse and speech are also affected, since the passage from the symbolic to the real focuses the analytical clinic on the 'phenomena of rupture in the symbolic chain' (Miller, unpublished, lesson of 23 March 1999) which can produce a disengagement from the enunciation, in other words, reintroduce a subject into knowledge.

Clinical and ethical aspects of psychoanalysis

The topic of ethics is regularly raised by Lacan and Miller when it comes to questioning the specificity of the clinic's psychoanalytical conceptions. The clinical and ethical aspects of psychoanalysis revolve around the principle of individuality, such that the clinic is not about example but about paradigm, about the event (Miller, unpublished, lesson of 12 March 2008) that can be rendered logical but impossible to universalize in terms of application (Miller, unpublished, lesson of 17 March 1982). On the question of individuality, Lacan first refers to Spinoza, then to Kantian ethics, traditionally indexed by ethical phrases of conviction or ethics of duty (Kant, 1993; Lacan, 1966). Kant's ethics of duty represents a continuity from the specific to the universal: the man of conviction exerts his influence on the course of time and testifies to his ability to take charge of the transformations of the world. Yet this ethic is incomplete – a space of interpretation that allows the subject to support his utterance and his responsibility within the social bond. The ethics of conviction is an ethics of reality if it does not respond to any morality, any ideal, or if it refers not to a predetermined object but rather to a core of the impossible at the heart of the subject: if your desire were the law, what could you desire? Kantian ethics – *Do your duty!* – thus opens onto the dizzying enigma of desire – *Which one?* It creates an imposition that becomes a mystery, to which the subject must find or invent his own solutions. It leads to the advent of an aesthetic, a creative formula that reconciles the singular being with the collective without being able to rely on the certainty of typical solutions. By bringing together the registers of individuality, conviction, responsibility and aesthetics, ethics and the clinic draw the political axis of psychoanalysis.

The clinic and the teaching of psychoanalysis

Miller comments extensively on the place of the clinic in the teaching of psychoanalysis and presents the clinician as the one who, in a complex narrative, is particularly skilled at revealing a constant that is not immediately obvious but reflects the unconscious text of the subject:

> In psychoanalysis, forced choice is what must be introduced to respond to the aberrations to which the concept of free alienation can lead. Free association is only there to reveal the subject's forced choice. Indeed, this is what makes clinical case histories successful when the analyst presents and constructs them. He builds them because he selects them. He does not give an exhaustive report, which in any case is impossible; rather, he selects and builds. What makes such narratives so successful [...] is that the analyst manages to present them as a series of forced choices. They are forced choices but choices nonetheless.
>
> (Miller, unpublished, lesson of 15 May 1985)

This reference to forced choices refers to a Lacanian conception of the unconscious as a discourse of the Other, of which the clinician becomes an amanuensis or secretary. Accordingly, the conjectural nature of clinical constructions in psychoanalysis no longer poses a problem insofar as they take up the logic of the subject's unconscious text. It is in this perspective that Miller mentions the scientific style of the account of the experiment, which is justified if each subject is his own mathema, in other words, his own formula or equation. However, he points out that not everything in the clinic is mathematicizable and invites us to undertake the narrative of clinical cases against a background of the incomprehensible, of opacity, or as an effort of poetry.

Issues in the practice and training of psychoanalytical conceptions of the clinic in the field of social intervention

I will now define the practical issues and training issues related to the psychoanalytical conceptions of the clinic in the field of social intervention by focusing first on the question of the handling of transference, then on the writing of the clinic in the training of social workers.

Clinic and practices in social work: the handling of transference in the educational relationship

The psychoanalytical conceptions of the clinic open up several perspectives in terms of social practices. Perhaps the most significant is the handling of transference in the educational relationship, the issues of which I propose to discuss via a famous case presented by Aichhorn[6] in 1925 to reflect the principles of his practice oriented by psychoanalysis in a center for young delinquents (Aichhorn, 2005).

Aichhorn received an 18-year-old man 'who, because he had been stealing from his classmates, had been excluded from school and who had also been guilty of theft at home and from foreigners' (Aichhorn, 2005, pp. 140–143). Aichhorn decided to entrust him with the cooperative fund used to buy tobacco for the young residents in the center – between 700 and 800 crowns, a relatively large sum at the time. The effects of this act were almost immediate: 450 crowns were reported missing. Inspired by something he had recently read, Aichhorn came up with a stratagem, the aim of which was to make the young man the hero of a drama to which the man himself would find the solution. He asked the young man to come to his office and to help him organize his books: he set the stage for a plausible scene that would trigger the ensuing drama. Gradually, Aichhorn brought up the tobacco money. 'How much money do you receive each week?' '700 to 800 crowns'. Aichhorn continued to organize his books: 'Does your cashbox always balance out?' The young man hesitated: 'Yes'. 'I'll have to check your cashbox nonetheless', Aichhorn replied. The young man became worried, but Aichhorn did not give up and started talking about the tobacco fund once again. Deciding the time had come, he said: 'When we are done here, I will go and see your cashbox'. Obviously ill at ease as he moved crates of books, the young man continued to work, took out a book to dust it off and dropped it. 'What's the matter with you?' asked Aichhorn. 'Nothing'. Aichhorn then suddenly shouted: 'How much is missing from your cashbox?' The theft had now been revealed, and the young man's face became distorted: '450 crowns'. Aichhorn spontaneously took out his wallet and silently handed him the corresponding sum. The young man looked back at him in shock and tried to say something, but Aichhorn did not let him speak, and sent him away from the office with a friendly wave of his hand. Ten minutes later, the young man burst into the office: 'Lock me up,' he shouted, 'I don't deserve your help, I'll steal again'. He burst into tears. Aichhorn had him sit down and talked to him. He did not lecture him but rather listened with interest to what this young man told him about his life, his family, his relationship with others and his torments. After the initial anxiety came emotion. At the end of this exchange, Aichhorn confided the 450 crowns to him again, stating that he did not believe he would steal again. Crucially, he did not offer the amount freely but asked to be reimbursed gradually. Within two months, he had his money back. In the end, the young man spent only a short time in the institution before securing himself a job as an accountant in a furniture factory.

First of all, it should be noted that while Aichhorn is guided by theoretical assumptions, he remains a fierce clinician, counting on surprise and novelty. He gives the subject the chance to transform the situation based on an act which becomes an event: he entrusts the cash box to a thief. Aichhorn admitted that, although he had some idea about what had occurred, he did not know exactly what he was doing. From a technical point of view, this clinical situation highlights the concepts of historization, displacement and know-how that can contribute to the formalization of the handling of transference in social practices: (1) historization – in the transferential situation, the educator is set up as a subject who is 'supposed to know how' with respect to culture, norms, knowledge or social relations: learning, understanding, speaking, exchanging and finding a place. The subject addresses his questions, requests, complaints and symptoms, and the educational relationship consists in listening to these words so that the subject takes ownership of his story and becomes responsible for it; (2) displacement – the consideration of transference in social practices leads to the emergence of a dynamic that consists in shifting the emotional burden borne by the educator towards other objects (expression, creation, learning, training and work) which serve as anchors within the social fabric; (3) know-how – the handling of the transference in social practices aims to transmit a certain know-how of the subject with regard to his symptom and the social fabric (Ponnou, 2016, pp. 72–79).

Let us review our case in light of these elements: Aichhorn relies on the subject's symptom (theft) to build a mediation space (the organization of the library) in which he can put his desire for work and his own ignorance into play. The strategy did not fail: the theft is brought out into the open, but in such a way that Aichhorn manages to transform the tension into intention by literally taking a chance on the young man. The subject buys into the situation. He returns to see Aichhorn – a narrative of life, historization, and in the end he consents to the meaningful displacement proposed to him by the educator: from the thief that he represented himself as until then, he becomes a debtor. And this move reflects the development of a particular know-how of the subject with regard to his *jouissance* and his symptom: he becomes an accountant

$$\text{in a furniture factory. The journey} \quad \frac{\text{Thief} - \text{Debtor} - \text{Accountant}}{\$ \quad \quad \$ \quad \quad \$} \quad \text{bears}$$

witness to the lasting effects of handling transference in social practices. This clinical situation also highlights the link between psychoanalytic clinics, transference management and symptom politics in the field of social work. Aichhorn does not simply adopt a clinical posture and activate the lever of transference: rather, he follows a political line that never relies on the suppression of the symptom, however painful and disturbing it may be. On the contrary, he builds a practice based on the acceptance of the symptom and putting it to work, via the subject himself, within the framework of a helping relationship. The ethical dimension underlying his intervention is clearly based on the dimensions of individuality, desire and responsibility.

Writing, formalization and transmission of the social work clinic

In terms of training, a recurring question concerns the writing of clinical studies in social work. In this respect, the results highlighted in the psychoanalytical corpora lead to formulate three main proposals: (1) the first consists in taking the clinician's responsibility for the formalization of the symptom literally; this perspective involves including the presence and intervention of the practitioner in the framework of the clinical narrative and dislodges social workers from the risks of objectification at work in their practice; (2) the second consists in considering the clinician as a scribe and secretary of the subject; in this perspective, the narratives of clinical situations must reflect the manifest content of what it said, but even more essentially, the structure of the subject's speech, in other words, the meaningful articulation that governs his choices and controls his words and actions; (3) the writing of the case or clinical situation is thus based on a paradox – the need to take into account or even assume the clinician's subjectivity and the need to distinguish or even identify the individuality of the subject's unconscious text.

Once the elements for collecting clinical data have been determined, I suggest an analysis of the situation based on four main axes: (1) writing the clinical situation according to the methods previously discussed; (2) highlighting the keywords in the situation; (3) transforming keywords into concepts within the framework of one or more theoretical prisms; and (4) problematizing and then putting the clinical situation to work via the invention of concepts that can condense or identify its logic and challenges. The interest of the clinical approach consists in building knowledge specific to each situation. It is based on an impossible assumption, that of covering the individuality of the case with a given theoretical model, even if it is inherited from psychoanalysis. This does not imply ignoring the theoretical models at work; rather, it implies demonstrating creativity – not referring to existing knowledge, but banking on that knowledge that remains to be invented.

Conclusion

Where evidence-based approaches suffer from obvious limitations or saturation effects, clinical approaches offer social workers the theoretical support they need to build a practice that can respond to contemporary socio-educational issues. From an ethical point of view, the clinical approach is part of a maieutic version of social work, where the subject is accompanied so that he might find his answer within himself and in the world, to seize upon his opportunity to create and to contribute to the social fabric (Maisonneuve, 1990).

The reference to psychoanalytic theory makes it possible to engage several perspectives that contribute to the clinical approaches used by social intervention professionals and practitioners: consideration of the dimension of transference, politics of the symptom and the writing of the clinic. These indications can shed new light on the register of individuality and the dimensions of an encounter, of the unexplored and of creativity while at the same time providing these perspectives with a theoretical and scientific basis that can support the paradigm of clinical-based practice. From this perspective, one of the challenges in the coming years is to structure networks of practice as well as institutional and research networks that can complement these clinical-based approaches and promote their relevance and scope to public authorities.

Notes

1   Given the constraints of a chapter of this length, the reader is referred to the bibliographic references of data concerning ADHD (biological etiology, social factors, treatment effects, etc.) in Ponnou, Kohout-Diaz & Gonon, 2015; Ponnou & Gonon, 2017; Ponnou, Haliday & Gonon, 2019; Gonon, Dumas-Mallet & Ponnou, 2019. For references to the psychoanalytical conceptions of the clinic see Ponnou, 2016.
2   This proposal provoked strong reactions in the fields of psychiatry, psychology, education and early childhood. It gave impulse to the creation of the collective 'Pas de 0 de conduite pour les enfants de 3 ans!' (www.pasde0deconduite.org).
3   Conners rating scales are standardized tests for assessing child behavior. Completed by a child's teachers and parents, they help to guide the doctor's diagnosis (Conners, 1969). The use of these scales therefore implies a form of responsibility on the part of teachers and parents in diagnosing ADHD, whereas they have neither the training nor the necessary information to make informed judgments.
4   In France, the MDPH (*Maison Départementale des Personnes Handicapées*, or French Departmental Center for Handicapped Persons) is a territorial public agency in charge of the administrative management and guidance of people with disabilities. The MDPH also has the authority to implement financial or human compensation benefits.
5   'The child fulfills the presence of what Jacques Lacan refers to as object *a* in the fantasy. By replacing this object, he saturates the mode of lack in which the mother's desire is specified' (Lacan, 2001, pp. 373–374).
6   August Aichhorn was a psychoanalyst, educator and disciple of Freud as well as one of the main contributors to the psychoanalytical pedagogical movement. After the war, he was head of the Vienna Psychoanalytical Society until his death in 1949.

References

Aichhorn, A. (2005). *Jeunesse à l'abandon*. Nîmes: Champ social.
ANSM (2013). Méthylphénidate: données d'utilisation et de sécurité d'emploi en France. https://ansm.sante.fr/var/ansm_site/storage/original/application/8dd1277a386715 5547b4dce58fc0db00.pdf

ANSM (2017). Méthylphénidate: données d'utilisation et de sécurité d'emploi en France. www.ansm.sante.fr/S-informer/Points-d-information-Points-d-information/Methylphenidate-donnees-d-utilisation-et-de-securite-d-emploi-en-France-Point-d-Information

Barbaresi, W. J., Katusic, S. K., Colligan, R. C., Weaver, A. L., & Jacobsen, S. J. (2007). Long-term school outcomes for children with attention-deficit/hyperactivity disorder: a population-based perspective. *Journal of Developmental and Behavioral Pediatrics, 28*(4), 265–273.

Biederman, J., Faraone, S. V., & Monuteaux, M. C. (2002). Differential effect of environmental adversity by gender: Rutter's index of adversity in a group of boys and girls with and without ADHD. *American Journal of Psychiatry, 159*(9), 1556–1562.

Biederman, J., Milberger, S., Faraone, S. V., Kiely, K., Guite, J., Mick, E., … Reed, E. (1995). Family–environment risk factors for attention-deficit hyperactivity disorder. A test of Rutter's indicators of adversity. *Archives of General Psychiatry, 52*(6), 464–470.

Bokhari, F. A., & Schneider, H. (2011). School accountability laws and the consumption of psychostimulants. *Journal of Health Economics, 30*(2), 355–372.

Bonati, M., & Reale, L. (2013). Reducing overdiagnosis and disease mongering in ADHD in Lombardy. *British Medical Journal, 347*, f7474.

Bourdaa, M., Konsman, J. P., Sécail, C., Venturini, T., Veyrat-Masson, I., & Gonon, F. (2015). Does television reflect the evolution of scientific knowledge? The case of attention deficit hyperactivity disorder coverage on French television. *Public Understanding of Science, 24*(2), 200–209.

Canguilhem, G. (1966). *Le normal et le pathologique.* Paris: PUF.

Christakis, D. A., Zimmerman, F. J., DiGiuseppe, D. L., & McCarty, C. A. (2004). Early television exposure and subsequent attentional problems in children. *Pediatrics, 113*(4), 708–713.

Conners, C. K. (1969). A teacher rating scale for use in drug studies with children. *American Journal of Psychiatry, 126*(6), 884–888.

Cottet, S. (2012). *L'inconscient de papa et le nôtre: contribution à la clinique lacanienne.* Paris: Éd. Michèle.

Currie, J., Stabile, M., & Jones, L. (2014). Do stimulant medications improve educational and behavioral outcomes for children with ADHD?. *Journal of Health Economics, 37*, 58–69.

Dougherty, D. D., Bonab, A. A., Spencer, T. J., Rauch, S. L., Madras, B. K., & Fischman, A. J. (1999). Dopamine transporter density in patients with attention deficit hyperactivity disorder. *Lancet, 354*(9196), 2132–2133.

Elder, T. E. (2010). The importance of relative standards in ADHD diagnoses: evidence based on exact birth dates. *Journal of Health Economics, 29*(5), 641–656.

Evans, W. N., Morrill, M. S., & Parente, S. T. (2010). Measuring inappropriate medical diagnosis and treatment in survey data: The case of ADHD among school-age children. *Journal of Health Economics, 29*(5), 657–673.

Faraone, S. V., Sergeant, J., Gillberg, C., & Biederman, J. (2003). The worldwide prevalence of ADHD: Is it an American condition?. *World Psychiatry, 2*(2), 104.

Foucault M. (1963) *Naissance de la clinique.* Paris: PUF.

Frances, A. J., & Widiger, T. (2012). Psychiatric diagnosis: lessons from the DSM-IV past and cautions for the DSM-5 future. *Annual review of clinical psychology, 8*, 109–130.

Froehlich, T. E., Lanphear, B. P., Epstein, J. N., Barbaresi, W. J., Katusic, S. K., & Kahn, R. S. (2007). Prevalence, recognition, and treatment of attention-deficit/hyperactivity disorder in a national sample of US children. *Archives of Pediatrics and Adolescent Medicine*, 161(9), 857–864.

Galéra, C., Côté, S. M., Bouvard, M. P., Pingault, J. B., Melchior, M., Michel, G., ... Tremblay, R. E. (2011). Early risk factors for hyperactivity-impulsivity and inattention trajectories from age 17 months to 8 years. *Archives of General Psychiatry*, 68(12), 1267–1275.

Gaugler, T., Klei, L., Sanders, S. J., Bodea, C. A., Goldberg, A. P., Lee, A. B., ... Buxbaum, J. D. (2014). Most genetic risk for autism resides with common variation. *Nature Genetics*, 46(8), 881–885.

Gizer, I. R., Ficks, C., & Waldman, I. D. (2009). Candidate gene studies of ADHD: a meta-analytic review. *Hum Genet*, 126(1), 51–90.

Gonon, F. (2009). The dopaminergic hypothesis of attention-deficit/hyperactivity disorder needs re-examining. *Trends in Neurosciences*, 32(1), 2–8.

Gonon, F. (2011). La psychiatrie biologique: une bulle spéculative ? *Esprit*, 11, 54–73.

Gonon, F., Dumas-Mallet, E., & Ponnou, S. (2019). Médiatisation des observations scientifiques concernant les troubles mentaux: analyse des biais, distorsions et omissions. *Les Cahiers du Journalisme*, 2(3), 45–64.

Gonon, F., Guilé, J. M., & Cohen, D. (2010). Le trouble déficitaire de l'attention avec hyperactivité: données récentes des neurosciences et de l'expérience nord-américaine. *Neuropsychiatrie de l'Enfance et de l'Adolescence*, 58, 273–281.

Gonon, F., Konsman, J. P., Cohen, D., et al. (2012). Why most biomedical findings echoed by newspapers turn out to be false: The case of attention deficit hyperactivity disorder. *PLoS ONE*, 7(9), e44275.

Harlé, B., & Desmurget, M. (2012). Effets de l'exposition chronique aux écrans sur le développement cognitif de l'enfant. *Archives de Pédiatrie*, 19(7), 772–776.

Humphreys, K. L., Eng, T., & Lee, S. S. (2013). Stimulant medication and substance use outcomes: a meta-analysis. *JAMA Psychiatry*, 70(7), 740–749.

INSERM, Expertise Collective (2005). *Trouble des conduites chez l'enfant et l'adolescent*. Paris: Éditions INSERM.

Jupille, J. (2011). Le trouble déficitaire de l'attention avec hyperactivité – Le rôle des associations de parents. *Médecine/sciences*, 27(3), 318–322.

Kant, E. (1993). *Fondements de la métaphysique des mœurs*. Paris: Livre de poche.

Kohout-Diaz, M. (2013). Usages des catégories de santé mentale par l'école. Que diffusent les Inspections Académiques sur le T.D.A./H.? *Proceedings for the Actualité de la Recherche en Éducation et Formation (AREF & AECSE)*, Laboratoire LIRDEF – EA 3749 – Universités de Montpellier, 26–30 August 2013.

Lacan, J. (2001). *Autres écrits*. Paris: Seuil.

Lacan, J. (1966). *Écrits*. Paris: Seuil.

Lacan, J. (n.d.). *L'objet de la psychanalyse*, séminaire XIII, unpublished, 1965–1966. Online: www.goagao.free.fr, consulted 10 January 2014.

Lacan, J. (1977). Ouverture de la section clinique. *Ornicar?*, 9, 7–14.

Lefort, R., & Lefort, R. (1988). *Les structures de la psychose: l'enfant au loup et le président*. Paris: Seuil.

Lecendreux, M., Konofal, E., & Faraone, S. V. (2011). Prevalence of attention deficit hyperactivity disorder and associated features among children in France. *Journal of Attention Disorders*, 15(6), 516–524.

LeFever, G. B., Dawson, K. V., & Morrow, A. L. (1999). The extent of drug therapy for attention deficit-hyperactivity disorder among children in public schools. *American Journal of Public Health*, 89(9), 1359–1364.

Li, Z., Chang S. H., Zhang, L. Y., Gao, L., & Wang, J. (2014). Molecular genetic studies of ADHD and its candidate genes: a review. *Psychiatry Research*, *219*(1), 10–24.

Linnet, K. M., Wisborg, K., Agerbo, E., Secher, N. J., Thomsen, P. H., & Henriksen, T. B. (2006). Gestational age, birth weight, and the risk of hyperkinetic disorder. *Archives of Disease in Childhood*, *91*(8), 655–660.

Loe, I. M., & Feldman, H. M. (2007). Academic and educational outcomes of children with ADHD. *Journal of Pediatric Psychology*, *32*(6), 643–654.

Maisonneuve, J. (1990). Réflexions autour du changement et de l'intervention psycho-sociologique. *Théories du Changement Social Intentionnel. Participation, Expertise et Contraintes*, *5*, 81.

Miller, J-A. 1, 2, 3, 4. Unpublished, 1984–1985. Online: www.jonathanleroy.be/2016/02/orientation-lacanienne-jacques-alain-miller, consulted 10 January 2014.

Miller, J-A. La clinique lacanienne. Unpublished, 1981–1982. Online: www.jonathanleroy.be/2016/02/orientation-lacanienne-jacques-alain-miller, consulted 10 January 2014.

Morrow, R. L., Garland, E. J., Wright, J. M., Maclure, M., Taylor, S., & Dormuth, C. R. (2012). Influence of relative age on diagnosis and treatment of attention-deficit/hyper-activity disorder in children. *CMAJ*, *184*(7), 755–762.

Needleman, H. L., Gunnoe, C., Leviton, A., Reed, R., Peresie, H., Maher, C., & Barrett, P. (1979). Deficits in psychologic and classroom performance of children with elevated dentine lead levels. *New England Journal of Medecine*, *300*(13), 689–695.

Nau, J-Y. (1995). Autorisation de mise sur le marché français du lundi 31 juillet 1995. *Le Monde*, 15 December, p. 11.

Parazelli, M., Hébert, J., Huot, F., Bourgon, M., Gélinas, C., Laurin, C., Lévesque, S., Rhéaume, M., & Gagnon, S. (2003). Les programmes de prévention précoce: fonde-ments théoriques et pièges démocratiques. *Service Social*, *50*(1), 81–121.

Phillips, C. B. (2006). Medicine goes to school: teachers as sickness brokers for ADHD. *PLoS Med*, *3*(4), e182.

Polanczyk, G. V., Willcutt, E. G., Salum, G. A., Kieling, C., & Rohde, L. A. (2014). ADHD prevalence estimates across three decades: an updated systematic review and meta-regression analysis. *International Journal of Epidemiology*, *43*(2), 434–442.

Ponnou, S. (2016). *Le travail social à l'épreuve de la clinique psychanalytique*. Paris: L'Harmattan.

Ponnou, S., & Gonon, F. (2017). How French media have portrayed ADHD to the lay public and to social workers. *International Journal of Qualitative Studies on Health and Well-being*, *12*(sup1), 1298244.

Ponnou, S., Haliday, H., & Gonon, F. (2020). Where to find accurate information on ADHD? A study of scientific distortions among French websites, newspapers and television programs. *Health*, *24*(6), 684–700.

Ponnou, S., Kohout-Diaz, M., & Gonon, F. (2015). Le trouble déficitaire de l'attention avec hyperactivité dans la presse spécialisée destinée aux travailleurs sociaux: évolution des discours psychanalytiques et biomédicaux. *Les dossiers des sciences de l'éducation*, p-139.

Roebroeck, E., & Ponnou, S. (2018). Conceptions biomédicales et psychosociales des trou-bles mentaux chez les étudiants éducateurs spécialisés: un analyseur des enjeux de formation en travail social. *Éducation, Santé, Société*, *5*(1). www.educationsantesocietes.net/publications/9782813003348

Sharpe, K. (2014). Medication: the smart-pill oversell. *Nature*, *506*(7487), 146–149.

Shaw, P., Gornick, M., Lerch, J., Addington, A., Seal, J., Greenstein, D., ... Rapoport, J. L. (2007). Polymorphisms of the dopamine D4 receptor, clinical outcome, and cortical structure in attention-deficit/hyperactivity disorder. *Archives of General Psychiatry*, 64(8), 921–931.

Smith, T. F. (2010). Meta-analysis of the heterogeneity in association of DRD4 7-repeat allele and AD/HD: Stronger association with AD/HD combined type. *American Journal of Medical Genetics. Part B, Neuropsychiatric Genetics*, 153(6), 1189–1199.

Swing, E. L., Gentile, D. A., Anderson, C. A., & Walsh, D. A. (2010). Television and video game exposure and the development of attention problems. *Pediatrics*, 126(2), 214–221.

Szatmari, P., Saigal, S., Rosenbaum, P., Campbell, D., & King, S. (1990). Psychiatric disorders at five years among children with birthweights less than 1000g: a regional perspective. *Developmental Medicine and Child Neurology*, 32(11), 954–962.

Tallmadge, J., & Barkley, R. A. (1983). The interactions of hyperactive and normal boys with their fathers and mothers. *Journal of Abnormal Child Psychology*, 11(4), 565–579.

The MTA Cooperative Group. (1999). A 14-month randomized clinical trial of treatment strategies for attention-deficit/hyperactivity disorder. *Archives of General Psychiatry*, 56(12), 1073–1086.

Visser, S. N., Bitsko, R. H., Danielson, M. L., Perou, R., & Blumberg, S. J. (2010). Increasing prevalence of parent-reported attention-deficit/hyperactivity disorder among children-United States, 2003 and 2007. *Morbidity and Mortality Weekly Report*, 59(44), 1439–1443.

Weyandt, L., Swentosky, A., & Gudmundsdottir, B. G. (2013). Neuroimaging and ADHD: fMRI, PET, DTI findings, and methodological limitations. *Development Neuropsychology*, 38(4), 211–225.

Starting from the ground **6**
The transcultural approach

Marie Rose Moro and Rahmet Radjack

Introduction

The transcultural approach has been developed in France for nearly thirty years now with an eye to better understanding and treating migrants and their children. France is a country of immigration with an important colonial past, one which it must now transform into the ability to build social cohesion in a multicultural society. This field-based approach has been influenced by the Canadian School[1] and has also been developed in various European countries such as Italy, Switzerland, Germany and Belgium.[2]

A question arises: is the cultural difference between the patient and the therapist a theoretical, clinical and pragmatic fact that is important to reflect upon and relevant in psychotherapy? Any psychotherapy presupposes an implicit knowledge common to both partners, patient and therapist. Minimally, this type of knowledge exists even before any communication has taken place, given the cultural and linguistic proximity between the psychotherapist and his patient. When it comes to the psychotherapy of migrants and their children, however, these assumptions are not necessarily shared. For each individual, the conditions for the emergence of their subjectivity are dependent upon conditions that they choose or believe that they choose – in

DOI: 10.4324/9781003296416-9

any case, they are their own: we cannot impose ours upon them. In some situations where such transcultural complexity is highlighted by the patient, more complex plans for care must be devised in order to make it possible to construct what is usually implicit: the cultural 'container' wherein interaction takes place. Only then does the stage of psychological universality, which belongs to everyone, emerge. And it is in the name of this shared psychological universality that we must consider the transcultural dimension of any psychotherapy.

All relationships are cultural and transcultural

For some time now, the question of culture has been raised by psychotherapy – in particular by psychoanalysis. Freud did so throughout his work, particularly in *Totem and Taboo* (1968), but also, for example, Roheim, Winnicott, Bion, Lacan and Kristeva. This question not only lies at the heart of the suffering of our migrant patients and their children, but it is also decisive for the creation of relevant and effective psychotherapeutic care facilities for these modern families coming from beyond our borders. This already well-established tradition should have encouraged clinicians to question the reciprocal interactions between the outside (culture, in the anthropological sense) and the inside (the psychological functioning of the individual), and more generally on the construction of identity and the links that unite us to each other. The recognition of the cultural dimension of any interaction – including the therapeutic relationship – has been long and confrontational, particularly in France. Thus, psychoanalysis and anthropology have sought for too long to assert their differences and avoid dialogue, although there do exist well-known counter-examples such as the collective work carried out under the impetus of Lévi-Strauss on identity (1977), to mention only the first of them. Despite this reluctance, the disciplines have influenced each other enough for a movement to crystallize. Today, we can consider that the clinic is an anthropology and that cultural data are the key ingredients of any human relationship.

And yet even among those who accept the cultural assumptions that constitute the therapeutic relationship as well as the conscious and unconscious emotional elements, there are two different epistemological positions. Some have chosen an essentially comparative perspective: what are the invariants found in a given culture of our patients and in our own? This comparative perspective leads to the construction of equivalences and parallels between cultural elements of distinct worlds but also between cultural elements of one group and pathological behaviors of individuals belonging to other groups. This option was present in Freud's *Totem and Taboo* (1968). At the clinical level, this perspective leads to the introduction of the patient's own language into certain practices or even to learning about the patient's cultural representations. But all these elements are posited as a mere variant of the clinical relationship, the core (the efficient part) being the same as that which would be established in any intracultural situation (patient and therapist belonging to the same cultural world). Others, following Devereux, have taken a complementary perspective. Complementarity then gave rise to ethno-psychiatry, which in France is essentially ethno-psychoanalytic, a perspective that will serve as a basis for the question of the transcultural clinic: some draw inspiration from it and propose specific measures to welcome and treat migrants. This perspective, which focuses on the status of patients' cultural representations in the clinic, is internationally known as 'transcultural'.

The foundations of ethno-psychoanalysis and ethno-psychiatry

Complementarist rigor

Devereux is the founder of ethno-psychoanalysis (1970, 1980, 1985). He built the theoretical foundations, constituted it as a discipline and defined its original and, yet today, subversive method: complementarism. He developed the field based on anthropology and psychoanalysis. The discipline should therefore be called ethno-psychoanalysis. However, there has been, from the beginning, a hesitation in the actual name of the discipline (Devereux himself sometimes called it ethno-psychiatry, sometimes ethno-psychoanalysis). For our part, we consider it and practice it as psychotherapy with a psychoanalytical orientation.

Devereux recognizes three types of therapies in ethno-psychiatry:

> 1. *Intracultural*: the therapist and the patient belong to the same culture, but the therapist takes into account the socio-cultural dimensions of both the patient's problems and the progress of the therapy. 2. *Intercultural*: although the patient and the therapist do not belong to the same culture, the therapist is familiar with the patient's ethnic culture and uses it as a therapeutic lever [...]. 3. *Metacultural*: the therapist and the patient belong to two different cultures. The therapist does not know the culture of the patient's ethnicity; however, he fully understands the concept of "culture" and uses it in the diagnosis and treatment process.
>
> (Devereux, 1978, pp. 11–12)

Based on this classification, a distinction is made between *cross-cultural* (or *intercultural*) *psychiatry* and *transcultural* (or *metacultural*) *psychiatry*.

Devereux highlights the importance metacultural therapies hold for him. The term 'metacultural' is based on 'a systematic recognition of the general meaning and variability of culture, rather than on knowledge of the specific cultural backgrounds of the patient and therapist' (Devereux, 1978, p. 11). This makes it possible to consider treatments for patients belonging to 'the therapist's cultural subgroup' as well as 'individuals from foreign or marginal cultures' (Devereux, 1978, p. 11). Devereux was the first to conceptualize the use of cultural levers to facilitate introspection and associations of ideas – thus for therapeutic purposes – as early as 1951. However, he insists throughout his work on the importance of narrative: cultural levers are not ends in themselves and disappear when they no longer fulfill their role as potentiators of narratives, transferences or affects.

Regardless of its orientation, this perspective can be built into any psychotherapy. This is why we prefer the term ethno-psychiatry to that of ethno-psychoanalysis. And to better communicate with specialists around the world, we have adopted the name transcultural psychiatry, which the English-speaking specialists now also call cultural psychiatry (Kirmayer et al., 2014) to emphasize that all psychiatry is part of a culture, whether it is applied to care, the social field or research.

Theory: psychological universality, cultural specificity and human diversity

For Devereux, ethno-psychiatry is based on two principles. The first is that of psychological universality: what defines a human being is his psychological functioning. It is the same for everyone. From this premise emerges the need to grant the same status to all human beings, to their cultural and psychological productions and to their ways of living and thinking, even if these ways are different and at times disconcerting (Devereux 1970). It may seem obvious to state such a principle, but the implications of much so-called scientific research, both past and present, remind us that this theoretical principle is not always respected. What Devereux is referring to here are a universality of functioning, processes, structural universality and *de facto* universality. But if humans tend towards the universal, they each tend towards it through the particularities of the culture they belong to. This encoding is part of our language and of the categories we have at our disposal that allow us to read the world in a certain way, in our body and in our way of perceiving and feeling through the process of enculturation (Mead, 1963) and in our relationship to the world through our systems of interpretation and construction of meaning. Illness does not escape this cultural encoding.

A methodological revolution

Ethno-psychiatry was also built on the basis of a second methodological principle: complementarism. 'Complementarism does not exclude any method or valid theory – it coordinates them' (Devereux 1972, p. 27). It is futile to forcefully integrate certain human phenomena into the field of either psychoanalysis or anthropology to the exclusion of the other. The specificity of these data lies in 'a non-merging pluridisciplinarity that is "not simultaneous": that of necessarily double discourse' (Devereux, 1972, p. 14). The two obligatorily present, non-simultaneous forms of discourse are then called complementary. This double discourse is a prerequisite for obtaining data. But the question is how to occupy two different places successively in relation to the object without reducing one to the other and without confusing them. Learning how to 'decenter' is a necessary, but difficult, task here. We must get rid of those somewhat careless habits in the human sciences that lead us to relate all data to ourselves or to what we already know and to be wary of the otherness of the object of study (Moro, 1993). The principle of complementarism is simple and obvious, but the real difficulty remains the implementation of complementarism in the clinic by therapists who must be able to decenter and work constantly on two levels without confusing them – the cultural level and the individual level – and on the necessary and sometimes conflicting interactions between these two levels.

A technical mechanism

An examination of Devereux's work reveals no specific mechanism in his theory and method that can be used with patients. Nonetheless, it naturally leads us to regard this cultural material as a potential transitory therapeutic lever, one that is both original and particularly effective. It also posits that culture is not systematically a facilitator for care. In some cases, cultural mechanisms may even function as obstacles.

For Devereux, the use of cultural representations in psychoanalytical treatments is not an ideological *a priori*, nor is it a purely theoretical act. On the contrary, it is a nuanced, critical and complex act, which is accomplished with complementarist rigor – in spite of its limits, it is particularly suited to creating complexity and depth. The purpose of focusing on the cultural aspect is to access that which is universal in each of us, the universal embodied in the particular and not in the universal – or what is decreed as such by the one who is designated as the giver of meaning: in other words, the universality of the subject, the enigmatic and sublime approximation of being.

The pragmatics of mixed origins

A plural theoretical contribution

While relying confidently on Devereux's theories – especially his theorization of psychological universality – and then on certain concepts borrowed from Nathan such as the psychological and cultural container, our clinical experience with children of second generation migrants has led us to reflect more deeply on the notion of mixing people, thoughts and techniques (Moro 2000; Moro, 2007). Indeed, for us, every migrant is in essence a person of mixed 'origins' insofar as his journey has led him to another world that will act upon him as he will act upon it. What is true for the first generation is even truer for the second generation, whose destiny is to mix, to become women, men, citizens of 'here' even if their parents came from elsewhere. Although 'migratory trauma' is neither systematic nor inevitable, it is nevertheless a major part of the migratory experience from which the parents' own migratory experience and transmission thereof to their children is structured, be it harmoniously or not. All these data lead us to be eclectic: multiple contributions and adaptations of the framework are necessary, as is the creation of links and bridges. For us, ethno-psychoanalysis is above all a pragmatic approach to links and intermixing. This complementary perspective takes psychoanalysis and anthropology as points of departure, but then opens up to other disciplines – in particular linguistics and philosophy but also history and literature – with an eye to accessing the complexity of changing, plural identities, intermixing and new outward-looking clinical perspectives.[3]

With regard to theory, the focus must be placed on a parameter that until now has been neglected: the development of otherness itself. Otherness is a feeling that is felt more or less by every migrant and by every child of migrants insofar as there is no immediate, perceivable, logical coherence, no systematic adequacy between the transmitted and the experienced, the inside and the outside. Whether for the patients via their requests, the construction of the alliance and the transference they establish – or for the therapists in their counter-transference and their experience of cultural difference – the elaboration of this otherness appears to us as a period which is often necessary for enabling deep and lasting changes. This experienced otherness, both internal and external, can be seen as consubstantial with the migratory situation; it is to be linked to the notion of intermixing. But in order to elaborate it, it is still necessary that the therapist recognize it in his patient and therefore first of all in himself. Second, our ethno-psychoanalytical practice is based on decentering and on the knowledge of diversity. Quality decentering is achieved through rigorous training, daily work with migrant families, supervision and regular work with anthropologists who specialize in the cultures of our patients as part of cross-cultural consultation, in joint research or in the field. Leaving is also what I advise apprentice ethno-psychiatrists – indeed, all psychotherapists – to do: leave in order to learn how to decenter.

A psychotherapeutic practice

The practice takes on any number of forms and depends on each situation. The framework is proposed by the therapist but negotiated with the patient. It is therefore by definition flexible and multifaceted.

GROUPS, IF NECESSARY

Either the patient is received by a single therapist in the presence of an interpreter, if necessary, or in co-therapy (two therapists who are used to working together) or with groups of therapists. It is this last configuration that we will analyze here because it is the most specific, but in no way is it meant to summarize the proposed psychotherapeutic approach. The group of co-therapists is a psychotherapeutic space for training and research. It enables experimentation with ways of working that can then be used at an individual level. It is only a small part of the proposed cross-cultural framework. The main therapist is surrounded by a group of co-therapists (doctors and psychologists with psychoanalytical training) from multiple cultural and linguistic backgrounds, trained at the psychoanalytical clinic and familiar with anthropology. The system is group-based, given that in some so-called traditional societies the individual is understood as being in constant interaction with his or her membership group.[4] In addition, the disorder can sometimes be considered an event that concerns not only the individual affected but also the family and the group (Thomas & Luneau, 1975). As a result, the person is cared for in a group setting and, with the patient's consent, the whole family can be invited to the consultation. Caregivers involved with the family also participate in this consultation insofar as they are carriers of a 'piece of the family history'. This active presence of the family and the care team means that ethno-psychiatric care does not become a new fracture in the long and often chaotic journey of these families.

LANGUAGE AND RULES OF THE EXCHANGE

To explore the complexity and breadth of the processes, the patient's mother tongue is necessarily present during the consultation. The patient has the opportunity to speak his native language (or languages), in which case an interpreter translates word for word. The process is efficient thanks to the possibility of moving from one language to another. What is sought here is the link between languages.[5]

The patient, his family, and the team accompanying him therefore settle themselves within the context of the consultation. To initiate the exchange, cultural rules are respected. Everyone is first introduced. The subject of the family's journey is then raised (that is, for example, the family's origin, the languages spoken and the migrations experienced). Once the context has been made explicit, the disorder for which the consultation has been organized is brought to the fore and the related cultural representations are discussed. A sense for the culture is thus established. This will serve as an associative support for an individual narrative that integrates defenses, psychological conflicts, ambivalences, fantasies, childhood memories, dream narratives and so on. It is this individual narrative that will be treated, as would be the case for any analytical psychotherapy material (including reactivation, complementation and interpretation).

The process that seems most efficient is the possibility to switch from one language to another rather than the sometimes artificial reference to a 'fossilized' mother tongue. Depending on his wishes and his capabilities, and on the nature of the narrative that the patient constructs, he uses this possibility to speak, or not to speak, in his native language. Here again, it is the link between languages that is being sought.

Given the importance of translation, we have undertaken studies on translation modalities in clinical situations. The first of these, carried out in collaboration with the linguist Sybille de Pury Toumi, consisted in having the words uttered by the patient translated, outside the therapeutic situation, by a second translator who reviewed the recording of the consultation and translated under conditions that were quite different from the clinical situation. He had much more time than in a natural situation, stopping when he wanted, going back, seeking outside assistance. Above all, however, he was not included in the therapeutic relationship. This totally changed his position (Moro & De Pury Toumi, 1994). Once this re-translation had been completed, we compared the two versions and highlighted the fact that there were many differences between *in vivo* and *a posteriori* translation, but that the overall meaning of the discourse was nonetheless shared by the patient–translator–therapist triad. This fact contradicts the widespread, though inaccurate, view that therapy with a translator is impossible. It is certainly a complex enterprise, but it remains possible and even comfortable to work with a translator – while he translates, the others think or dream. This process of translating is possible if therapist, translator and patient do not disregard literal, word-for-word translation, that is, the precious, irreplaceable nature of each word uttered and shared in the psychotherapeutic framework. For this to be possible, the translator must be well-schooled in clinic-based translation, and this requires training and supervision.

Beyond the general observation that translation in clinical situations is indeed feasible, the study also highlighted the importance of several processes that have now changed the way we work during a bilingual interview. We interviewed the clinic-based translator on what had led to these differences between the two translations, which allowed us to better understand the translator's share in the system as well as his choice and decision-making mechanisms at the actual moment of the interview. Thus, 'shared cultural knowledge' makes it possible to express oneself through innuendo and tacit knowledge, both of which are fundamental when dealing with difficult subjects – sexuality, intimate relationships between women and men, even between parents and children. In France, this also includes everything related to the domain of the sacred.

It must be borne in mind that we are first and foremost working on *translated* discourse (patient–therapist–patient), that is, a discourse mediated through the translator, which implies fully integrating the translator into the therapeutic system – thus, training him in the transcultural clinical exchange.

Finally, this study and subsequent research (Abdelhak & Moro, 2006; Moro, 2017) have highlighted for therapists the importance of associations related to the materiality of language expressed directly by the patient: even if one does not understand the meaning, one allows oneself to be affected by the sound itself of the language: its prosody, its rhythms, its accelerations and its silences. This total immersion in the language provokes in us images and associations linked to the direct effect of words, the way they are stated and the sounds of the patient's sentences, for example. The interaction is with the meaning but also with the language itself and the universe it carries.

Translation is therefore not simply a means to an end, but rather is a part of the interactive process of psychotherapy in a transcultural situation.

THE CO-CONSTRUCTION OF CULTURAL MEANING

Three specific levels must be explored to co-construct a culturally relevant framework:[6]

1. The ontological level – What representation does the patient have of himself, his identity, his origin and his function?
2. The etiological level, the meaning – What meaning should be given to the disorder that inhabits the patient? How can one attempt to answer questions about the disorder? How can one understand the consequences of this disorder? There are many etiological theories, such as witchcraft, *maraboutage* and possession.
3. Therapeutic logics – What is the logic behind the care to be undertaken? How can the world be reordered after the chaos brought upon by the disorder? What logic must the transformation follow for healing to occur?

To this process of co-construction of meaning linked to the culture of origin must be added the dynamic perspective of the migratory event, its potentially traumatic consequences for the individual and the acculturation secondary to this migration (such as loss of the group and doubt about or ambivalence to life in the country of origin). By migrating, the individual loses his external cultural framework and enters a world where he knows neither the language nor the rules, a world of 'nonsense' and precariousness. Migration therefore can bring with it certain psychological consequences that must be taken into account.

For this psychotherapeutic method to work, there remains one factor linked to the co-therapists themselves: decentering and analysis of the complexity of their individual and cultural counter-transference.

CULTURAL COUNTER-TRANSFERENCE

The clinician must seek to understand himself as a person who is part of an individual history, a profession, a theory, a society or a culture. In counter-transference, one can then differentiate what belongs to the clinician's singular identity, but also to his professional, social and cultural identity. It is therefore necessary to take into account the therapist's reactions as someone from a given culture who then meets and relates with a person from another culture.

These reactions derive from the therapist's history, sociology, politics, ethics, myths, family history and personal history, but also sometimes from implicit stereotypes and ideologies. It is therefore crucial to know how to identify them and in so doing be willing to recognize and develop them as an integral part of the approach.

In the therapeutic process, it is therefore necessary to recognize several parameters: the cultural and migratory dimension, the family dynamics and the individual perspective.

FOLLOW-UP AND TIMELINE

Another factor which is modified when compared to the traditional system is that of time: consultations last about two hours, which seems to be the time necessary for a narrative to unfold given the traditional representation of time, the encounter and the therapeutic journey. Similarly, follow-ups generally take the form of therapeutic consultations or brief therapies of less than one year at the rate of one session every two months or so. Although long-term therapies can be carried out in this context, they remain quite rare. In addition, longer therapies can take place individually with one of the co-therapists after a few ethno-psychiatric consultations that provide a framework for the family's suffering and initiate the process. Finally, psychotherapies can, and frequently do, resume with the teams that referred the patient and his family after a sense of otherness in the patient himself has developed, a kind of intermediate space that will allow individual therapies to resume in a traditional setting. Cross-cultural consultation then serves as therapeutic consultation for the patient and his family. It also serves as a third space for developing therapists' positions (individual and cultural counter-transference, and the need for an indirect development space for the team).

Therapeutic indications and limitations

These patients are migrants. They come from sub-Saharan Africa, the Maghreb, Southeast Asia, the West Indies, Turkey or elsewhere. But not all migrants need specific care. After an initial evaluation, therapeutic indications are established.

Broadly speaking, we will identify two specific types of therapeutic indications:

1. As a first step, it is possible to offer this type of cross-cultural psychotherapy:
    *   to patients whose symptomatology appears to be a direct consequence of migration in the short, medium or long term;

- to patients who present a culturally encoded symptomatology (emphasis on a cultural etiological theory such as witchcraft or possession) or when the symptom itself is directly encoded in its very form, such as trance and communication with cultural beings (such genies or spirits);
- finally, to patients who explicitly ask for this cultural decentering: they mention the need to work via their language, to explore aspects from 'back there'.

2. Second, this type of psychotherapeutic approach is proposed:
   - to patients who go back and forth aimlessly between a Western system of care with psychiatrists and psychotherapists, for example, and a traditional system with healers (either local or from their country) without the tools that would enable them to establish links between the two and without either system leading to any real work being done to develop and transform the situation;
   - finally, to migrant patients in transit whose clinical pathways have often been chaotic and who are *de facto* excluded from places providing psychotherapeutic care.

These indications concern both first- and second-generation migrants provided that one of these parameters mentioned exists (Moro et al., 2006), that is, provided that the transcultural dimension exists.

Finally, like any psychotherapeutic technique, there are limitations: general limitations, common to psychotherapy in general, and more specific limitations: in some cases, for example, the patient and his family are unprepared for the development of cultural otherness that is denied or repressed; in other cases, patients have broken away from their membership group; there are also patients for whom an individual development of psychological suffering is absolutely necessary.

Therapeutic effectiveness

Current work in ethno-psychoanalysis shows that this technique is well suited to the migrant clinic and achieves profound and lasting therapeutic results.[7] Multiple etiological hypotheses result from the following: the existence of a complex therapeutic approach that can be adapted to each situation; the cultural decentering that forces us to defer a diagnosis that is often too quick when it is made from our Western categories (this can stem, for example, from a confusion between cultural material such as bewitchment and delirium or from a lack of perception of a melancholic affect behind a cultural discourse centered on witchcraft); and the use of complementarism. All these undoubtedly constitute an efficient factor of this approach. Current work on the evaluation of psychotherapies has shown that the therapist's ability to make several diagnostic hypotheses and modify them is a general factor of effectiveness, regardless of the technique used.[8]

We have conducted several studies on the effectiveness of ethno-psychoanalytic techniques for cross-cultural mother–baby therapies (Moro, 1994; Moro, 2007), for school-age children and adolescents, and for children of migrants (Moro, 1998, Moro, 2004; De Plaen & Moro, 1999). In addition to the parameters already identified by the previous teams, we have highlighted some of the following aspects: the importance of developing cultural otherness; co-constructing meaning with the family; the impact of exploring ontological, etiological and therapeutic levels for each situation on the quality of the narrative; the importance of articulating a singular and contextualized narrative in the mechanisms of change; the need to work on imaginary productions made real by the therapeutic relationship to reconstruct parent-to-child transmission; and the interest of working on the internal conflict of children subjected to a certain degree of dissociation between filiation and affiliation. This psychotherapeutic technique thus includes factors common to any psychotherapy such as the setting up of a framework and the construction of a narrative, but also specific factors related to the very nature of the technique with elements that facilitate the construction of the framework, the manner in which associations unfold, the construction of the narrative and, in certain cases, the emergence of conflictuality.

The data gathered from this clinical research lead us to eclecticism within the consultation itself, the final step being the construction of links between these hypotheses of meaning and above all the possibility for the patient to construct his own story based on these different representations. Thus, this care system, which integrates the psychological and cultural dimension of any human dysfunction, is not strictly speaking a specific system in our view. It would be more accurate to say that it is a complex, mixed psychotherapeutic framework that allows therapists to be decentered and, consequently, to take into account the cultural otherness of migrant patients. It can be interesting for anyone, be they migrants (or not), or of mixed origins (or not).

The patients' language, their cultural representations, the cultural logics that permeate them, and their migratory paths are thus not obstacles. On the contrary, they become elements of the therapeutic framework and sources of creativity for both therapists and patients.

The cultural representations of patients are thus not an epiphenomenon, an exotic coloration devoid of clinical or even epistemological value. Such a position would deny cultural otherness and abrogate human complexity by reducing the unknown to the known and presupposing that knowledge resides in the science of the West and in those who embody it. It is with an eye to rising above the ill-conceived debate on ethno-psychoanalysis that we have chosen to discuss transcultural psychotherapy, an approach which broadens the perspective and relates it to other disciplines, to society as a whole and to the world. This perspective is common to all forms of psychotherapy.

A psychotherapy for each patient even outside a specific cross-cultural approach

Cultural representations thus provide a preform for individual representations and serve as a semantic channel for the construction of the narrative. These are veritable principles of narrativity. The intricacies of human desires and conflicts, in this field as in many others, account for the extraordinary diversity found in humans. Neither magical nor demonic, ethno-psychoanalysis recognizes indications and limitations that we must clarify without being influenced by ideological passions. The cross-cultural clinic is not a clinic for experts or travelers only. It belongs to all those who take the trouble to undergo rigorous, multifaceted training.

However, the challenge that remains is the introduction of this type of cultural representation into our toolbox and beyond, into our ways of understanding the world so that French society is able to embrace all its children, regardless of their history and the color of their skin.

The conditions of subjectivity

This raises the important question of how to set up the necessary framework outside the cross-cultural framework for certain migrant patients and their children. This framework is not essential for all migrants, and yet for others healing cannot take place without it. Consequently, the need for it must be assessed. Certain unshared cultural elements are tacit and can require reorganization even in a non-specific context: the dual relationship is not self-evident for a patient from a non-Western culture where the individual is thought of in constant interaction with his membership groups (including family and community). This dual relationship is therefore sometimes experienced by the patient as violent and intrusive. When this is the case, it is necessary to re-establish with him the conditions of his intimacy and of the expression of his subjectivity. It is then important to introduce the notion of group by asking the patient to come with someone he chooses; one must then set up interviews with another person who monitors the patient's progress. This is easy enough to organize in an institutional setting.

Similarly, the interview technique including the questions asked must be well thought out. This is especially true for direct questions concerning intimacy, the inside of the house, life with a partner and more private matters, but also questions on cultural aspects held to be self-evident for patients such as polygamy and certain customs and rituals – in short, all interrogative formulations which presuppose an implicit cultural bias on our part, without which we would not be asking the questions. Such questions are often experienced as violent, intrusive, displaced or preposterous, but also sometimes impolite because they do not respect the cultural rules of exchange: these include the hierarchy of generations, differences between the sexes and the respective place of children and adults. The questions are often excessive, and rather than asking them, it is more useful to propose one's own representations in order to encourage a story to unfold at the patient's pace. Similarly, again to help the narrative to move forward, it is important to respect the cultural order of the family: it can at times be difficult to have access to a wife or a mother without first asking the husband's permission – she may be eager to remain loyal to her husband, and therefore may not be able to express herself freely. It is thus advisable to negotiate this authorization so that she can come to the interviews, to the school or to the dispensary, and express herself as she wishes. These examples should not be set up as rules or recipes to follow, or as new restrictions for women, men, migrant families and their children. These basic elements must be known and included in the negotiation of the framework for any work. There are, of course, other points such as the introduction of the patient's mother tongue and the analysis of our own cultural counter-transference. All of this is possible in any care setting, or can at least become possible, provided we are convinced of its effectiveness. Here as elsewhere, thought must precede action.

Experimenting with differences

Other parameters from the cross-cultural framework (changing the timeline – for instance, offering longer consultations – or setting up a small group of co-therapists) can be integrated in non-specific places depending on the clinician's personality, his comfort with a particular aspect and the place of practice. But to gradually introduce all these changes into our prevention and care frameworks, we must explore their relevance and effectiveness based on the experience of others or by giving ourselves the means to experience them. But what about social differences? And how does this social perspective influence the implementation of individual or institutional psychotherapy with a migrant patient?

Racism and exclusion

For a large proportion of migrants in Europe, confrontation with more or less open manifestations of racism is part of daily life. In a 1999 campaign, the French organization SOS-Racisme documented numerous types of racist exclusion in France: nightclubs that do not allow 'blacks' or 'Arabs' to enter, landlords who inform real estate agencies that they do not rent to foreigners, or employers who prefer a 'real French person' to a candidate who much better meets the required conditions but who has an Arabic name.

Given such situations, therapists must be made aware of how racism works, especially when they work with migrants. First and foremost, it is necessary to identify the mechanisms of exclusion at work within the care settings. For example, if there is no possibility of involving translators in an institution that receives migrants, those who do not speak French will have difficulty accessing the services offered. This is a situation of exclusion. We must also be aware of the ethnocentric points of view that have entered psychiatric and psychological thinking. If we do not take into account the cultural diversity that can manifest itself in different values or forms of family organization, we risk describing any difference as a pathological deviance.

In addition, it is essential to become familiar with the challenges of cross-cultural communication. Sometimes, encountering cultural differences in migrants (real or imagined) can cause strong emotional reactions in the therapist, which can in extreme cases lead to rejection or abandonment of the patient. To avoid this kind of reaction, a reflection on the cultural aspects of counter-transference is necessary.

But racism does not only lead us to question our own reactions and the functioning of our institutions. It also forces us to question the place we give to the everyday reality of the patient in therapy. Confronting stereotypes, prejudices and situations of exclusion is often the daily bread of migrant patients. To ignore this reality would be to risk making patients understand that their sometimes extremely harsh experiences are being denied. We must therefore ask ourselves what place should be given to the social reality of patients in therapy.

From 'classic' racism to 'cultural difference' racism

The term 'racism', which first appeared between the two world wars, refers to ideologies and practices that refer to the 'nature' of others (which is considered inferior or 'incompatible' with the dominant society) to justify their submission or exclusion from society. For the sociologist Michel Wieviorka:

> Racism consists in characterizing a human whole by natural attributes, themselves associated with intellectual and moral characteristics that apply to each individual within that whole and, from there, implementing in certain cases practices of inferiorization and exclusion.
>
> (Wieviorka, 1998, p. 7)

Racism can appear in the form of attitudes (prejudices, stereotypical views), behaviors (exclusionary practices, racist violence), and in the form of ideology that justifies the exclusion or inferiorization of certain populations.

Since the 18th century, racist ideologies with a 'scientific' claim have had a strong impact on Western societies. This kind of ideology, also called 'classic' racism, implies a hierarchy of 'human races' and considers it a natural, biological fact. Historically, the emergence of these ideologies took place in the context of European expansion, colonization and the birth of nationalism (Wieviorka, 1998, p. 18). The ideology of 'classic' racism has therefore served to justify external domination. But at the same time, it was also the basis for an intra-European exclusion that concerned certain parts of society, in particular Jews and gypsies. German Nazism marked the height of racism based on a 'scientific' claim. Following the racist atrocities and anti-Semitism that marked the Nazi regime, 'scientific' racism fell into disrepute. Similarly, decolonization has helped to challenge the racist views that have structured the mindset of the colonizer with respect to the colonized, but also in a more subtle way the mindset of the colonized (Fanon, 1952).

At present, 'scientific' racism is hardly ever expressed explicitly in political or scientific debates. However, it still manifests itself, albeit in a less obvious way. For example, any research that aims to 'explain' social differences between 'races' by genetic factors can be described as racist. This type of research can be seen as a continuation of the comparative phrenology that was once used to 'demonstrate' the superiority of the 'Caucasian race' (Gould, 1981). Apart from scientific discourse, 'classic' racism also persists in the form of racist prejudices that still occupy an important place in ordinary discourse.

Since the 1950s, there has been a change in the racist discourse of the far right (Taguieff, 1988). The 'new right' no longer uses 'biological' theories to attribute one 'nature' to the other, but a static and stereotypical conception of its 'culture'. 'Culture' therefore takes the form of a 'natural feature'. It is presented as innate and static, and transmitted without change from generation to generation. By referring to 'insurmountable cultural differences', the spokespersons of the far right demand the exclusion of certain groups of migrants. Their presence is posed as a threat to the identity of European societies. The kinship between the two forms of racism is all the more apparent because the populations presented as 'culturally too different' by the new right are the same as those who had previously been presented as 'inferior races' (for example, Africans or North Africans).

'Classic' racism and 'cultural difference' racism follow two different logics. While the former claims a hierarchy between the different 'human races' and operates in a mode of domination, the latter assumes insurmountable differences between certain cultures and implements a logic of exclusion. Nevertheless, the two logics are closely linked. *De facto*, domination leads to exclusion because submissive populations do not have access to the social and political life of the dominant society. In this way, the colonized were excluded from important sectors of society because the positions of power were reserved for the colonizers. Similarly, exclusion goes hand in hand with domination and subjugation of the other, who is deprived of economic resources and participation in political activities. Through a policy of segregation, the *apartheid* regime in South Africa led to the submission of non-Whites, who were excluded from participation at the political level in particular.

However, it is necessary to distinguish the two logics of racism in order to be able to recognize them in their less obvious manifestations. We must be aware of both the functioning of 'classic' racism and its logic of domination and the racism of 'cultural difference' and its logic of exclusion. Shifting away from our own norms and stereotypes is necessary if we are to avoid ethnocentric views and the logic of domination in the field of psychiatry. To avoid the logic of exclusion, it is indispensable to conduct a critical analysis of the functioning of our institutions and to remove the mechanisms of institutional racism.

Ethnocentrism in psychiatry

Psychiatric thinking, like psychological thinking, is far from being culturally neutral. Psychiatry has developed in a specific historical and cultural context and integrates cultural assumptions (one might call these *ethno-theories*) into its basic categorizations and beliefs. These Western ethno-theories concern, for example, the character of the link between mind and body, the nature of emotions, personality elements and so on. Psychological theories also propagate norms when for example they define a child's normal development. If the therapist accepts these theories and puts them into practice in a cross-cultural situation without questioning their relevance, he risks distorting his patients' reality: any difference from the Western norm may appear as a pathological deviation. The cultural difference can therefore be misconstrued as a pathology.

Let us take the example of the body–psyche link. The clear distinction between the body and the psyche has been fundamental to modern Western medicine. It was even the basis for the creation of the professions of psychiatrist and psychologist. Yet a look at other forms of medical thought – for example, Chinese medicine (Kleinman, 1980) – shows us that this duality based on Cartesian thought is far from universal. The manner in which people understand humanity, disease and the social context in which it is played out can vary widely between different cultural systems of representation. In some cultures, suffering is expressed more by pain or discomfort attributed to body dysfunction, although it can be characterized as socio-psychological suffering (Gailly, 1997). If a therapist cannot decipher such 'non-Western' forms of the expression of suffering, he may find that the patient is 'somatizing' psychological suffering (a theory that implies body–mind duality), or even deduce an inability of the patient to elaborate. Through this kind of misunderstanding, the patient may be deprived of care on the pretext that psychotherapy is not offered to those who are not able to enter into a process requiring such elaboration.

Even the basic concepts of psychology – especially those about emotions – are not universal. Anthropologist Catherine Lutz (1985) confronts the notion of emotion as it exists in the West (as a subjective, inner, quasi-corporeal experience opposed to thought) with another conception she encountered in her research among the Ifaluk, a population living in the South Pacific Ocean. In this cultural group, thought–emotions are said to circulate between people and to designate situations rather than inner experiences. To understand the way in which the Ifaluk conceptualize these thought–emotions, it is necessary to enter into an exchange that takes into account the symbolic context of their thinking. Cross-cultural research on emotions invites us to think of them as processes that must be analyzed in the context of the scenarios and associations they evoke (Rosaldo, 1984). To access these scenarios and associations, it is essential to explore the cultural systems of representation to which patients refer.

It is also important to question the norms that underlie the goals of psychotherapy. Fernando (1995) points out that these goals imply Western values such as autonomy, control (of emotions, for example) and understanding through analysis. Fernando confronts these values with the values that dominate in Asian cultures: acceptance, harmony and understanding are sought through contemplation. If we want to avoid imposing Western values on patients, we must define the goals to be achieved in therapy with the patient while at the same time accepting the values to which he refers.

Sometimes, a lack of detachment from Western thinking in the mind of the therapist may lead him to ignore important resources the patient possesses. These resources can be both symbolic and social in nature. Knowledge of common forms of family organization in the patient's cultural context can help to explore and mobilize resources. With regard to symbolic resources, Obeyesekere (1985) takes the example of Buddhist thought. It provides extremely rich possibilities for developing situations of loss, failure or distress. Obeyeskere suggests that these characteristics can have a protective effect against depressive decompensations in people who live in cultures steeped in Buddhism. This hypothesis remains to be examined, but the example shows that an exploration of the patient's symbolic references can mobilize significant resources. Ignoring these resources would contribute to making patients more vulnerable.

To develop psychological theories that avoid ethnocentrism and the dominant view that describes cultural difference as a deviation from the Western norm, a confrontation of psychology with anthropological theories and data can be extremely useful. In current psychology and psychiatry, there is significant ongoing research aimed at overcoming the ethnocentric views inherent in psychological and psychiatric theories, including (1) research on basic conceptions of psychology (Stigler, Shweder & Herdt, 1990); (2) research on the cross-cultural validity of psychiatric categories (Kleinman & Good, 1985); and (3) collaborations between psychologists, anthropologists and historians who attempt to exchange on different ways of accompanying children in their development (Guidetti, Lallemand & Morel, 1997). These types of research can help to shift our psychological and psychiatric thinking. To understand the human psyche and the universal aspects of its functioning, we must first examine the diversity of its manifestations. To bypass this step by declaring that Western categories in psychology are universal would be tantamount to remaining in a logic of domination.

Institutional racism

The term 'institutional racism' refers to a form of institutional functioning that causes inequalities or even exclusion of certain populations in important sectors of society. This functioning is not necessarily based on a racist conviction of the professionals and can sometimes even be maintained with good intentions. It may be the consequence of specific intervention measures that become exclusionary practices.

To avoid the mechanisms of institutional racism, it is first necessary to ensure that care services are accessible to all migrants and that the means are provided to effectively care for this population. Access to translation services is essential to do this work. In addition, care teams must be trained in the challenges of cross-cultural communication. This is essential in psychological care, but also in other places of care that are often the first to encounter patients in psychological distress. It is often during visits to the general practitioner, the gynecologist or maternal and child welfare centers[9] that psychological suffering of migrant patients can be detected. Good communication in all health institutions is therefore crucial to ensure that migrants receive the necessary care in a timely manner.

With regard to the establishment of specialized services for migrant patients, extreme caution must be exercised to ensure that these places do not turn into spaces of exclusion: if all migrant patients are systematically referred to specialized services (perhaps with the intention of providing them with better care), they are at the same time excluded from regular care. Ordinary institutions will then no longer be obliged to adapt their services to migrant patients. When setting up specific services for migrants, it is therefore necessary to clearly define their tasks and formulate guidelines for this type of care. It is essential to ensure their integration into all institutions; otherwise a new segregation logic will emerge. Any division between specialized services and ordinary care should be avoided.

Lack of knowledge of the cultural representations that patients use can sometimes lead to misdiagnosis. Thus, a discourse organized around fears of witchcraft can be taken as a psychiatric symptom indicating psychosis without further exploration of the patient's psychological functioning. Fernando cites studies in England that have shown that Afro-Caribbean patients are more frequently interned than other patients (1995, p. 34). The diagnosis of schizophrenia is also more frequently given, and referral to psychotherapy is rarer. There are distorted and stereotypical perceptions at the root of this institutional dysfunction: Afro-Caribbean people are considered violent, the cultural encodings present in their discourse are qualified as psychotic symptoms, schizophrenia is too hastily diagnosed and their capacity for introspection and psychological development is also denied. For these reasons, they are not given access to psychotherapies.

Sometimes extremely violent situations can occur when the mechanisms of institutional racism combine with stereotypical perceptions of professionals towards migrant patients. Patients may not get the care they need because their mental suffering has not been detected due to a lack of a translator. Others may be hospitalized because of the anguish that their difference generates in the workers. There are also situations where children are too quickly placed in care without specialists' having attempted to identify the resources of a family organized differently from Western norms or certain reports of abuse on the basis of misunderstandings that could have been prevented by good cross-cultural communication.

A clinical history: Aminata

Aminata grew up with her grandparents in West Africa. At the age of eight, she came to France to join her parents, whom she hardly knew. Aminata was having trouble finding her way around in this new context. At school, she always stayed close to the teacher. Every time he took care of the other children, she would become restless. Over time, Aminata developed significant behavioral problems that caused great concern to her teachers. After three years in France, conventional schooling had become impossible, with major learning delays and behavioral problems.

The teachers began to have doubts about the ability of Aminata's parents to take care of their daughter. As a result, they attributed great importance to rather banal incidents: at school, Aminata often smelled bad, so the teachers wondered if she was washing herself at home. She stole food from her classmates and there was immediate talk of malnutrition. One day, the gym teacher noticed traces of burns on Aminata's arm and, since the teachers were already alarmed, the school reported suspicions of negligence and abuse. The parents were overwhelmed by these accusations and were unable to defend themselves adequately against the report. Aminata was placed in a home. The parents' efforts to deal with this situation with dignity and calm turned against them, reinforcing the judge's perception that the parents were neglecting their daughter's needs. The dialogue between the family and institutions became extremely difficult. The parents were so afraid that their own words would be used against them that they stopped explaining anything: neither the fact that Aminata had a form of urinary incontinence and had trouble changing properly at school if she soiled her clothes, nor the existence of burn scars prior to her migration. Currently, the family is awaiting a favorable court decision that would allow Aminata to return home (a solution strongly desired by the parents, but also by the team at the center taking care of Aminata). It was more than six months after Aminata's placement that the family was welcomed by a team specializing in cross-cultural work to give an opinion on the situation. With regard to Aminata's scars, many questions remain unanswered: are these traces of trauma suffered in Africa? Or perhaps traces of traditional care? Given the distress of the family and the feelings of distrust that have settled in them, these issues are still difficult to address.

This clinical situation raises the question of why the intervention of the cross-cultural care team was not requested before Aminata's placement. It is also questionable why there was no dialogue between the school and her parents that would have put the suspicion of negligence into perspective. Aminata's behavioral disorders clearly show her psychological suffering, probably linked to her complicated trajectory (including migration, change of family and cultural context and confrontation with the French school system). Psychotherapeutic care would have been preferable for Aminata and her family. In this case, the intervention of the institutions only worsened the family's situation. Adequate care was not provided at the right time, and later on, the already fragile relationship between Aminata and her parents was further destabilized due to her precipitate removal from home.

To avoid such dysfunctions in institutions, it is important to facilitate migrant populations' access to care through the availability of translation services and the distribution of information about existing services. In addition, good cross-cultural communication is necessary between professionals and users. Finally, professionals must become familiar with the complexity of the lives of migrant families, which include their migratory trajectories and their lives in transnational family networks as well as the cultural representations of multiple origins that they bring to the consultation.

Research based on clinical and social data

Based on these care mechanisms and within the framework of the National Institute of Health and Medical Research (INSERM) and the University,[10] we have set up studies in a natural environment (children of migrants in child protection units, in maternal and child welfare centers and at schools and high schools) and in a clinical population (children of migrants who consult in child psychiatry or in our cross-cultural consultations to monitor the development of the child in a cross-cultural situation).

In the general population, we have worked on children's language development and language paths and have developed a tool to promote children's mother tongues, the ELAL d'Avicenne (Moro et al., 2018a, 2018b).[11] We have also worked on the vulnerability and creativity of all migrant children (Moro, 2007) and on the consequences for the prevention of school failure and for the development of these special-needs children.

In clinical populations, using the cross-cultural method described in this chapter, we are still working today on different populations and issues related to care in the field:

- children of second- and third-generation migrants and children of mixed couples (Moro, 1994, 2000, 2004, 2007);
- internationally adopted children (work coordinated by Harf et al., 2015);
- unaccompanied minors who arrive without parents and without papers in our regions and consultations (work coordinated by R. Radjack, F. Toumahi and S. Minassian: Radjack, Guzman & Moro, 2014; Minassian et al., 2017);
- radicalized adolescents (Lenjalley & Moro, 2019; Touhami et al., 2018);
- all those who, for one reason or another, have traveled across languages, worlds or traumas, such as children in the context of war (Moro, 2003) or expatriate children (Moro, 2011).

Finally, the third category of studies concerns the cross-cultural psychotherapeutic technique itself. The processes of its effectiveness are studied – both the factors common to any psychotherapy and the specific factors of cross-cultural technique (timelines, groups of co-therapists, the presence and effects of the translator on children and adults, the effects of taking into account patients' cultural representations – etiological, ontological and pragmatic). A major cross-cultural study has recently been accredited by the Hospital Clinical Research Program (PHRC)[12] on the effects of cross-cultural psychotherapy on depressed children (Moro, 2020).

Whatever the type of cross-cultural research, it is based on data from families and children and serves to better understand and care for them. We involve families in this work and discuss with them both our research axes and our results.

We also publish many life and therapy stories that are submitted to families and discussed in the presence of an interpreter. Translators are also involved in these discussions, either in interviews with families or afterwards, during seminars.

Conclusion

With regard to the adaptation of psychological and psychiatric theories to the complex issues that may arise in working with patients from migration, there is still much work to be done in both care and research. We are still far from an understanding of the consequences of the current transformations of our societies on the psychological life of children and their families (including globalization, migration and creolization phenomena and establishment of transnational networks between migrants). In this context, research is essential, but it has to be a type of research that starts on the ground and returns to the ground, that starts from the stories and lives of migrant families and returns to them.

Notes

1   The McGill School, with Cecile Rousseau, Laurence Kirmayer and colleagues, and the journal *Transcultural*.
2   There are several cross-cultural associations that bring these teams together, such as the International Association of Ethnopsychoanalysis (www.cliniquetransculturelle.eu).
3   This led the Bobigny group to create a multidisciplinary journal in 2000: *L'autre, Cliniques, Cultures et Sociétés*, which serves as a forum for exchange in this transcultural field (www.revuelautre.com).
4   At least this is the case for the majority of our patients from Africa and around the Mediterranean. This is less useful for Asian patients for whom the question must be asked individually.
5   For a detailed study of translation processes in psychotherapy, see Moro & De Pury Toumi, 1994.
6   For a more detailed definition of these three levels, see Moro, 1994 and Moro, 2011.
7   For an extensive bibliography on this subject, see Moro, 1994, Moro, 2004 and Moro, 2007.
8   On this subject, see Moro & Lachal, 2006.
9   The French PMI (*Protection Maternelle Infantile*, or Maternal and Child Welfare Centers) is a system of social and health protection for mothers and children. It was created in 1945 and its mission is to provide: (1) Medical, psychological, social and health education prevention measures for parents and children. (2) Preventive actions and screening for disabilities in children under six years of age and counseling for families facing issues related to disability. (3) The supervision and monitoring of establishments and services for the care of children under six years of age as well as of childcare assistants. (4) Help to families.
10   Unit 1178, Methods and Cultures Team and the Transcultural Team of the University of Paris (PCPP).
11   The Avicenne ELAL (*Evaluation Langagière pour ALlophones et primo arrivants*, or Linguistic Evaluation for Non-Native Speakers and Newly Arrived Immigrants) is the first transcultural tool available in the world to evaluate the linguistic and cultural skills of migrant children. This test responds to a growing need of psychological, medical and educational professionals to evaluate and enhance the language and cultural skills of multilingual children.
12   The PHRC (*Programme Hospitalier de Recherche Clinique*, Hospital Program for Clinical Research) is a public research program aimed at improving care techniques in hospitals.

References

Abdelhak, M. A., & Moro, M. R. (2006). L'interprète en psychothérapie transculturelle. In Moro, M. R., De La Noë, Q., & Mouchenik, Y. (Eds.), *Manuel de psychiatrie transculturelle. Travail clinique, travail social* (pp. 239–248). Grenoble: La Pensée Sauvage.

De Plaen, S., & Moro, M. R. (1999). Œdipe polyglotte. Analyse transculturelle. *Journal de la psychanalyse de l'enfant*, 24, 19–44. Republished in C. Geissmann, & D. Houzel (Eds.), *Psychothérapies de l'enfant et de l'adolescent* (pp. 642–660). Paris: Bayard.

Devereux, G. (1980). *De l'angoisse à la méthode*. Paris: Flammarion.

Devereux, G. (1970). *Essais d'ethnopsychiatrie générale*. Paris: Gallimard.

Devereux, G. (1985). *Ethnopsychanalyse complémentariste*. Paris: Flammarion (original version 1973).

Devereux, G. (1978). L'ethnopsychiatrie. *Ethnopsychiatrica*, 1(1), 7–13.

Fanon, F. (1952). *Peau noire, masques blancs*. Paris: Le Seuil.

Fernando, S. (1995). *Mental health in a multi-ethnic society: A multi-disciplinary handbook*. London: Routledge.

Freud, S. (1968). *Totem et tabou* (French translation). Paris: Payot (original version 1912).

Gailly, A. (1997). Turkish immigrants in Belgium. In Al-Issa, I. & Tousignant, M. (Eds.), *Ethnicity, immigration and psychopathology*. New York: Plenum Press.

Gould, S. J. (1981). *The mismeasure of man*. New York: W.W. Norton.

Guidetti, M., Lallemand, S., & Morel, M. F. (1997). *Enfances d'ailleurs, d'hier et d'aujourd'hui*. Paris: Armand Colin.

Harf, A., Skandrani, S., Sibeoni, J., Pontvert, C., Revah Levy, A., Moro, M. R. (2015). Cultural identity and internationally adopted children: qualitative approach to parental representations *Plos One*, 10(3), 1–9.

Kirmayer, L. J., Guzder, J., & Rousseau, C. (Eds.) (2014). *Cultural consultation: Encountering the other in mental health care*. New York: Springer.

Kleinman, A. (1980). *Patients and healers in the context of culture: An exploration of the borderland between anthropology, medecine and psychiatry*. Berkeley: University of California Press.

Kleinman, A., & Good, B. (Eds.) (1985). *Culture and depression. Studies in the anthropology and cross-cultural psychiatry of affect and disorder*. Berkeley: University of California Press.

Lenjalley A., & Moro M. R. (2019). *A l'adolescence, s'engager c'est exister!* Brussels: Yakapa.

Lévi-Strauss, C. (1977). *L'identité*. Paris: Grasset.

Lutz, C. (1985). Depression and the translation of emotional worlds. In A. Kleinman, A. & Good, B. (Eds.), *Culture and depression*. Berkeley: University of California Press.

Mead, M. (1963). Papers in honor of Melville J. Herskovits: Socialization and enculturation. *Current anthropology*, 4(2), 184–188.

Minassian, S., Touhami, F., Radjack, R., Baubet T., & Moro, M. R. (2017). Les détours du trauma lors de la prise en charge des mineurs isolés étrangers. *Enfances et Psy*, 74, 115–125.

Moro, M. R. (1993). Les méthodes cliniques. In R. Ghiglione & J. R. Richard (eds.), Cours de psychologie II. Bases, méthodes, épistémologie. Paris: Dunod.

Moro, M. R. (1994). *Parents en exil. Psychopathologie et migrations*. Paris: PUF.

Moro, M. R. (1998). Aspects psychiatriques transculturels chez l'enfant. *Encyclopédie Médico-chirurgicale Psychiatrie* (Fascicule 37–200 G-40). Paris: Elsevier.

Moro, M. R. (2000). *Psychothérapie transculturelle des enfants et des adolescents*. Paris: Dunod.

Moro M. R. (2003). Parler d'amour en temps de guerre. *L'autre, Cliniques, Cultures et Sociétés*, 4(2), 165–166.

Moro, M. R. (2004). *Enfants d'ici venus d'ailleurs. Naître et grandir en France.* Paris: Hachette Littératures.

Moro, M. R. (2007). *Aimer ses enfants ici et ailleurs. Histoires transculturelles.* Paris: Odile Jacob.

Moro, M. R. (2011). Nos enfants demain. Pour une société multiculturelle. Paris: Odile Jacob.

Moro, M. R. (2017). *Enfants d'ici venus d'ailleurs.* Paris: La Découverte.

Moro, M. R. (Ed.) (2018a). *Manuel ELAL d'Avicenne. Evaluation Langagière pour ALlophones et primo-arrivants.* Paris: AIEP/Babel. www.transculturel.eu;www.transculturel.eu/L-ELAL-d-Avicenne--un-outil-novateur-pour-valoriser-les-langues-de-tous-les-enfants-plurilingues_a933.html

Moro, M. R. (Ed.) (2018b). L'ELAL d'Avicenne, un outil transculturel très attendu pour évaluer et soutenir les compétences en langues maternelles des enfants. *L'autre, Cliniques, Cultures et Sociétés*, 19(2), 138–41.

Moro M. R. (Ed.). (2020). *Guide de psychothérapie transculturelle. Soigner les enfants.* Paris: collection Hospitalités.

Moro, M. R., De la Noë, Q., Mouchenik, Y. (Eds.) (2006). *Manuel de psychiatrie transculturelle. Travail clinique, travail social.* Grenoble: La Pensée sauvage.

Moro, M. R., & De Pury Toumi, S. (1994). Essai d'analyse des processus interactifs de la traduction dans un entretien ethnopsychiatrique. *Nouvelle Revue d'Ethnopsychiatrie*, 25/26, Traduction en psychothérapie, 47–85.

Moro, M. R., & Lachal, C. (2006). *Les psychothérapies. Modèles, méthodes et indications.* Paris: Armand Colin.

Obeyesekere, G. (1985). Depression, Buddhism and the work of culture in Sri Lanka. In Kleinman, A. & Good, B. (Eds.), *Culture and depression.* Berkeley: University of California Press.

Radjack, R., Guzman, G., & Moro, M. R. (2014). Enfants mineurs isolés. *Adolescence*, 32(3), 531–539.

Rosaldo, M. Z. (1984). Toward an anthropology of self and feeling. In Shweder, R. A. & LeVine, R. A. (Eds.), *Culture theory: Essays on mind, self and emotion.* Cambridge: Cambridge University Press.

Stigler, J. W., Shweder, R. A., & Herdt, G. (Eds.) (1990). *Cultural psychology: Essays on comparative human development.* Cambridge: Cambridge University Press.

Touhami, F., Minassian, S., Radjack, R., Lenjalley, A., Lachal, J., El Husseini, M., & Moro, M. R. (2018). Les voies de Khalthoum. *Adolescence*, 36(2), 275–290.

Taguieff, P. A. (1988). La force du préjugé. Essai sur le racisme et ses doubles. Paris: La Découverte.

Thomas, L. V. & Luneau, R. (1975). *La terre africaine et ses religions.* Paris: Larousse Universités.

Wieviorka, M. (1998). *Le racisme. Une introduction.* Paris: La Découverte.

Part III

Clinical approaches in social work
Between professionalization and training

The circulation and emergence of knowledge and practices between youth professionals
The central issue of collaborative clinical research

7

Pascal Fugier

Introduction

The involvement of human relationship professionals in participatory and clinical research schemes, and more particularly here professionals in the educational, health and social sectors working with young people, contributes to the defense and recognition of their core professional activity: a relationship aimed at assistance and support (Cifali & Périlleux, 2012; Doucet & Viviers, 2016). It also facilitates the circulation and emergence of knowledge and meanings which can (re)think, (re)found and (re)problematize the issues at stake in their professional positions, practices and cultures. This is the position we will support in this chapter, basing our demonstration on the results of an action research project on preventing young people from getting involved in drug trafficking.

DOI: 10.4324/9781003296416-11

We will first focus on describing the basic modalities and principles of this Collaborative Action Research (CAR) scheme, which borrows some of its concepts and methods from clinical approaches in the social sciences, in particular the use of collective interviews and the establishment of restitution and resurgence sessions dedicated to exploring the resonances (understandings and emotions) generated by the action research scheme (Vandevelde-Rougale, 2011). We will then focus on reporting on a number of research results and on the effects produced by this type of scheme. Their participatory nature involves professionals in a clinic of change inasmuch as 'the work of shared knowledge is a condition for change: it is in itself action through analysis' (Rhéaume, 2010). In doing so, participatory and clinical action-research works towards the emergence of reflexive practitioners (Schön, 1994) or research practitioners (Kohn, 2001), but also, at the collective level, towards the development of reflexive organizations (Herreros, 2012a).

'Coming between' youth professionals

At the request of the youth group organization of a Priority District of City Policy of a town in the Pays de la Loire region in France, we conducted in 2015 and 2016 an action research aimed at questioning the involvement of young people in drug trafficking and the support provided to these young people by professionals from the educational and social sectors (such as social workers, facilitators and teachers). This action research was carried out with Pierre Roche, who had already organized exchanges of professional practices on the prevention of young people's involvement in trafficking (2013). The youth group that initiated the commissioning of this action research has been in existence since 2007 and is the brainchild of a social and socio-cultural center and a child protection association.

As part of this action research, a multidisciplinary working group was set up on the initiative of professionals from the youth group and researchers. It is composed of specialized prevention educators, a Judicial Protection of Young People (PJJ, in French)[1] educator, an educator from a Non-Institutional Educational Action Service (AEMO, in French),[2] socio-cultural and sports coordinators, integration counsellors, social service workers, a night-time mediator, the person in charge of the youth programs at the social and cultural center, and also a school nurse and a primary school teacher. These professionals work in various structures and establishments: a social and cultural center, a child protection association, a local mission, a high school, a middle school, a primary school, a Maison Départementale des Solidarités (MDS),[3] a neighborhood development committee, a PJJ and an AEMO service. What they all have in common is a 'public' (young people, some of whom are involved in drug trafficking) and a territory (a Priority District of City Policy of a town in the Pays de la Loire region).

The multidisciplinary and multi-professional composition (Emery, 2017) of this working group reflects the process of decompartmentalization that professionals from the health, social and educational sectors are strongly encouraged to promote (Jaeger, 2012; Depaulis, 2013). That said, the form of participation that such an action research system entails does not simply fall within the scope of 'symbolic cooperation', as often do partnership mechanisms in which professionals, persons receiving support or citizens are 'informed', 'consulted' or 'reassured', without exercising or increasing their 'effective power' (Arnstein, 1969; Donzelot & Epstein, 2006). Similarly, as pointed out by professionals in the working group when referring to their collaborations with local and regional authorities, partnership work can sometimes be experienced as prescriptive (an imposed rather than desired partnership) or as an element of external communication (a façade partnership rather than a genuine collaborative experience). Following the example of the 'as if management' described by Michel Feynie, that is, 'management that acts as if everything was fine, ignores problems and does not seek to address them' (Feynie, 2012, p. 8), many professionals in the educational and social sectors deplore what could be called 'as if partnership': the injunctions and partnership practices that do not require a reflexive analysis of the problems they cause and the necessary conditions for high-quality partnership work, co-constructed in its methods and purposes.

The system set up as part of this action research establishes 'collaborative practices between partners from different institutions or organizations' (Emery, 2017, p. 195), who are not gathered solely by the public and the territory of intervention they have in common. They are brought together in a system in which they carry out a common activity, a collaborative action research, which constitutes a shared experience of telling and debating their professional experiences and knowledge acquired by working with young people. A growing proportion of these young people are involved in drug trafficking. The common aim of the working group engaged in this collaborative action research is not to solve problems or find immediate solutions. Instead, research work literally 'intervenes', as it 'comes between' these professionals, their missions (such as education, treatment and prevention) and the defined objectives (such as satisfying the 'needs' of young people and evaluating the efficiency of prevention practices). There emerges a common aim of explaining and understanding, on the one hand, the problems in which young people are involved and, on the other hand, the problems with which the professionals who support them are faced: How is drug trafficking organized? What is the economic, ethnographic and sociological interpretation of this traffic? What meaning should be given to young people's involvement in this type of trafficking? What are the tools used but also the constraints and obstacles faced by these local professionals? Such are the questions that must be discussed, starting from their representations but also from their experiences: indeed, it is important to tap into the register of emotion as well as that of reflection. In addition, researchers also intervene: we have thus 'come between' professionals from different sectors (educational, social, health), playing the part of third parties. We supply support for symbolization, mediation, moderation or even translation. This is necessary because various kinds of rhetoric, professional cultures and other 'self-evident' elements of language specific to an activity sector (a professional group or a generation, for example) can sometimes become an obstacle to interprofessional communication.

Multiple problematization and restitution at the heart of a clinical sociology of human relationship professions

The methodological framework of this research is part of a clinical sociology that pays close attention to the connections between the individual and collective dimensions as well as between the psychological, affective and existential registers of experience (Gaulejac, Hanique & Roche, 2007). Thus, youth professionals were invited to:

- explain their professional practices (for example, to explain what they say to young people who talk to them about the extreme sensations caused by their involvement in drug trafficking in contrast to the boredom felt at school);
- express how their work affects them (what they may experience or how they may feel when young people express their disgust with school).

Our questions and hypotheses were also an invitation to re-contextualize the experiences of these youth professionals:

- in their personal life (how do young people's relations to work, money and school reflect their own relations to work, money and school?)
- in their emerging socio-historical context, by assuming, for example, that young people's appetite for trafficking and their correlative disgust with

school are linked to the 'spirit of the times', symptomatic of a hyper-modern society (Aubert, 2004) which enjoins us to push our limits in a quest for instant gratification and extreme sensations caused by urgency, pressure or risk.

As we can see, the interdisciplinary theoretical framework of clinical sociology (a meeting place for social sciences and psychology, the study of social and psychological processes) as well as the adoption of several levels of analysis (individual, group, organizational, institutional and socio-historical) encourage a multiple problematization of certain characteristics of the involvement of young people in drug trafficking. We also refer to Vincent de Gaulejac, who makes multiple problematization one of the characteristic features of clinical sociology, as opposed to disciplinary and theoretical compartmentalization. Stressing the heuristic forces of a clinical sociology of work, he proposes to 'put into perspective four registers usually approached separately: the macro-economic register [...] The political and ideological register [...] The organizational register [...] The existential register' (Gaulejac, 2014). However, this desire to involve people in a multi-pronged problematization of their real-life experiences does not mean that the clinical sociologist has the ambition to possess absolute, total or totalizing knowledge about a field or an object of research. Any multi-pronged problematization is embedded in a specific context; it is incomplete and concerns only certain features of the object studied, such as the extreme sensations caused by involvement in drug trafficking, to use the aforementioned example.

The participatory and clinical nature of the research system gives professionals the opportunity to address topics that tend to be excluded or even taboo in institutional spaces and writings (such as team meetings and activity reports), particularly because they refer to professional practices that are remote from 'good practices'. The discussions and reflections carried out between the professionals of the working group thus enabled some of them to be innovative in their prevention practices by allowing themselves (and by feeling authorized) to talk with young people about the money generated by drug trafficking. This risky initiative, uncertain in its effects, has nevertheless proved to be beneficial in the educational work carried out with young people. This has been confirmed by Karima Esseki, an educator at the PJJ, in an article about the involvement of young people in drug trafficking:

> Knowledge of the gains made in cannabis trafficking is also a factor that can positively influence the professional's work. This information allows the professional to demonstrate to young people that they do

not earn their money so easily. By calculating the hourly rate, a watch-man earns only about five euros an hour and a dealer about ten euros.

(Esseki, 2016, pp. 57–58)

Not only did the participatory and clinical mechanism of this research make it possible to expand the space of possible postures and educational tools for professionals, but it also enabled them to increase their individual and collective power to act (Roche, 2016). It did this by allowing them to experiment with creative professional practices (which were not 'already there', established in recommendations and other 'good practice' guides).

Clinical sociology is embodied in a certain posture: we did not claim to be experts in youth populations and drug trafficking, or more generally experts in the social and psychological fields; we were totally neutral in our approach to the situations studied and considered the professionals involved to be objects of study. The question was rather to involve them actively in each phase of the research and to engage them in a work of co-production of knowledge, combining academic knowledge, practical knowledge / experi-ence and existential knowledge (Rhéaume, 2007).

To this end, we recorded several group interviews, spaced a few weeks apart. This allowed us to transcribe each interview and categorize them into themes and sub-themes in a text file. The file was completed and mod-ified as the sessions progressed and then sent to the entire working group before the following session. This thematic reorganization facilitates the reappropriation and elaboration of everyone's words. Each transcription and thematic reordering of a session is an opportunity to complete and refine research issues and hypotheses – for example, following the transcrip-tion of a new session, we added further elements concerning the factors that, according to the professionals in the working group, encourage the involvement of young people in trafficking. We also added to the economic factor discussed in previous sessions another factor related to the disquali-fication of the urban space in which those young people live. The updated version of the thematic corpus, consisting of the sum of the collective interviews already carried out, is discussed at the beginning of each ses-sion during a period of restitution and resurgence. This step is decisive in that it promotes 'the distancing of the experience through self-reflection' (Vandevelde-Rougale, 2011).

This constant feedback of the data thus collected is the key element of the system. The return of these words, recorded, transcribed, reworked and grad-ually joined by interpretations and the hypotheses they raise, makes it possi-ble to work on the statements expressed by each professional and encourages the passage from narratives of experience to the development of knowledge of experience, to which can be added academic knowledge:

> The statements are therefore recorded, transcribed, returned, elaborated, perlaborated, conceptualized, re-conceptualized, and *in fine*, put into perspective, confronted with theories that have been constructed from other approaches in order to be able to be part of an increasingly complex thought process. The aim here is not consensus but the conflict of interpretations that pushes everyone to go as far as possible in their own elaboration. [...] In fact, it is a matter of returning to the players so that they can return to their thoughts, think their thoughts rather than being objects of thoughts.
>
> (Roche, 2007, p. 191)

In short, we invite participants to be the 'subjects' rather than the objects of their thoughts and experiences.

In addition, the multi-professional composition of the working group makes it possible for several experiential skills to be circulated and debated. For example, the sociological knowledge of young people in the neighborhood acquired by a school teacher joins the sociological knowledge acquired by a street educator or night watchman. This experiential knowledge is, in turn, circulated and confronted with academic knowledge that we proposed in the form of research leads and hypotheses.

The research report submitted at the end of the collaborative action research is the final version of the feedback sent to the working group. The last two meetings were devoted to a review of the entire report in order to make any final corrections deemed necessary. The working group also participated in the two public reports carried out at the end of the research. It is therefore the final product of this collaborative action research – its research report and public feedback – which was co-constructed with professionals from the beginning of the project. The research process undertaken is part of 'research in action' in the sense that it involves 'the participation of research subjects in the conduct of the research itself' (Dubost, 1987, p. 72) in all its stages (from the determination of its purpose and its initial questioning to the dissemination of its results).

Co-constructing a reading grid for drug trafficking

The elaboration and confrontation of experiential and academic knowledge relating to the involvement of young people in drug trafficking within this collaborative and clinical research-action system has led to the emergence of significant research results.[4] Two types can be identified:

- A qualitative reading grid of drug trafficking, aimed at reflecting its complexity and concerning the main characteristics of trafficking, the various factors that encourage young people's involvement in trafficking, the meaning that young people can give to their involvement, their life course and the positions and attitudes of their parents.
- Alternatives in the support provided to these young people and their entourage. From this collaborative action research a reorganization of the space of possible practices emerges for each professional so that they can better identify what can hinder their prevention actions, make better use of their positioning as local professionals, support the young person's family environment, develop local partnerships and, ultimately, offer young people credible alternatives to drug trafficking.

Thus, one of the main characteristics of drug trafficking is that it appears to be a neoliberal-type organization of labor, in which there seems to be a division of labor typical of capitalism, with management positions monopolized by a few 'heads' of networks. Between them, both struggles and alliances take place with the aim of capturing the profits generated by the sale of goods within a regional market. Precariousness and competition are exacerbated among the masses of front-line 'field' workers confined to execution posts (lookouts, dealers). These networks operate like commercial companies, with wholesalers, semi-wholesalers and retailers. Certain current trends can be highlighted, such as the increasingly younger age of those involved in trafficking (those in watch positions may be eight or nine years old). Professionals note their propensity to talk more and more openly about their involvement in trafficking, a sign of its trivialization. They also highlight the evolution in the relationship that 'big' people have with 'small' people, from protection to instrumentalization and the manipulation of those identified as the 'weakest'.

The succession of working sessions makes it possible to better understand the interdependence of several factors that encourage the involvement of young people in trafficking. Financially, the cost of integrating them into a consumer society incites some young people to invest in drug trafficking as a source of income. On the territorial level, the isolated life within a given neighborhood or district prevents them from participating in social activities that take place elsewhere. Moreover, although neighborhoods are discredited, they can be represented as enveloping, protective spaces, as opposed to the outside world, which is perceived as hostile, cold and distressing. In addition, the discredit suffered by neighborhoods, compounded by the discrimination suffered by these young people regarding, for example, access to employment, housing and health care, results in some young people's feeling trapped in low self-esteem and turns them towards the activities of the underground economy. At the family level, parents are known to be passive and silent, although it is true that the role of father is put to the test or even doomed to failure by unemployment, poverty and miserable living conditions. To this is further added an intergenerational conflict concerning collective norms and values. At the academic level, the experience of middle school and adolescence creates a sense of emotional insecurity that can lead to forms of addiction and entry into the drug trade. Teachers point to the nostalgic and idealized image that some young people have of primary school, perceived as a safe place where adults paid attention to them. School drop-out, which rises sharply during the high school years, also seems to be linked in the eyes of professionals to the fact that young people are insufficiently supported by their families, who delegate school work to the teaching teams at a time in the young people's lives when school is less restrictive. Finally, ideologically speaking, many young people seem to be sensitive to the neoliberal fantasy of the self-made man. A link appears between their 'culture of narcissism' (Lasch, 2006[1979]) and their use of violence: young people push the limits of violence further and further, whether it is directed against themselves or against others. This can also be understood as a way of responding to the hypermodern injunction of surpassing oneself.

The involvement of young people in drug trafficking has several meanings. First among these is an economic meaning. Money acquired through trafficking can represent additional income for their families, a capital that enable them to afford independent housing and trendy consumer goods, or a way to finance drug use or to pay off a debt resulting from drug use. But more subjective reasons for their involvement also appear: trafficking constitutes a space of affiliation and recognition that they lack in other social universes. Since it is a source of profit, prestige, power and privilege, the high-risk activity of traffickers even allows them to experience a narcissistic sense of omnipotence. Drug use also appears to be a defensive set-up, allowing them to put an end to and turn away from a situation of suffering. But the meaning of their involvement and the sensations it creates changes over time: if pride and excitement predominate at first, the balance seems to gradually tip the other way and the young people involved end up with the sense of having ruined their lives. Anger with themselves is compounded by low self-esteem. This process is similar, although not identical, to the process known in the professional world as burnout. Faced with the urgency of the profit to be acquired, the bodies of young traffickers become exhausted and their personalities waste away.

Creating alternatives in the support provided to young people and their entourage

The collective interviews are an opportunity for the professionals of the working group to reaffirm the principle of unconditional local support, necessary for building and maintaining social ties with young people: the deviant acts in which they are engaged (drug-dealing) and their sometimes aggressive and violent attitudes towards ordinary citizens and figures of authority (such as teachers, social workers and police officers) do not constitute sufficient grounds to question this principle. On the contrary, in the presence of vulnerable young outsiders who are faced with the indifference or stigmatization of adults, it is imperative for community professionals to take care of these young people and to show concern for them (with reference to a care ethic) so that they can modify their representations of and attitudes towards adults.

Based on compliance with this principle of unconditional local support, professionals can now propose alternatives. In particular, questions are asked during the working sessions about what could encourage encounters with young people and the establishment of a lasting relationship with them. One of the effects that this action research has on the posture of professionals is that they feel authorized and thus allow themselves to engage more in exchanges with young people on the strictly economic dimension of trafficking, a subject of discussion that now seems legitimate to them. This does not go without causing some surprise, or even concern, on the part of some young people, who are not used to being questioned on this subject by educators, social service workers, facilitators and counsellors. These local professionals explained to them that this unprecedented questioning was to be linked to their involvement in action research, bringing together various people for whom the involvement of young people in drug trafficking is a concern. This contributed to the positive reception of this approach by young people, who appreciate the interest and attention that adults pay to them. Daring to broach the subject of the strictly economic dimension of trafficking, to calculate the gains actually obtained and to list all the disadvantages associated with it makes it possible to put the notion of easy money into perspective. For example, in some cases, their earnings ultimately only allow them to continue using drugs. The fact of then putting the results of this calculation in perspective with the amount of the educator's own salary and the benefits associated with it makes it possible to put the notion of easy money into even greater perspective. Once initiated, the exchange about the economic dimension (gain/cost) is fruitful because it totally ignores the moral (permit/defended) or even sanitary (normal/pathological) dimensions.

There is another point worth highlighting among the significant results of this action research: professionals know how much the presence of new identifying figures among young people can impact the construction of their identity and invite them to explore a 'becoming an adult' process other than that of a drug trafficker. However, while some professionals regret in this regard that the city's most renowned high-level athletes are not engaged in such a local approach towards young people, certain perverse effects caused by the visibility of such identification models can also be noticed: the promotion of top athletes also refers to 'outstanding', 'extraordinary' and therefore rare human beings, structurally belonging to the domain of exception rather than the rule. It is in fact impossible to build a common world composed of beings who are perceived and perceive themselves as 'extraordinary'. Promoting both the merits of living together and the status of 'exceptional being' is somewhat contradictory on the part of youth professionals.[5] However, at the end of the working sessions, they do not conclude that such identification models should be dispensed with, but rather that top-level athletes should not be the only models offered to young people. One of the challenges consists in not engaging them in a merciless 'struggle for positions' (Gaulejac, Blondel & Taboada-Leonetti, 1994) which, inevitably, will cause far more failures than successes: these failures can prove all the more brutal when the young people invest their entire reason for living in this opportunity to become 'extraordinary'. On the other hand, by offering them a 'space of possible identities' in which 'extraordinary' identifying figures (top athletes) and 'ordinary' ones (attesting to the professional success of young people from priority neighborhoods in various sectors of activity) coexist, another challenge has emerged during the course of this action research: that of putting to work the 'ideological implications' (Lamihi & Monceau, 2002) of professionals as much as of young people, and more precisely the way in which everyone can be 'trapped' in a neoliberal vision of the world, composed of an 'excellent', 'efficient', 'extraordinary' elite and an anonymous, invisible mass, confined to execution tasks or even reduced to the status of 'useless to the world' or of 'supernumeraries', to use Robert Castel's terms (1995).

In the context of this action research, reflecting on how professionals as well as assisted young people can be involved in such ideological issues has made it possible to initiate professional posture and positioning shifts that can encourage identity shifts among assisted young people. It thus seemed appropriate to rely not only on top athletes from the city as role models, but also on people who were once involved in trafficking and who, at one time or another, took action to get out and get by. Indeed, these people converted their knowledge, skills and know-how acquired in the context of drug trafficking (that is, their economic, cultural and relational capital (Bourdieu, 1979)) into professional training and 'ordinary' jobs. For example, one young man who was asked to speak about his life course and how he managed to escape trafficking explained how he became a civic service coordinator.

Finally, among the possibilities for action developed at the end of this collaborative and clinical action research, we will retain the importance of involving young people's families and helping them to reclaim their neighborhood and to inhabit the public space (Bonetti, 1994). Indeed, in today's context, it looks as though everyone is expected to remain confined in their own space and not encroach on that of other people. Dealers are in the main square of the district and in the hidden corners; children are in the public garden most of the time; families never remain in one place for long – they just come and go on their way to the supermarket. Thus, the respect on each side for the other's territory results in confinement. The goal is to help families to reclaim the entire space of their neighborhood. Such an aim runs counter to the ideal of a calm, peaceful civil society, where the public space is only a 'non-place' (Augé, 1992), a space of transit between work, home and places of consumption. Similarly, the question for professionals is not so much to protect children from a public space perceived as dangerous and to support parents absorbed by their educational role in the private home as it is to encourage children and parents to inhabit the public space. The problem is not that young people are outside but rather that they are the only ones there and that adults do not join them. Laurent Ott explains this in his work devoted to educational work in an open environment with families:

> If we set ourselves the objective of mobilizing parents and children around coeducation projects, working essentially in public spaces takes on a completely different meaning: outdoor spaces are no longer just a space for meeting and detection, a diagnostic space or a 'zone' to be 'pacified'; they become somehow a possible work space recognized and valued for what it is: a 'forum space', an 'agora space', a 'citizen space'. The question is not to send children back home or to institutions, but on the contrary to become positively active in collective spaces and to create opportunities for exchanges, meetings and common actions [...]. We see how working with families in an 'open environment' contravenes the security-oriented vision of society that the practice of 'curfews' conveys; the scandal is no longer that children are 'outside' but rather that they are alone and that adults do not join them there.
>
> (Ott, 2008, p. 73)

It is clear here how such a conception of social and educational work does not reduce the exercise of parenting to the restricted circle of the family. The family is only one link in a community chain in which other links are made up of friends, neighbors, bystanders, the extended family, social workers, volunteers, and local elected officials as well as economic, political, cultural key-players.

Research as a space for expressing the work of negativity

Collaborative action research such as the one conducted with these youth professionals constitutes a form of clinical support that is manifested in particular by our involvement and proximity to the experiences, hardships and difficulties they encounter in their profession. We have ensured that the uniqueness of each person's experience is not denied or dissolved by the potentially generalizing nature of a hypothesis proposed during the conduct of the research. Each hypothesis or interpretation is discussed insofar as it gives a (different) meaning to the experiences reported by the professionals, sometimes constituting a 'milestone event' or at least putting them in motion: subjective shifts (Roche, 2013), which can result in changes of posture and professional positioning, and new implementations, through which they reappropriate their power to act and the meaning of their real-life experiences (the meanings, sensations and directions that their professional experiences take).

In this type of research system, it is essential to move away from the position of 'supposedly knowing subject' to which we are often assigned as sociologists or psychosociologists 'specialized' in youth work or drug trafficking. The circulation of professional, experiential and academic knowledge, without any hierarchy between these different forms of knowledge, is decisive in this respect. Similarly, in order to avoid playing the role of spokesperson that can also be ascribed to us, it was important that the professionals of the working group participate in the two public reports carried out at the end of this action research and during which our statements were kept separate from theirs.

Contrary to the opinion that grants the researcher the status of expert, it is important not to yield to the temptation to return verdicts (literally 'true statements') on the practices and representations professionals tell us about – here on the organization of trafficking, social and educational support for young people and their entourage, as well as the various alternatives that emerge from the discussions and reflections conducted within the working group. On the contrary, we encouraged professionals to be constantly vigilant, both within the research space and in their profession, with regard to anything that takes the form of a verdict, a 'true statement', a 'truth' that is undisputed because it is supposedly indisputable. Such is the paradoxical function of research, its constant vigilance towards what seems 'obvious' and 'self-evident' (*doxa*). This paradoxical function given to research, shared by researchers and their audience, can also be defined as a 'work of criticism', a place of expression for *disputatio*, for the confrontation of representations, for their deconstruction, but also for the emergence of a creative imagination and instituting forces, redesigning the space of possible representations and professional practices.

On this point, we agree with Gilles Herreros, who insists, as part of his action research, on engaging people in a 'work of negativity and intranquility' (Herreros, 2012b). Referring in particular to George Bataille's reflections within the College of Sociology and to the supporters of the Frankfurt School (Adorno, Horckeimer), he defines this work as a permanent challenge and action, a systematic doubt that invites each professional to question the norms instituted in their organization and everything that tends to smooth the rough edges and contradictions that exist in organizations. This also includes the role that managers can play there, such as the person in charge of the youth service of the social center; this person initiated the commission of this collaborative action research and played a leading role in the negativity work carried out within the group by allowing its participants to take a reflexive look not only at themselves and their professional practices, but also at the organizational and institutional conditions in which they carry out their work:

> Giving a place to negativity in organizations, expecting executives and managers to be users of it, means expecting them to have a capacity for systematic doubt. Doubt is not intended to paralyze the action but to question it. Negativity is an invitation to intelligence, understood as a desire to render intelligible those situations which, rather than being perceived as smooth and homogeneous, in accordance with what the institutional discourse claims they are, deserve to be understood in their complexities, with their rough edges.
>
> (Herreros, 2012b, p. 53)

We are therefore far away from – if not totally at odds with – the 'culture of proof' promoted in social policies and public action in France that expects professionals to base their practices on 'proof', 'facts' and 'evidence' (that is, evidence-based practice), with its endless list of figures and statistics that leave little room for the kind of qualitative and clinical research results we present here. In the same way, the self-reflection expected of professionals, as it appears in particular in the various recommendations for good practice published by the High Authority of Health, tends to leave 'off-limits' a critical analysis of the institutional frameworks of their practice, reducing the expression of their self-reflection to 'technical acts in an organizational context that is often perceived as immutable or at least unquestionable' (Monceau, 2013).

Conclusion

The establishment of clinical co-research spaces that promote self-reflection invites professionals to revisit their practices: they should aim to transform these practices without submitting them to the implicit or explicit imperatives of managerial and control logics. These tend to institute them as supposedly knowing subjects – veritable supervisors of living beings – applying competency frameworks and following the prescriptions of 'good practice recommendations'. Such recommendations aim, for example, to prevent and reduce the slightest 'risk', the slightest disorder, whether in the functioning of teams and services or in the support relationship. Participatory and clinical action research, such as the kind we conducted with Pierre Roche with youth professionals, creates another dynamic, in which the explanation, understanding and analysis of professional experiences based on 'proven knowledge' leaves room for negativity, intranquility and collective action in organizations (Herreros, 2012b). The regulatory ideal towards which these participatory research mechanisms tend to work is the institutionalization of reflexive organizations, which is a necessary condition for the expression and analysis of their complexity.

Notes

1   In France, the PJJ (*Protection Judiciaire de la Jeunesse*, or Judicial Protection of Young People) refers to all the measures for the protection of minors implemented by the Ministry of Justice whether for children at risk or for juvenile offenders.

2   The AEMO (*Aide Educative en Milieu Ouvert*, or Non-Institutional Educational Action Service) is an educational assistance measure that the juvenile judge recommends when the holders of parental authority are no longer able to protect and educate a child whose health, morality, safety, educational conditions or development are seriously compromised.

3   In France, the role of MDSs (*Maisons du Département Solidarité*, or Solidarity Departmental Centers) is to participate in the elaboration and implementation within their territory of the departmental policies of solidarity and social development: policies dedicated to social and professional integration, to the support of children and

families, of the elderly, of people with disabilities and of vulnerable people, and also of cross-cutting policies relating to health and housing

4   In this section, we reproduce some of the research results presented in the final report of this action research coordinated by Pierre Roche (CEREQ –*Centre d'Etudes et de Recherches sur les Qualifications*, or Center for Studies and Research on Qualifications) and sent to its sponsors in June 2016. For reasons of confidentiality, we provide no further details.

5   In this regard, note that politicians also tend to make top athletes idols, as evidenced by the work done by Aude Harlé with advisors in ministerial cabinets who would like to see extraordinary sporting performances duplicated at the level of all citizens, one of them confiding, for example, that '*France would be ideal if populated by sixty million Manaudous*' (Harlé, 2010, p. 254).

References

Arnstein, S. R. (1969). A ladder of citizen participation. *Journal of the American Institute of Planners, 35*(4), 216–224.

Aubert, N. (Ed.) (2004). *L'individu hypermoderne.* Toulouse: Érès.

Augé, M. (1992). *Non-lieux. Introduction à une anthropologie de la surmodernité.* Paris: Seuil.

Bonetti, M. (1994). *Habiter. Le bricolage imaginaire de l'espace.* Paris: Hommes et perspectives.

Bourdieu, P. (1979). *La distinction. Critique sociale du jugement.* Paris: Les Éditions de Minuit.

Castel, R. (1995). *Les métamorphoses de la question sociale. Une chronique du salariat.* Paris: Fayard.

Cifali, M., & Périlleux, T. (Ed.) (2012). *Les métiers de la relation malmenés. Répliques cliniques.* Paris: L'Harmattan.

Depaulis, A. (2013). *Travailler ensemble, un défi pour le médicosocial. Complexité et altérité.* Toulouse: Érès.

Donzelot, J. & Epstein, R. (2006). Démocratie et participation: l'exemple de la rénovation urbaine. *Esprit, 7,* 5–34.

Doucet, M-C., & Viviers, S. (Ed.) (2016). *Métiers de la relation, nouvelles logiques et nouvelles épreuves du travail.* Presses universitaires Laval: Quebec.

Dubost, J. (1987). *L'intervention psychosociologique.* Paris: PUF.

Emery, R. (2017). La collaboration multiprofessionnelle dans les contextes d'institution spécialisée. Dimensions thématiques et concepts convoqués pour l'étude des pratiques. *La nouvelle revue de l'adaptation et de la scolarisation, 78*(2), 193–209.

Esseki, K. (2016). Implication du mineur dans le trafic de cannabis: des postures et des outils pour améliorer le travail éducatif. *Nouvelle revue de psychosociologie, 21*(1), 49–62.

Feynie, M. (2012). *Le "as if" management. Regard sur le mal-être au travail.* Lormont: Le Bord de l'eau.

Gaulejac, V. de. (2014). Pour une sociologie clinique du travail. *La nouvelle revue du travail.* 4. Online: http://journals.openedition.org/nrt/1576

Gaulejac, V. de, Blondel, F., & Taboada-Leonetti, I. (1994). *La lutte des places.* Paris: Desclée de Brouwer, 2015.

Gaulejac, V. de, Hanique, F., & Roche, P. (Eds.) (2007). *La sociologie clinique. Enjeux théoriques et méthodologiques.* Toulouse: Érès, 2012.

Harlé, A. (2010). *Le Coût et le goût du pouvoir : le désenchantement politique face à l'épreuve managériale. Sociologie clinique des cabinets ministériels.* Paris: Dalloz-Sirey.

Herreros, G. (2012a). *La violence ordinaire dans les organisations. Plaidoyer pour des organisations réflexives.* Toulouse: Érès.

Herreros, G. (2012b). Vers des organisations réflexives: pour un autre management, *Nouvelle Revue de Psychosociologie, 13*, 43–58.

Jaeger, M. (2012). *L'articulation du sanitaire et du social. Travail social et psychiatrie.* Paris: Dunod.

Kohn, R. C. (2001). Les positions enchevêtrées du praticien qui devient chercheur. In M-P. Mackiewicz, M-P. (Ed.), *Praticien et chercheur. Parcours dans le champ social* (pp.15–38). Paris: L'Harmattan.

Lamihi, A., & Monceau, G. (Eds.). (2002). *Institution et implication. L'œuvre de René Lourau.* Paris: Syllepse.

Lasch, C. (2006). *La Culture du narcissisme.* Paris: Flammarion (1st American edition, 1979).

Monceau, G. (2013). Institutionnalisation de la réflexivité et obstacles à l'analyse de l'implication. Dans Béziat, J. (Ed.). *Analyse de pratiques et réflexivité. Regards sur la formation, la recherche et l'intervention socio-éducative* (pp. 21–32). Paris: L'Harmattan.

Ott, L. (2008). *Travailler avec les familles. Parents-professionnels: un nouveau partage de la relation éducative.* Toulouse: Érès.

Rhéaume, J. (2007). L'enjeu d'une épistémologie pluraliste. In V. de Gaulejac, V., Hanique, F., & Roche, P. (Eds.), *La sociologie clinique. Enjeux théoriques et méthodologiques* (pp. 68–87). Toulouse: Érès, 2012.

Rhéaume, J. (2010). La démarche clinique en psychodynamique du travail, en psychosociologie et sociologie clinique du travail. In Clot, Y. (Ed.), *Agir en clinique du travail* (pp. 169–183). Toulouse: Érès.

Roche, P. (2007). La subjectivation. Dans de Gaulejac, V., Hanique, F., & Roche, P. (Eds.), *La sociologie clinique. Enjeux théoriques et méthodologiques* (pp. 161–185). Toulouse: Érès, 2012.

Roche, P. (2013). Espaces interqualifiants et prévention de l'implication des jeunes dans le trafic de drogues. *Nouvelle Revue de Psychosociologie, 15*, 207–224.

Roche, P. (2016). *La puissance d'agir au travail. Recherches et interventions cliniques.* Toulouse: Érès.

Schön, D. A. (1994). *Le praticien réflexif. À la recherche du savoir caché dans l'agir professionnel.* Paris: Les éditions logiques.

Vandevelde-Rougale, A. (2011). La co-construction de la posture clinique dans une recherche sociologique. *Revue ¿Interrogations?, 13.* Online: www.revue-interrogations.org/La-co-construction-de-la-posture

Building oneself as a professional

8

Florence Giust-Desprairies

Introduction

This chapter is an introduction to the daily reality of the work of medical–psychological aides (MPAs)[1] in organizations that receive people with multiple disabilities in day care or day and night care. It is the result of an intervention research project based on a clinical system involving, over a period of one year, some twenty professionals working towards the elucidation and development of their professional identity as MPAs.

The process involves training two groups of MPAs in five two-day seminars. Everyone is invited to share their experience based on the links between their personal and professional itinerary and the reality of their work. Because the approach is both individual and group-based, the system offers trainees a social space where a story is elaborated with a facilitator and the group members. It is part of a voluntary process focused on personal involvement (Cifali & Giust-Desprairies, 2006; Cifali & Giust-Desprairies, 2008; Giust-Desprairies, 2013).

As an illustration of the clinical approach, we have chosen to return in this chapter to certain sequences of this work of elaboration that have made it possible to shed light on a continuous construction of oneself as a professional

DOI: 10.4324/9781003296416-12

through a story; this work has also revealed modes of being and doing that can be heard rather than seen in a personal involvement that goes beyond what is required, observable or utterable.

A psychosocial clinical approach

This intervention research is part of a psychosocial clinical practice concerning in particular the processes of identity building and the weakening of these processes, captured in the institutional and organizational contexts in which they are formed.

The clinical psychosocial approach focuses on the study of the experience of one or more subjects in social situations, the meanings of this experience and how these meanings are formed (Barus-Michel & Giust-Desprairies, 2000). The reference to the notion of subject is central. The subject is considered to be under construction and under tension. The individual is not a unit in a series, but a unique person. The notion of subject is thus to be taken not as a personality model with normative value or as a philosophical figure, but as a clinical psychological notion defined as a privileged figure in the construction of subjective spaces at the intersection of the psychological dimension and the social dimension. He is a divided subject, the site of intrapsychic conflicts, regarded as a being who speaks, thinks, identifies and gets fully involved outside and in himself as an 'apprentice historian' of his own life (Aulagnier, 1986). He is also the subject of an intersubjectivity, that is, taking a part in the interplay of relationships and grappling with collective realities in a continuous effort to construct meaning in relationships where the question of exchanges and recognition is at stake.

Clinical social psychology is thus recognized in a definition of social experience that integrates subjectivity into its conscious and unconscious dimensions and links it to social logic, constructions and meanings in ways that are always potentially conflictual and changing. Its aim is to understand the specificity of situations of exchanges and practices that bring individuals into contact with each other in space and time. It mainly concerns situations and phenomena linked to or caused by relationships that involve representations, involvements and positions, and their evolution. Social situations are regarded as scenes where individuals repeat, improvise, recite old, proposed or co-produced scenarios, build a representation of themselves, others and the world, and participate in collective representations. This constructive dynamic of representation places the subject in a history.

The social situations examined include family, school and professional scenes, for example. The structures that form them fulfill (or prove deficient in doing so) the functions of underpinning identities and propose (or impose) social objects to be explored that engage the subjective dynamics in repetition, reparation, disruption or creation.

Clinical social psychology does not propose to reveal facts as such or to objectify what is given as experience, but to analyze the complex processes by which experience is constructed meaningfully. The analysis of processes involves uncovering ways of combining and sequencing the factors that contribute to making current or evolving situations what they are for individuals or groups. This analysis is done by taking into account this complexity and the subject's experience in a real-life social situation that either allows him self-realization or raises obstacles, creates unease or poses challenges. The intervention research system is thus an offer for the elucidation and the elaboration of the experience.

The clinical postulate is that the words that are spoken in the clinical space established for their reception are words addressed to another person or other people. These words succeed in linking affects and representations, and give access to the meaning of a personal history, promoting a work of awareness and elaboration that enables the renewal of meanings. It is this process of renewal of meaning that gives access to the specificity of the processes and their challenges. These processes are activated by the stories solicited in the space of clinical listening and lead to the analysis of the complexity of the registers of the stories: individual, collective, institutional and social, but also symbolic, imaginary and functional.

In the research undertaken, the aim is to develop an understanding of the identity of MPAs and the complexity of their profession as well as the evolution of this identity: the processes of linking, untying and re-linking these identities during a career path are observed through a description that takes place from within a relationship. This relationship, in the research situation that has been set up, takes place in a group which provides the methodological framework. This group-based framework is important because it enables us to implement a practice of analysis aimed at elucidating the history of each of its members, thus contributing to the construction of their professional identities.

The clinical system creates a space in which people can feel listened to and supported without being subjected to leading questions and pre-formulated hypotheses conceived by the researcher. Particular attention is paid to the construction of an open space, a space for play, doubt and discovery, where analysis progresses through stories that express suffering, obstacles, difficulties and constraints but also the possibilities found and the satisfactions experienced in the situations mentioned through their specific context. From one period of life to another, connections are made that link the present to the past and allow the emergence of new meanings. The material is therefore made up of the stories told, which testify to the relationships established in professional situations. It is this link that partly gives it its coherence: 'the place of the process is the discourse that constitutes the fabric of existence, accompanies and punctuates acts and relationships and extends them' (Lévy, 1997).

The clinical analysis identifies the various ways in which the subject negotiates his internal psychological reality and the external reality so that he might find a place in the situations that he encounters. The question is to identify how the subject constructs his own representations in a constant confrontation with those resulting from the context.

An approach based on stories

To enter the real-life experiences seen in their development and to approach the conscious and unconscious processes in individual journeys, we have chosen to use the narrative method. These stories are reconstructions that allow us to listen to subjective problems in social situations where intersubjective relationships are at play. Attention is focused on discourse as the creation of the speaking subject and on the transactional and adaptive modalities developed by the speaking subject in his environment. The story is thus appreciated in its specificity and situated in diverse contexts, thus giving access to a set of dynamically linked meanings.

The theoretical hypothesis, supported by psychoanalysis, is that intersubjectivity is required as a constitutive condition of human psychological life. The subject is constituted in the necessity and conflict of being an individual entity while at the same time being irreducibly dependent on an organized pre-existing whole from which he takes his place and value: 'the individual actually leads a double existence: he is both an end unto himself and a link in a chain to which he is subjected against his will or at least without the intervention of his will' (Freud, 1999). The consequence is that the subject is 'condemned to become involved' (Aulagnier, 1986), that is, he cannot escape this involvement with objects and other people, since any act of representation is an extension of an act of involvement.

We started from the premise that professional identity is to be seen in the construction of a narrative, conceiving our project as a narrative, temporal process for the unfolding of an individual and collective history allowing us to approach the professional worlds of the MPAs from within, the structuring role of identifications and the dynamic function of their involvement in work.

Identity as a process

The aim of this research is therefore to develop an understanding of the MPAs' construction of their identities observed in the specific organizational context of their work within an institution. Any activity is a compromise to be found between three elements: an intention related to a history and a project; exogenous requests and constraints (coming from the material and relational environment); and endogenous constraints (resulting from the physiological and psychological state of the subject). Work can be defined as the set of activities carried out by everyone to deal with what is not given in the prescribed organization of work – Who does what and how? According to which modalities, which procedures, which means, which types of skills? (Dejours, 2000) – in order to question the forms of coordination and the levels of responsibility, power or autonomy.

There is a discrepancy between prescribed work and real work (what people really do and how they do it); our research focuses on this discrepancy so as to highlight the skills used by professionals as they confront on-the-ground realities and difficulties. This compromise is of course unstable since it is subjected to unexpected, ever-changing factors, but it is possible to identify shared constructs that enable us to draw the outlines of a professional identity and its demands. Real-life experience always exceeds the framework that formalizes it; the approach consists in capturing this experience analytically by dissociating and separating the levels and registers that form the complexity of what is to be captured as a whole. We start from the experience of professionals and remain as close to it as possible; therefore, the analysis goes beyond that of the actual organization of work. It is more a question of understanding an organization of work as experienced by the players themselves. This objective justifies the choice we made to take into account the processes of subjectivation that govern the construction of the self as a professional through analytical work that includes the role that social subjects play in this construction.

Professional behaviors can sometimes be seen through direct observation and present themselves directly to the consciousness of the players, but a significant part of them and their logic remains unknown. Understanding them can be made easier by analytical work in a co-construction of meaning between the clinician and the professionals themselves. The storytelling approach can thus allow access to what was not known; the story acquires new meaning when it is addressed to and listened to by another person. The stories told by social players about their work situations are not limited to collections of facts, but can also be interpreted. Meaning is constructed, derived from a set of representations and experiences that are forged in the confrontation with professional reality, and made up of tasks, procedures, instructions, functions, norms and relationships.

In the conception that supports the approach, identity is understood as a complex process of continuous adjustment between psychological and social constructs. These adjustments may reach a certain balance, but identity can become threatened with the loss of what makes sense and is coherent, or when the subject fails to be recognized in what gives him consistency.

At the psychological level, identity obviously concerns the particular modalities of conflict resolution, self-realization and avoidance of displeasure and anxiety through processes of protection and defense that are specific to each individual. However, it can also be collective and part of a culture of the profession. The subject's experience, seen through the prism of his history, shows the emotional positions, the conflict resolution methods and the identifications and ideals which make up the relationship that each person has with his professional activity.

At the social level, identity shows how the subject discovers or is offered goals, an activity or relationships, all of which may seem constraining to him or, on the contrary, leave room for creation and initiative. Social organizations propose codes and benchmarks that may or may not include the subject in a dynamic of exchange and recognition by validating (or not) his representations and ideals. In his personal journey, the individual relies on these codes and benchmarks (or struggles to do so) to build a sufficiently coherent and meaningful representation of himself and of his action. This construction of professional identity develops in time, in spaces and in situations. It is the result of a constantly renewed negotiation between the reality of the situations that arise and expectations, desires and ideals – a negotiation whose results will guide the projects in terms of choice and renouncements.

Identity is therefore the result of a potentially conflictual tension between social logics and the psychological needs of individuals. This tension, contained in the inevitable gaps between social logics and individual needs, constitutes the dynamic pole of identity that is made up of constantly renewed readjustments. The weakening of identity and the resulting unease are due to the fact that the gap is widening between the individual, on the one hand, and expectations, norms and organizational, institutional or social prescriptions, on the other. When these are too high, the individual is obliged to use his own resources. He is led to situate himself in his personal itinerary, to formulate the meaning that this itinerary takes on or that he gives it, to rethink his objectives or to resign himself to renouncing them. The representation of the self is questioned and entails both suffering and hope.

The MPA seemed to us to be living at the crossroads of two requirements. The first one is the concrete, material, physical and bodily care of the person with multiple disabilities who needs, at all times, the arms and body of another to get up, stand, sit, lie down and provide for his vital needs.

The second one concerns the bond that bodily care involves and through which the MPA mobilizes his psychological and cognitive qualities to meet the other person, who at first appears enigmatic and with whom social interaction must be re-established through this intersubjective relationship:

- Finding a path to language, building shareable representations, helping to express affects and suppress impulses;
- Hearing, seeing, translating the invisible and the inexpressible; being their interpreters, so that life can take hold and a project be formed.

Given the existence of these two requirements, the social representation of MPAs oscillates between two extremes leading to a contradictory image of the profession that MPAs experience as a tension: sometimes it is seen as having a mothering function that requires no specific skills, but just a good natural disposition; sometimes it is the object of excessive admiration on account of MPAs' ability to grasp the difficulties of the person with multiple disabilities and to become part of the world of people trapped in their suffering bodies: 'I can't know, but I can feel. I can feel that, from the start of the day, this person is in pain even if he doesn't speak'.

At the heart of the profession

The various themes presented above were the subject of further group work. Depending on the specific clinical approach adopted, the method encouraged participants not only to move forward in their reflection but also to circle back. In other words, the analytical dynamic has favored the emergence of elements that recur and lead to new elucidations of what lay behind more conscious discourses but was hitherto little understood, denied or totally unknown.

The first encounter with a person with multiple disabilities

A SENSE OF STRANGENESS

The first encounter an MPA has with a person with multiple disabilities most often takes place at the time of his first professional experience. At the moment of first contact, MPAs are rarely prepared to deal with the 'otherness' of multiple disability. The shock comes both from 'the way the bodies are all wrapped up' in equipment and from the unusual nature of their bodies and their extreme fragility. The overwhelming presence of the bodies initially causes fear – they have the impression that they are not up to the task. MPAs then see themselves as small, young and inexperienced. One of them even said that he wished he could 'become invisible' so that residents would not come near him.

With no degree, no training, no familiarity with the world of disability, the MPA is 'afraid he won't manage'. He is confronted with a daunting strangeness that makes him wonder if he will be able to 'actually do something' and whether he will 'ever succeed in doing the job like the professionals he sees around him'. His fear can be brought under control once he agrees to let himself be approached, touched and looked at, and finally 'monopolized without even noticing it' by the resident, who slowly leads him into his world. First tormented by questions about his 'competence to do for' the other person, he is eventually surprised by his 'capacity to be with' someone who is so different from him.

The encounter is rarely isolated from the context of life at the institution. However, the activity room is often deserted and puts the future MPA in a face-to-face relationship with someone he does not yet know. Thus 'landed', sometimes without any information about what is going to happen and haunted by a deep sense of loneliness, he is attentive to what he sees and feels. He finds it difficult to look at the person with multiple disabilities with a 'really cute' face, with 'a beautiful gaze ' but trapped in 'support devices, lifts, corsets, hand and foot braces'. He finds this environment intimidating: 'It took me a long time to be able to see beyond this'. Though this equipment shocks by its barbarity, it also gives substance to the person who wears it. It provides information on the nature of disability and dependence, but also on the professionals involved, on the scope of their specificities and on the importance of their cooperation.

The MPA finds it difficult to communicate with this other person, who produces sounds, but most of the time few words, 'in a loud voice'. The young MPA often has a sense of indefinable discomfort; he 'understands nothing at all', is surprised by what he does not know and disturbed in expectations which cannot be satisfied: 'I wondered what I was there for', 'I am not familiar with it all'. The initial meeting is at first an upheaval. This feeling of disgust mingled with curiosity gradually gives way to an aptitude, as the MPA gets used to other ways of being. The lack of response in communication is such that some MPAs want to enter into the relationship further. This encounter cannot take place according to the usual social codes; it thus arouses curiosity.

This feeling of strangeness is followed by another impression, that of gaining access slowly and smoothly: 'It just happened, the children took my hand', 'That's how it happened, diapers just needed to be changed'.

A POSSIBLE ENCOUNTER

Once familiarized with the new environment, the MPA is surprised when he feels confident in a relationship that relies to some extent on sensoriality: 'The second time, I let myself be touched, and it was very pleasant. I was preparing his clothes. I didn't realize that he was deaf and mute'. The professional describes a different kind of communication, which gives 'the impression of being in a world where [we] are accepted' for what we are. A sense of well-being results from feeling valuable and not judged: 'If I said something stupid, they didn't pay attention'. The person with multiple disabilities also knows how to listen to him in a 'quiet attitude that is not morbid'. The guilelessness of these fragile and speechless beings strikes the MPA, who in turn feels protected from his own inhibitions about a social world seen as threatening. Being with people with multiple disabilities appears to be a 'good way to exist'.

Because he has so many deficiencies, the person with multiple disabilities seems helpless, and the future MPA is ready to 'do anything' to help him. Nevertheless, the MPA has no choice but to let himself be guided. The other person takes his hands, invites him to stand near and overcome his own fears. If at first he has the 'impression that people with multiple disabilities cannot do anything alone', experience ultimately shows him that his position is one of 'support and guidance' and that he need not 'do anything in the resident's stead'. The MPA 'tends to want to do too much', but he should instead focus on providing benchmarks that can make everyday life easier. At the same time, the person with multiple disabilities guides the MPA in his discovery of a new capacity to take care of the other person. Contrary to what one might expect, the person with multiple disabilities does not expect a constant presence at his side. A certain distance is necessary to understand situations of all sorts, especially given the episodes of violence which people with multiple disabilities can have.

The person with multiple disabilities becomes in turns an enigmatic figure or a familiar one. One MPA recounted that he was struck 'on the first day' by the beauty of the gaze of a young teenage girl who had tripped over an imaginary border into mental illness and become psychotic. The encounter therefore occurs if the MPA takes a step back and overcomes his initial apprehensions. The person with multiple disabilities strikes one as a figure of strangeness that remains enigmatic in his way of being, and at the same time makes one feel intimately familiar because of his vulnerability.

Keeping balance between yourself and the other: a rickety bridge

'If you get dizzy easily, you can't walk across a rickety bridge.' With this metaphor, MPAs try to identify this very specific constructive capacity that they develop and without which 'you cannot be an MPA'. It is a fragile, unstable construction which constantly needs to be rebuilt and depends on a number of attentions and gestures supported by permanent readjustments of one's own body and one's own moods. It is vital to support this structure since it is constantly threatened by a collapse of the necessary and sufficient balances of the person under their care.

Maintaining balance on the rickety bridge between oneself and the other implies vigorously and constantly searching for an understanding of what first appears as incomprehensible, invisible or unspeakable. Thus, psycho-affective involvement and strong commitment to the profession are anchored in the necessity to decipher what is immediately perceived as enigmatic. Because he truly wants to go further and to give form and meaning to what cannot be approached by appearances or to what escapes any direct grasp, it is enough for the MPA to maintain support simply by being there.

The stories show the extent to which cognitive functions are largely stimulated by this search for meaning. They also show how this stimulation can outweigh technical professional knowledge with respect to the way each one views the expansion of his skills. MPAs are true researchers at the service of an expertise based on a desire to have the other person recognized as an equal, but these professionals are not named or recognized as such. This is because professional acknowledgment typically lies more in the recognition of a skill acquired through formalized knowledge. Thus, what can be perceived as solid competence on the part of MPAs is ascribed, at worst, to sheer common sense, and at best, to an admirable generous disposition, but without really taking into account their professional knowledge, which they apply and deepen through their practice.

Returning to the dynamics that govern their involvement in the profession, MPAs also say that they feel stimulated by the obligation to let themselves be questioned in their habits in order to enter into a relationship with the resident and have access to his needs and requests. Allowing the resident to find ways of expression implies surpassing oneself and this necessity to surpass and invent oneself is experienced as a source of continuous learning and renewal of skills: 'If the child won't participate, I will try to find other ways'.

The reflective and questioning skills that allow practices to be renewed and adjusted to the specific public they have to deal with are not officially part of

MPAs' professional skills. Such is the case even if these skills are sometimes mentioned by other key players in the institutions, particularly directors, when they express their appreciation of MPAs' work.

Finally, MPAs act as spokespersons for the person with multiple disabilities whom they seek to 'better represent outside'. This social function seems to underlie professional practice as a thread connecting MPAs, the person with multiple disabilities and the outside world, a necessary condition for not breaking the social fabric. This commonly shared competence is based on a commitment: the care they provide must be the link that obliges society to take disability into account and to remain committed to this responsibility.

Observing the infinitely small

The MPA is particularly attentive to the lifestyle and means of expression of the person with multiple disabilities. Since many people with multiple disabilities do not use symbolic language, communication is often limited to feelings. MPAs must learn to quickly interpret a different, very basic kind of message, since the capacity to interpret an incoming message is the first condition for effective communication. They explain how it is necessary for them to put themselves at the same emotional level as the resident when the resident is unable to express things by means of signs. This challenge places great responsibility on the professional in charge. MPAs are constantly evaluated on the use of this language of another kind – a symbolic violence that is applied to the actions and gestures of the other person or an expression that is accepted in its enigmatic forms. One MPA refers in this respect to the ritual of attendance that takes place in his children's institute every morning. At this particular moment, the professionals force themselves to keep their participation to a minimum in order to give free rein to the children as they move their fingers and to those micro-gestures that are their essential mode of expression. The satisfaction that characterizes the relationship to the profession lies less in the resolution of the enigma than in the density of the enigma itself.

Because the person with multiple disabilities does not always present signs of a medical problem, the MPA is both the receiver of the pain of the resident who is struggling to be heard and the transmitter of the interpretation that allows this expression to be conveyed to the team and passed on to the medical staff. Therefore, a slightly different attitude, such as 'closed eyes' or a rising temperature, are elements to be considered seriously. They can provide valuable clues that 'something is wrong'. The role of the MPA is then to turn the work over to the nursing staff, a situation which is not always self-evident.

Health professionals do not have the MPA's expertise, which consists in the observation of the infinitely small. The MPA does not use the professional tools that record standard elements of a person's state of health, such as the thermometer; he can only look at the person, an approach which proceeds from his capacity for fine-tuned clinical observation: 'Some people are wine experts. *We* are experts in poop and body odors'. The MPA is sensitive to abnormal odors that may indicate problems that are still invisible; he permanently ensures that people with multiple disabilities do not have 'some pain somewhere'. One MPA tells of an episode with a seventeen-year-old boy who kept screaming louder and louder, with 'tears rolling down his cheeks'. She could not bear to see him in this state and not relieve his pain. Among her team members, she was the one who made sure that he 'would no longer be contained and would feel his whole body in a privileged moment'. Noting that the young person loved hand-to-hand contact like a baby and that water could serve as a third party in this relationship, she suggested to her colleagues that balneotherapy sessions would help the boy. It was then that she realized how important her specific role was.

MPAs are remarkable for their ability to access the suffering of others. According to MPAs, other professionals consider that it is 'not possible to feel pain and not say anything'. In contrast, MPAs define themselves by their ability to imagine what cannot be expressed by the resident, something that cannot be seen by the naked eye. The ability to detect abnormal signs is sometimes negatively perceived by medical teams, who disparagingly describe it as 'healing boo-boos'. The MPA is something like 'a go-between for the doctor' to whom he reports his observations, but the serious message he conveys is not always well received due to the lack of recognition of his preventive work, perceived as an excess of emotional closeness. Seeing what cannot be seen and hearing what cannot be heard does not take place in the same time frame as the approach through diagnosis and the treatment of the symptom. Knowledge becomes more sensitive and intuitive, and the alert more permanent. This means that MPAs are perceived as 'moaners': 'I have the impression that we are a pain in the ass. When something goes wrong, there's always an MPA involved'. Since his professional skills are not recognized, the MPA may be seen as having an attitude that is part of his personality, and this has some impact on the recognition of his identity.

'Blurriness' as an area of experience

Through this clinical process, the group gradually experiences more ambivalent feelings: 'It is necessarily a blurry, ambiguous job'. Be it in the search for a more flexible separation between medical and educational functions or in actual experience on the ground, ambivalence at this stage of the analysis focuses on how MPAs relate to and confront the reality of multiple disability. The notion of blurriness refers to the need for self-preservation in the close bond between the MPA and the resident. 'To be in the blur' creates a sort of halo of distance, a double skin to protect oneself from the fear of 'losing a part of oneself', of one's identity. What is called 'blurriness' is necessary for everyday practice. It represents both the distance and flexibility required in situations where it is virtually impossible to evaluate what should be done. The group associates it with the close ties that the MPA establishes with residents at mealtimes – a central issue for everyone, in all institutions. Two positions clash, but most often this is an internal debate for each MPA: is it a therapeutic time or a time of pleasure for the resident?

The conception of the meal as a therapeutic time is associated with training norms: 'When you go to school, in the MPA training, the meal is a therapeutic time'. This official recommendation is at odds with what will be called an 'emotional moment' inasmuch as it reflects the pleasure, the trust and the bond created in this moment of intimacy. There is something ambiguous to be found in an act or a relationship, in which the meaning of what we do and what we are remains uncertain, whatever our proclaimed intentions – daily scenes, repetitive scenes whose repetition does not protect us from a confrontation with an unexpected situation that might become too involving. The therapeutic element here does not lie so much in the posture adopted as in the ability to let oneself be involved in this moment of sharing, when availability results in satisfaction.

Thus, each one tries to account for this indescribable part of a position that he is led to occupy in his own way, attached as he is to what seems right to him in a given situation.

What leads to the choice of the profession

The intimate experience of human disability

We worked on each person's individual path. Group work on these paths offers a unique and transversal perspective on the processes of self-building as professionals and the construction of their identity in childhood, within their family and then through their different social positions. It seeks to confront and identify the places where professional skills are rooted through a return to past experience.

Everyday life in childhood is often associated with parental care but also with a role held in early childhood which involves a parent in difficulty or a family strongly affected by illness or death. The stories recount these moments of disruption when the feeling of relative stability in an 'ordinary family' is gradually or suddenly broken. But within the closed environment of the family, everyone performs assigned functions related to the hardships of everyday life without questioning or complaining. This is because the family is also a cocoon in which the presence of parents and siblings binds and protects. The clan-like aspect of life behind closed doors contributes in some families to creating a somewhat suffocating atmosphere that the child is not yet able to grasp: the outside world is perceived as a threat by the parents (often of humble origins) and by the child through his school experience. But he does not have the words or the social legitimacy to express his anger, his indignation and his aggressiveness, which become internalized as negativity turned against himself and expressed by shame, depression, alcoholism, submission or a rigid defense against the unknown.

However, this humble family background is a place of belonging and strong references. It is a place where the importance of the values of humility and simplicity is stressed. These are shared values that predispose one to recognize, without reservation or complacency, one's own capacities and disabilities. Thus, entering the work force does not expose one to the anxieties of 'the right choice' because finding a job does not derive its essential driving force from processes of idealization of the self or of a profession. The consequence is that there is no real impediment or inhibition to embracing the profession. Finding a job is not associated with the search for a socially rewarding self-image but with the search for a place just for oneself, where one can feel good and 'be oneself'. Thus, the important question in adolescence does not revolve around surpassing oneself but around moving away, getting out of a stifling family environment to fend for oneself and to take charge of one's life.

Finding oneself so close to human disability does not necessarily mean that in the course of one's life one has been brought into contact with people with disabilities, even if this is the case for a number of MPAs. The connection is more indirect and involves strong emotional ties with people around them, in a family context and in a social context where the sharing of values, firmly rooted in each of them, takes presence and care for granted. Tolerance, courage, mutual aid, solidarity and trust are all values in whose name the hierarchy between those in good health and the others in our care is erased. The disadvantages brought upon us by the challenging situations that those with a disability experience give rise to respect and compassion that legitimize the need to put oneself at the service of their comfort.

The relationship to disability is thus rooted, for everyone, in the experience of familiar, highly valued and active support, provided by them or by members of their entourage to parents or relatives in a state of poverty or physical or moral disability. However, this closeness of ties in a context of increased dependence can confront one with major upheavals caused by the excessive suffering, agonies and deaths of those one cares for so lovingly. The ordeal also concerns what can be experienced as an excess of responsibility, which is difficult to cope with and which causes feelings of guilt, helplessness and discouragement that can have inhibiting effects on school and social life. For most MPAs, the teenage years are characterized by a difficulty in finding a grip on school work, resulting in fear of failure, isolation or marginalization. Involvement in domestic life often makes it feel absurd to take time for oneself and to consider that the effort to be made might only concern one's own development or success.

Becoming the interpreters of the inexpressible

Although one may not be fully aware of what is happening, it becomes necessary at the end of adolescence to free oneself of family ties that have come to feel very much like a constraint. One must release oneself from a system that appears to claim too much time, too many energies and affects. The values that have supported identifications to family figures, such as the early, constantly renewed capacity to take on responsibilities, will be the levers of empowerment. Entering adulthood means finding work quickly and settling in; obstacles, whatever they may be, can be overcome. There is adversity for poorly educated and often poorly socialized young people. But what is striking in their stories is how much each one finds in himself the capacities, the will and the energy to face the harshness of social and professional integration without feeling threatened, weakened or hindered.

It is in this context that MPAs become aware of what it means to have multiple disabilities. Be it at the beginning of their professional life or later, they find a way to cope with their own deficiencies, and a renewed self-construction that enables them to both accept their personal history and move beyond it gradually emerges. In these stories, we learn about individual situations where each MPA evolves professionally and is led to assist those who are the most in need. By sharing how they experience lack, inadequacy or failure brings consistency to what they do, thus allowing them to develop a true professional competence and recognize themselves in it. The more fragile parts of the self, as well as the resources that have developed in relation to them, have come to coexist where revisited family values can be re-appropriated and self-invention can be achieved in a social activity of help and care.

But the ability to stay as close as possible to people with multiple disabilities and to accompany them in their daily lives does not depend solely on an ability to accept, tolerate and cope with the adversity to which their situation exposes them. Important support for involvement is provided by the specific conditions attached to the institutional construction of care for those having multiple disabilities.

Through the stories that recount the youth of each person, a recurrent problem emerges. In each unique family and relational context, there is always a history of suffering, of uneasiness in the face of what appears to be hindered or forbidden speech, inhibited as one is by humiliation, the need to repress family episodes, the supposed risks incurred by its expression, or the requirement of silence imposed on children. The often painful experience of living in a family without a place to speak, to communicate, to exchange, to make oneself heard or to find a listener seeks to restore itself in a new experience that gives access to speech. This unformulated expectation will find satisfaction in an activity that cannot fail to take into account a shared speech that questions, explores, explains, elaborates and supports. Helping severely disabled people who for the most part can hardly speak requires careful listening at all times so as to hear and understand without the use of words and thus to become 'the voice' of the other person, who does not have access to speech. Establishing a 'talking team' is absolutely necessary.

This necessity, which guarantees a place for the expression of everyone's speech as a space for exchange and listening, provides a compensation and contributes to job satisfaction. The associative project, which in its founding principles attaches great value to speech and collective exchange, is particularly attractive with respect to this expectation.

The desire to express oneself is related to an interest in deciphering the often enigmatic, difficult way in which the people they are supporting express themselves and communicate their daily need to be helped. We have already stressed how much the dynamics of involvement are rooted in the necessity to decipher what is perceived as incomprehensible, invisible or inexpressible.

The environment of multiple disabilities thus offers itself as a possible way to restore a means of communicating that was initially experienced as deficient. It becomes a space open to the expression of flaws where fragilities can instead be experienced as resources. It forms an alliance with the part of the self that tolerates its own inability to transform reality without losing consistency. It encourages one to surpass oneself by following the imperceptible paths that lead across impossible boundaries: 'You can't change someone, you can just do your best'.

The fragile construction of an inventive appreciation of the relationship

'Somehow, we're proud to be MPAs, it's not a dead-end job'. At the heart of MPAs' identity construction is a double image, that of a job in turns under-estimated and overestimated by their professional and personal environment. This is an image they internalize in part. They experience their entry into the world of the person with multiple disabilities as the entry into a world of ever-challenging questions, a world that escapes the certainties of under-standing. Facing the obscure density of the other's enigma requires presence, bonds and sharing.

The experience of a thought that seeks to build meaningful connections is constantly required, as is the experience of a sensoriality that tends to feel inex-pressible feelings (intranquillity, even daunting anxiety at times) which MPAs have to come to terms with on a daily basis. Through listening, speaking and touching – not so much to translate what cannot be said and shown as to wel-come and make contact – MPAs reach the limits of expression.

Helping the resident to get out of the stranglehold of the multiple disabil-ities that lock him in his own body without subjecting him to constraining behavioral or technical restraint, and allowing him to enter into a meaningful life, is the fragile process that characterizes the ultimate competence as expe-rienced by the MPA.

The sense of identity is experienced thanks to the slow approach to knowledge through experience, success being only a sign that the MPA keeps moving forward, deepening a knowledge that comes through the ordeal of everyday life.

If he finds the right distance, it is through a concrete bond: at first, making contact and establishing the closeness of a presence, and then, each time, con-structing the fragile, inventive appreciation of the relationship.

The need for group work also emerges: it makes it possible to find acces-sible paths when one becomes overwhelmed. The group has a capacity for alerting and controlling that makes it possible to take a break, adopt a differ-ent perspective and lighten the constraints: the unpredictable or unbearable requires a place to lay down the heavy burden of tension and get back on track, a necessary condition to preserve the bond with the person with mul-tiple disabilities.

There is also the burden of the parents, whose perfectly legitimate suffering and anxiety must be borne when anxiety takes the form of an often unconscious reluctance to leave their child in the care of an institution.

Finally, there is the need for the specific nature of the profession to be recognized, a recognition commensurate with the importance of the positions held, which runs counter to the usual hierarchy of professions and social recognition: 'We do everything but we are nothing'.

Professional identity thus redraws its contours as changes occur between the subject's own dispositions and external realities, logics and constructs, in particular the organization of work and the exercise of power, but also the hierarchy of activities and professions. Interpersonal conflicts arise from the discrepancies between one's sense of identity and other people's opinion. The challenges of recognition are at the heart of professional life. The need for recognition is based on the need to receive confirmation of the value of self-building as a professional, a confirmation which is necessary to maintain sufficient self-esteem.

Identity is also nourished by the place found in a team, in the professional organization and frames of reference and in shared values and representations. The challenge is to find a sufficiently stable balance, but this stability is always potentially weakened, subject to internal and external turbulence.

Working to elucidate the identity of the different professionals who work together in an establishment cannot aim to build a homogeneous and transparent organization by strictly delimiting the place of each. What allows the creation of a shared collective space is not just a delimitation of individual identities but also that which makes each identity different: common ground is not characterized by specific elements but rather by a certain disappropriation that creates a different perspective. It is about the sharing of a burden or a task, and this involves maintaining tension.

The social bond is not strengthened in the individual affirmation of strictly separated competences. It is because there is opacity, strangeness and inadequacy that there is actually a task and a necessity to share.

The social bond is a common and plural space, not a fragmented territory with transparent borders. Open identities are needed to build solidarity. Uncertainty is productive when it comes to approaching the enigmatic and the unexpected provided it can be worked on. It is unsustainable if it is used as evidence of the incompetence of others.

'They are strong in their desire to live,', the MPAs point out somewhat admiringly when talking about people with multiple disabilities. The task to be shared when helping residents requires the pooling of the professional specificities of each person, but it depends very much on this ability to come to terms with what exists and to accept deficiency.

Conclusion

In contexts of change where it is more difficult for social structures to fulfill their function as supports of identity and reference points, individuals and groups must situate themselves in the very place where the contradictions with which they are confronted exist. Indeed, the feeling of disruption is linked to changes in external reality, but it is not enough to explain the feeling of discontinuity in the representation of oneself. The feeling of weakening identity, of weakening of the self in one's professional activity, is due to the fact that structures do not only exist as external to individuals and groups but that they are the subject of internalization processes. The part of the self which is engaged in social and institutional structures is affected, and everyone's previous balances become destabilized. The question of adaptability is raised in the encounter between constructs outside oneself and the constructs that are one's own to find a place in one's work. The feeling of unease, being shared, is most of the time observed from the outside, that is, objectivized instead of being analyzed from the point of view of individual subjects. Yet it is they, alone or with others, who are in a position to reshape their representations, question their positions, challenge and renew their relationships and practices.

The question of professionalization is now almost exclusively judged by skills. This focus on the action of each individual in the service of overall efficiency, dictated by the race for performance, is not well suited to the complexity of work situations, all the more so when they concern assistance, care and support activities. The conception and management of jobs by identifying skills alone does not make it possible to take into account the intricate cognitive, relational and subjective qualities that professionals demonstrate in their work in relation to the specific conditions of material and human contexts.

Within the framework of an individual approach and groupwork based on elaboration and sharing, this intervention research has allowed professionals to approach the way they exist in their activity. It has enabled them to comprehend the complexity of the situations they face and has led them to identify the breaking-points or stumbling blocks that can lead to the weakening of their ties to themselves, to work, to residents and to their colleagues. It has made it possible for them to identify the resources that allow them to develop a representation of themselves as competent professionals: 'In this work there is a lot of instinct, something that cannot be explained. We were able to find the words to express this'.

Note

1 Medical–psychological aides (MPAs) work with diverse populations in hospitals, psychiatric institutions as well as other institutions for children, adults and the elderly. In this research, we are talking exclusively about professionals who provide daily assistance and support to a population of people – children and adults – with multiple disabilities. Throughout the text, the acronym MPA will be used to refer to medical–psychological aids because it corresponds to the name given by professionals themselves. In 2016, the State Diploma of Educational and Social Accompaniment merged the diplomas of MPA and Auxiliary of Social Life. It is now divided into three areas of specialization: intervention in institutions, at home and in ordinary settings (schools). At the time of writing, it is still too early to say whether these changes have led to a real change in the profession and professional identities.

References

Aulagnier, P. (1986). *Un interprète en quête de sens*. Paris: Ramsay.

Barus-Michel, J., & Giust-Desprairies, F. (2000). Pour une épistémologie de la psychologie sociale clinique. *Bulletin de Psychologie, 51*, 317–323.

Cifali, M., & Giust-Desprairies, F. (2006). *De la clinique. Un engagement pour la formation et la recherche*. Brussels: De Boeck.

Cifali, M., & Giust-Desprairies, F. (2008) *Mettre la pensée au travail: approche clinique*. Brussels, de Boeck.

Dejours, C. (2000[1980]). *Travail, usure mentale – De la psychopathologie à la psychodynamique du travail*. Paris: Bayard.

Freud, S. (1999). *Métapsychologie*. Paris: PUF.

Giust-Desprairies, F. (2013). *Le métier d'AMP*. Paris: Dunod.

Lévy, A. (1997). *Sciences cliniques et organisations sociales*. Paris: PUF.

Clinical ethics applied to training

9

Mireille Cifali

Introduction

A clinical approach is an art of research, intervention and training aimed at change and specific to each situation encountered. It does not belong to a single discipline and does not constitute a specific field. It therefore concerns the professional who tries to think about his action as well as the researcher accompanying the professional in his desire to understand, and the participant seeking to change a situation, a structure or an institution.

When we are confronted with situations where the primary goal is not to build generalizable knowledge but to allow others to access knowledge, overcome a disabling difficulty, free themselves or regain a foothold in a particular social and historical context, or when we develop, with the people involved, an active understanding of what is happening and a co-construction of meaning that can provoke change, then we find ourselves in a space called 'clinical' (Cifali & Giust-Desprairies, 2006).

A clinician in a social space is not only able to show consideration and pay attention to another person but is also, first and foremost, a practitioner reflecting on his own action when he *encounters* this other person. He builds his decision and knowledge in interaction with this person and does not deny

DOI: 10.4324/9781003296416-13

his suffering but welcomes it by letting himself be guided by it. He chooses to constantly adjust his distance from this person so that the feelings that accompany his action are not only projection or introjection. In this way, he accepts being confronted with dilemmas, almost always without invoking his powerlessness. He has at his disposal tools, theories and techniques, which he puts at the service of the relationship and of the other person, seeking not to use them as defenses against this person. Although he uses these techniques, he refuses to be subjected to them and does not regard techniques as a goal but as a means.

On a certain register

In this chapter, I will restrict myself to drawing the broad lines of a training program for relationship professions that is based on such a clinical posture. For many years, this was my field of research and action (Cifali, 2018).

Thinking as a daily routine

What can be transmitted? Not generalities, but particularities. Not statistics but the importance of a look, a presence, an interest for the specificity of the situations encountered. Everyday life, with its accidents, its multiple influences, its events, its surprises and its wonders is what must be talked about. It is in everyday life that the actions that have an effect on another person are possible. Hence the importance of thinking in a specific situation and therefore of thinking after integrating knowledge without necessarily 'applying' it. A trainer then transmits knowledge related to specificities; he obeys an ethic of the use of acquired knowledge so that it is not used to hold power over another person.

In doing so, we are guided by a conviction: although our knowledge is necessary, the essential thing is that another person be able to build an understanding of the situation that he alone is going through. This can be done through sharing, exchanges and common research around what sometimes blocks a path and makes it dangerous for oneself and others. In training, the concern is to restore an interest in the banality of everyday life so that another person, who may have put himself in danger, can get back into motion, that is, to affirm that understanding is a construction elaborated by several people and not a prerequisite held by a single person (Cifali & Giust-Desprairies, 2008).

Theory is preliminary, of course, but it must be suspended to build something that might contradict it. There is neither application nor reduction of the living subject to a hypothesis, but rather a type of work based on hypotheses that need to be put to the test and above all be allowed to evolve. Ideally, hypotheses never pre-exist; they result from field work. This reverses the research process insofar as we regard theory as a guide, not as a constraint. Having a clinical posture therefore implies questioning all the application processes of theories and taking into account the existing gap between a theoretical contribution and the ability for a subject to build knowledge from his action. The transmission of theory as such is not enough if one is to elaborate a reflection on action: it contains traps likely to result in being locked in preconceptions that may even hinder it.

The question, therefore, is to promote a reflection on professional action, a reflection that each of us must develop. Yet some scientific policies or conceptions can lead to a 'prohibition of thinking' (Malherbe, 2001). They reduce us to the role of executors, making us believe that it is impossible for us to think because others have already thought everything through. They thus enjoin us to stick to only one thought (whether a theory, a discipline or a technique) and to renounce our own. However, in action, such disengagement is disastrous. It is field work that makes a scientific discovery a source of hope for those who are in a particularly difficult situation. Thinking in the solitude of the moment, but also thinking and being intelligent together, is then a joy. We will get through the most difficult situations if we can think together.

A constructed subjectivity

Involvement in professional action requires us to recognize that our subjectivity is part of it and that it needs to be worked on. There is therefore an affirmation of a subjectivity necessary for action. The recognition that this subjectivity exists concerns both the professional in action and the one who builds with him an understanding of what is happening. It establishes a position that seeks to achieve objectivity by confronting subjectivities, not by excluding them. It therefore defines a clinical posture, preserving even in professional acts an interiority marked by unconscious processes.

However, this subjectivity must be worked on and not be confused with ego or identity. One could indeed suspect a clinical approach of reinforcing the process of an individualization that reduces the subject to his psychology, making him the center of the world and thus weakening the norm and the social bond. Conversely, recognizing and working on subjectivity means, in this context, starting from an 'I' so as not to end up with just 'I'.

In training, it is up to us to talk about these subjective processes, to encourage a professional to review his practice both when it has good effects and when it fails in order to try to understand the different dimensions of his actions with their intimate resonances. Naming and talking about these processes as ordinary processes may be a safeguard against overinvolvement and errors leading a professional to situations that are dangerous for him.

This part of the training is delicate and requires many precautions to be taken by building mechanisms that protect a professional, or a student, from the misuse of what he has said or written in his quest for understanding; institutional supervision should not interfere with these particular mechanisms. It is in the best interest of an institution to preserve these spaces and make them available without controlling them; this is a guarantee of its confidence in such work and the skills of its trainers. We can then pursue this type of 'self-analysis' in our own way because we are constantly confronted with the enigmas hidden in our actions, our positions and our beliefs. Sometimes without realizing it, we contribute to preserving the qualities of our presence, so vital for those who meet us.

Similarly, it is important for a clinical trainer not to neglect his own subjectivity. On the contrary, he must put it into work and thoughts, write about it and introduce it into a community, not so that it becomes a model, but so that it is confronted with other practices. This would allow professionals to recognize themselves, to reassure themselves, not to have the impression they are the only ones experiencing such a feeling. Among other things, this requires paying attention to one's physical involvement. It is not only one's knowledge that is beneficial but also how one's body participates in the transmission (Cifali, Grossmann & Périlleux, 2018).

A preservation of the relationship

If we retain a 'constructed subjectivity' as the basis of a clinical position, it follows that we must also pay particular attention to intersubjectivity, that is, take into account the relational dimension of the professions and recognize the importance of an 'encounter' that draws people out of themselves. Paying attention to the relationship means trying to understand that its driving forces can be both constructive and destructive. The relationship with another person (singular or plural) is often painful, and admitting this preserves each partner in a given institutional context.

It is in a relationship that our actions take place, so it is important to analyze its components. As a result, we do not only focus on the other person (to define, diagnose and control him), not only on ourselves, but on what happens between our professional self and that other person, indissociable, as we both are, from a social context. The strength of the relationship must be recognized, as it almost always plays a part in what has allowed this other person to overcome his difficulty. Conversely, professional violence in the relationship (contempt, rejection, humiliation) precludes evolution and leads to destructiveness. This may seem an obvious observation, but it can nonetheless be difficult to avoid such deviations. Let us at least admit that this could happen to any of us. It is not that we should be virtuous and just, but that at our level we should at all times strive for justice, equity and benevolence. This in no way excludes authority, strictness and constraint.

An emotional commitment

One conviction persists today among professionals working in the care, education or social work sectors: do not let your emotions be seen. Feelings are regarded as being harmful and subjective, the required condition being strict objectivity. The golden rule is that we should remain neutral. Affectivity is seen as parasitical; there is a belief that feelings are not of the same order as knowledge, that they must therefore be eliminated from professional action because they tarnish the ideal of self-control.

The question of feelings is what most surely separates the two approaches to professional action on either side of a dividing line: on the one hand is a romantic vision that allegedly does not honor reason; on the other hand is a rational stance based on a scientific application that is supposed to guarantee the effectiveness of action. These strong metaphors speak for themselves. However, a human being distinguishes himself in his action by the presence of both. Thinking is based on feeling; it is the first, necessary step that enables one to speak, argue and discuss. Feelings never leave a human being alone, and until the end they persist, color action and the reflection about action. In feelings, moreover, humanity can recognize itself. The disappearance of feelings would herald brutal times, the loss of response to the unbearable – in short, the possibility of the worst. Moral indifference is a sign of dehumanization. Simply being allowed to feel is therefore an important first step. Creating the space so that the expression of feelings can find a place and a framework to be welcomed and worked on is a second step. The effectiveness of a thought would therefore require an incarnate thought that does not attempt to control or silence the feelings experienced. Our reactions and affects are not unique, and yet we think they are when we experience them, for example, when we say: 'I alone feel this sense of helplessness'; there is almost always a human community behind us.

Today, cognitive neurosciences recognize that emotions have a place in learning and human relationships. However, their aim differs from a clinical approach by reducing emotions to cognitive processes and attempting to control them. In short, the important thing is to '*control* your emotions'. I prefer talking about feelings rather than emotions. I encourage people to welcome them when they occur. I advise colleagues or trainers to pause, to take a break, sometimes to write or speak with each other so as not to deny these feelings but instead to challenge the belief that so-called 'positive feelings' have a good effect, while so-called 'negative' ones should be banished (Cifali & Périlleux, 2013). I am grateful to them for informing us of what is happening in our relation to a situation. I do not advocate controlling, but listening and sometimes changing the way we position ourselves in the present.

A link between the individual and the social world

Most of the time, a clinical approach is seen as centered on the inner self, the individual psyche, and as totally uninterested in the social question. Therefore, it supposedly cannot contribute anything to the group or to social institutions and organizations. This criticism is not a new one. It denounces for example a failure on the part of psychoanalysts to take into account the group and its effects, but studies carried out today highlight three key notions: the construction of the subject only occurs in intersubjectivity; the interior and the exterior cannot be separated if we want to understand their construction; and the institution incites a constrained subject to undertake a lucid self-analysis to free himself from alienation. Some of these studies focus more particularly on putting the imaginary dimensions between subject and institution (Giust-Desprairies, 2003) into perspective. The group, the framework and the mediations are recognized as having a structuring effect: they make it possible to overcome difficulties, whether within a class, a school, an institution or a team.

Among the divisions that persist, the one between the individual level and the social level is deep-rooted (Cifali, 2015). Like clinical sociology or psychosociology, a clinical approach cannot accept this. Even if a training course is divided into parts corresponding to the different social sciences or techniques, a trainer must accept – and say – that his discipline alone cannot do anything. It is through coordination that we must seek understanding. The existence of 'practice analysis seminars' or 'integration seminars' becomes essential, but it requires that trainers obey some sort of an ethic in relation to their knowledge. Otherwise, a sociologist might reject a clinician; a neurologist might only swear by his MRI imagery and the potentialities of the brain, neglecting all the clinical knowledge accumulated before him; a cognitivist might come to make an ideal of reason and totally ignore unconscious psychological processes; a clinician, in turn, might not want to learn from the contributions of neurosciences.

A historian's approach

In current training, a historical perspective is very often missing. History is not a mere series of dates or a presentation of theories that we wave aside because we consider them outdated. Rather, historical research gives meaning to our present and preserves our roots in humanity. Thanks to it, we are sometimes able to detect where traps, dangerous repetitions and false innovations lie hidden and to say that dehumanization processes are still possible. Instead of making us believe that the present is what is best, that we are in constant progress, historical research sometimes enables us to highlight what must be preserved today and tomorrow and to describe the destructive processes that no society can avoid. By retracing the filiations, inventions and creations of the past, we are in a position to remain humble in relation to our knowledge. Any denial of history is alarming. A clinical approach is historical. It remembers its history, but also the history of others.

'Error', for example, is a major discovery made by the neurosciences. That is all very well, but for our part we turned error into a driving force for learning a long time ago. What is asserted, scientifically established, may reassure us – we were not in 'error' – but it is unfortunate that this assertion should be presented as a novel one. The recognition of knowledge built up by pedagogical movements, institutional pedagogy for example, and a dialogue between them, based on mutual respect, would be more beneficial.

An ethical debate

A clinical approach has developed an ethic of otherness and specificity. To pose its contribution in terms of ethics is to consider this approach from the point of view of a questioning, an opening for those who are constantly confronted with uncertainty. It thus contributes to the preservation of humanization processes. To use Marie Balmary's beautifully worded phrase, we should never forget that 'humanity is not hereditary'. This 'humanity' is transmitted, in the strongest sense of the word (2009, p. 23). It does so through work based on interiority – a sensitive, bodily, committed thought, capable of setting thought in motion. It can be seen as a particular style that has nothing to do with religious or scientific rhetoric. It is a style that uses language like a poem, with its rhythm, its cadence, its silences, its depths, its tremors and its escapes. It could also be the transmission of 'addressed knowledge' encouraging one to build 'transforming knowledge'.

It is not just a question of ethics, but of a debate between several people, or an internal debate, when our actions are confronted with dilemmas or dead ends, when we have to make a decision that we know is the least bad one but not 'the best', as we had hoped. There is constant doubt and torment, and also the risks taken to preserve one's dignity for another person and therefore also for oneself.

Psychological commitment

During the 20th century, so-called social professions appeared, created by a Western society to assist, help and support people confronted with a physical and/or psychological handicap, unable to provide for their daily lives, exiled from their land and their roots, separated from the world and in the process of becoming reintegrated. Mediation, support, regulation and control professions have also emerged. These stress the social dimension with its possibilities and impossibilities determined by regulations, with its political debates and their evolutions.

Is a clinical approach relevant to these professions? I will come back to it a little differently than before and obviously answer in the affirmative by giving, in what follows, some elements which prove that it is essential to preserve it.

A personal relationship to social work

What social workers accomplish in their everyday tasks is based on a number of external factors that they need to take into account: assumptions made by the human and social sciences; progress in the field of medicine; legal and judicial frameworks; the complexities of existing documents; the procedures to be followed; political injunctions; and the financial and economic state of a society. However, professionals are not 'neutral' with respect to these factors.

They either subscribe to them or do not, and when they do, their support may not be total. Their convictions, beliefs and militancy sometimes come into play. Certain mediation-focused professions put them in the position of having to comply with constraints imposed by their employer (most often the State), and these constraints affect the people they are helping. They are supposed to be at the service of society, with its norms and jurisprudence, but they find themselves in the presence of someone who may not understand these norms and thus sees them as unfair. If these social workers remain ambivalent to such constraints, the situation can become confused, and the consequences are not always positive.

How a social worker relates to the norms that he is supposed to transmit is only a first step, though it is a major one and may be difficult. Only then can he act in full knowledge of the facts and not blindly apply the rules. He may also have to break rules that seem unfair to him, playing with the letter of the law while respecting its spirit, but with an ability to explain his action and accept its consequences. It is sometimes by deviating, by taking by-paths, that we allow another person to regain their ability to act and to accept these requirements. This requires insight into what is at stake so as not to deceive or be deceived. It is important that such work can be preserved in the training period and continued in daily professional life.

An encounter within an institutional framework

These professions essentially consist in encounters. The professionals are a presence for other people, sometimes even the only presence that those who have lost their footing, or are close to losing it, can hold on to. Such encounters are more or less calibrated. The quality of a long-term relationship can only be preserved by keeping boredom and repetition at bay. But in the case of a single appointment, everything takes place in an instant. The challenges are not the same, nor are the difficulties. There is always an encounter, however: a mutual presence in a particular place, a bodily presence, words and silence.

An encounter brings out working-off mechanisms; it plays a part in any evolution of a person whose own action is required. One legacy of our 20th-century experience in the field is our ability to understand this now. A relationship supports and facilitates evolution. It is not all about good feelings. Rather, it is a reliable presence, one that supports yet constrains, is both patient and exacting, understands yet demands, accepts the aggressiveness of those who are angry yet asserts authority and wisdom. It does not just amount to constant empathy or meek benevolence. Nor is it limited to instant mistrust towards those who might lie and make promises that they will not keep. A relationship is built by two people; it involves confrontations, setbacks, progress and negotiations if it is not to be broken. Depending on the situation, it can take place in close proximity or at a distance. But it is a construction each time. It depends on the skills of the professional, but also on the way he welcomes the other person, on his voice, bodily posture, the words he addresses to the other person: in short, his qualities as a human being.

As we have seen, a professional encounter can generate violence, misunderstandings and humiliations and turn into a power game that the other person has no choice but to submit to. This can be avoided by re-thinking this relationship while keeping in mind its specificity: this is an absolute necessity when a relationship goes wrong. We often believe we can save ourselves the trouble of ensuring the quality of a relationship by setting out some sort of procedure. While this may exempt us from having to reason in terms of the specificities of the relationship, we risk missing what we are looking for. The relationship will then remain superficial (Cifali & Périlleux, 2012).

A personal history

Working on the relationship means thinking about how you relate to yourself, given the profession you have chosen and how this choice makes sense in your own history and psychological commitments. This personal history can negatively affect another person and create mishaps or even scandals that are all the more difficult to understand because they are caused by someone who is paid to take care of a person, but who in fact is satisfying their own impulses or inclinations and considers that this person is 'their' thing. Because he knows how fragile this other person is, the social worker must avoid two contradictory impulses. One is the impulse to identify with the suffering of a person who has experienced trauma: the professional then wears himself out vainly trying to 'save' the person, and then experiences his helplessness as personal grief. The other is the impulse to reject, which it is always possible to justify by saying it is the fault of the 'customer', who has not taken responsibility. The professional sometimes exhausts himself alternating between these two attitudes.

Does working in the social sphere save us the trouble of having to worry about psychological processes? This approach can be convenient in theory; in practice, it is destructive. When we work in the social sphere, we also commit ourselves psychologically. When we work on the psychological level, we cannot constantly ignore the social dimension. At least that is my position. Many authors define the subject as someone who cannot exist outside relationships, who – though constantly shaped by the world and its events – is not conditioned to be a pale replica of phenomena greater than him. He is not only a 'being spoken about', but also a 'speaking being', responding to the forces of destruction, transgressing norms that would lead to excessive submission in order to keep building and rebuilding himself.

Training programs

How can we reflect and work on the relational and emotional aspects of social work? This begins in initial training and continues throughout one's professional life. Obviously, much depends on whether or not what is described above is accepted. If the social dimension prevails and the impact of the encounter, of individual commitment and of self-analysis is denied, social work training does not leave room for the ins and outs of the complexity of such a relationship.

If a training course accepts this, then it makes sure to open up various spaces for reflection, experience and encounters. These include spaces for a philosophical questioning of its ethics, spaces for working on the relationship with oneself, with others and with the institution, in internships or in professional practice, with feedback on what has been experienced in a unique relationship, including feelings. More conventionally, the courses and seminars approach subjectivity at the workplace through the theories of human sciences and literature or through the use of different training techniques such as life stories or the writing of real-life experiences, and also including artistic practices such as visual arts, drama or poetry (Cifali, Giust-Desprairies & Périlleux, 2015). A clinical approach favors certain training methods that include writing – the story of an experience or autobiography, literature as a mode of knowledge, art with its creative processes and individual professional practices. That is, they associate science and philosophy as well as self-analysis and exercises so that certain technical gestures become automatic reflexes while we remain attentive to the reactions of another person to whom our technical gestures are addressed.

In my training activities, I use experience stories (Cifali & André, 2012). In order to make room for interiority, I have students or experienced professionals talk about work situations that, when put into words, become as captivating as a novel. These are stories of misfortune and happiness, stories about how they first bungled an encounter and then pulled it off, stories in which you can feel a presence, an availability – these words that are the core of our professions, but that we have difficulty qualifying and, of course, quantifying. They tell, express, share these fragments of action to build a thought together. It is important to be able to share what has made us suffer, to write about these situations in which we experience doubt – these stories that Paul Ricoeur calls 'the laboratory of moral judgment' (1985, p. 74), in which we cannot decide according to principles and must develop this capacity for instantaneous thinking. These training situations give us – both myself and the participants – something to think about. I then use them to explain what the daily life of these professions is all about, stressing the importance of the 'I', the 'you' – in the singular or in the plural – time and events. They sensitize us to how life is lived, to how a dialogue is held, to how the moment occurs, to what is experienced inside us and is not predictable.

These telling and writing methods require time and maturation; they do not claim to teach interiority in three lessons. They set a different pace that allows one to make a pause, a break and then go on (Billeter, 2015). They allow everyone to revert to more humility, to think about their professional actions and to constantly question what they thought they knew. This is what is at stake. Initial training can give a taste for thinking, reading and self-analysis, all of which are essential.

Tomorrow, or even today?

A question arises: is it conceivable that in a not-so-distant future a clinical approach will be rendered obsolete by a scientific and social policy that gives priority to figures, efficiency, standardized procedures, computerized quality systems or neuroscientific approaches, for example? This is what many think, erasing the very history of such an approach and what it has generated in terms of techniques and ethical practices in the relationship professions.

If we decide that training no longer needs trainers or that the Internet and screens are enough to transmit knowledge, if we argue that the assessment of acquired knowledge can be satisfied with 'right-or-wrong' quizzes, if we decree that the years of training can be reduced because there are enough rational procedures and ready-to-use models so that professionals are only asked to conscientiously apply procedures, if we believe that someone working in a relationship profession must become like a researcher in his laboratory – then yes, the clinical approach will be put at risk, until human reality puts a brake on such hegemonic claims. That is what history teaches us. When we repress reality, it always returns in the form of symptoms, and we can no longer pretend it does not exist. We may have already reached this point in history.

References

Balmary, M. (2009). Le désir à la recherche de ses sources. In *Le sacré, cet obscur objet de désir* (pp. 157–173). Paris: Albin Michel.

Billeter, J. F. (2015). *Esquisses*. Paris: Alia.

Cifali, M., & Giust-Desprairies, F. (Eds.) (2006). *De la clinique. Un engagement pour la formation et la recherche*. Brussels: De Boeck.

Cifali, M., & Giust-Desprairies, F. (2008). *Formation clinique et travail de la pensée (Clinical training and thought work)*. Brussels: De Boeck Supérieur.

Cifali, M., & André, A. (2012). *Écrire l'expérience. Vers une reconnaissance des pratiques professionnelles*. Paris: PUF (1st ed. 2007).

Cifali, M., & Périlleux, T. (Eds.) (2012). *Les métiers de la relation malmenés. Répliques clinique*. Paris: L'Harmattan.

Cifali, M., & Périlleux, T. (Eds.) (2013). Clinique du négatif, enseignement et formation en tension. *Cahiers de Psychologie Clinique*, 41, 7–190.

Cifali, M., Giust-Desprairies, F., & Périlleux, T. (Eds.) (2015). *Processus de création et processus cliniques*. Paris: PUF.

Cifali, M. (2015). L'entre-deux de la littérature: de la psychanalyse à la sociologie. In Arnaud, G. & Fugier, P. (Eds.), *Sociologie et psychanalyse. De l'échange de vues à la transformation du regard. Clinique du changement social*, vol. 20 (pp. 75–97). Paris: L'Harmattan.

Cifali, M., Grossmann S., & Périlleux, T. (Eds.) (2018). *Présences du corps dans l'enseignement et la formation. Approches cliniques*. Paris: L'Harmattan.

Cifali, M. (2018). *S'engager pour accompagner. Valeurs des métiers de la formation*. Paris: PUF.

Giust-Desprairies, F. (2003). *L'imaginaire collectif*. Paris: Érès.

Malherbe, J-F. (2001). *Déjouer l'interdit de penser. Essais d'éthique critique*. Montreal: Liber.

Ricœur, P. (1985). *Temps et récit 3. Le temps raconté*. Paris: Seuil, Point.

Part IV

The clinic and ethics in social work

Psychoanalytical dissent **10**

Guy de Villers

Introduction

The purpose of the analyses we propose is to highlight the urgency of restoring a speech clinic in a context where a clinic based on 'scientifically' verifiable facts continues to prevail. We will first go back to the origins of evidence-based medicine (EBM) and then analyze how the hegemonic position that this orientation now occupies in social workers' practices took shape. We will end this survey by pointing out the relevance of psychoanalytical orientation to establish a practice that goes against the evidence of the facts established by the verification procedures advocated by the supporters of EBM.

The origins of evidence-based medicine

The pre-history of EBM

Several authors agree that the roots of EBM can be found in the work of Philippe Pinel[1] on the probability of cure of the insane (1808) and Dr. Pierre-Charles-Alexandre Louis[2] in the 1830s. Between 1821 and 1827, Dr. Louis

DOI: 10.4324/9781003296416-15

observed hundreds of patients. 'He developed a method for collecting observations according to a plan that would be taught to generations of physicians: the patient's medical history, history of the disease, physical examination, evolution and *post-mortem* examination results if necessary' (Fagot-Largeault, 2018). He classified, listed and compared. For example, his 'numerical method' allowed him to distinguish the typhoid fever syndrome from other febrile syndromes. And it is the statistical tool that was to prove the ineffectiveness of bleeding in the treatment of pneumonia (Morabia, 2006, pp. 158–160).[3]

A 'revolutionary' project therefore began to emerge: the use of the knowledge gained from medical science to support the practice of patient care. This project required a new approach in the training of clinical physicians and the provision of new information resources for practitioners. It also required creating a new link between scientific data obtained from medical research and the questions that physicians face in their practice, such as inequalities regarding the cost of medical care.

An edifying intention

The purpose of EBM is to base each patient's care on the most robust data from scientific research so that he benefits from the best possible evolution. The target of EBM is the *clinical decision-making process*, the objective of which is to identify ways to render effective and efficient the application of scientific research results to care. Archie Cochrane expressed this in 1971 when he recommended that forms of health care that have proven effective through well-designed evaluations should be provided equitably (Cochrane, 1972).[4] This is what we recognize under the label of 'good practices'. To this end, he stressed the importance of using data from randomized controlled trials (RCTs), [5] since they could provide much more reliable information than other data sources. These other data sources, considered less reliable, were clinical impressions, anecdotal experience, 'expert opinion' or tradition. The choice was clear: it was either a clinical decision based on data from RCTs or data based on 'clinical impressions', that is, the clinician's subjectivity.

It should be noted that, from the outset, EBM has been part of a negative critical perspective towards the clinic. A rough estimate suggests that nearly 30% of patients in the United States, irrespective of the pathology they suffer from, receive inappropriate treatment (Schuster et al., 1998; Masson et al., 2008).

Towards a hegemony of medicine based on well-established facts

Perino (2013) has noted that the phrase 'evidence-based medicine' bears in its very formulation the mark of its hegemonic position. Indeed, scientific medicine covers three fields:

- descriptive sciences, such as anatomy, physiology, histology, biology or genetics;
- pathology and the clinic (nosography and diagnosis);
- therapeutics, which prescribes treatment and evaluates actions aimed at modifying the evolution of diseases (prognosis).

It is therefore through a misuse of language that all medicine is placed under the EBM banner, whereas it only covers its therapeutic aspect. This violent seizure of power is not without consequences for the critical distance that we should keep with regard to how we consider a dimension of medicine. It is as if there were no choice: it is either evidence-based medicine or nothing. That is, there is pre-evidence medicine[6] (for instance, Vesalius's anatomy, Laennec's anatomo-clinical method, Claude Bernard and Carl Ludwig's physiology, Virchow's cellular pathology, Jenner and Pasteur's vaccinations and Dr. Louis's counting) and the evidence-dominated medicine that is now the sole accepted norm. This is a first effect of the abuse of a dominant position. The second effect, more pernicious, derives from the first. The only scientific subject worthy of interest is the physiological efficacy of therapies, provided that these therapies are tested in randomized clinical trials. Thus, it can be said that the dispossession of medicine by EBM in favor of therapy alone is coupled with another dispossession, one that recognizes no other scientific therapy than that based on solid evidence (EBM), whereas many treatments proved their worth long before the EBM procedures were established. Let it suffice to mention 'insulin, cortisone, sex hormones, heparin, VKAs, diuretics, neuroleptics, most vaccines, vitamins and antibiotics and so many other drugs that were discovered and validated without resorting to EBM' (Perino, 2013).

How then can we understand the almost absolute hegemony of EBM in the therapeutic decision-making process? There are no doubt strictly medical reasons for this *de facto* monopoly. Among the reasons for its domination is the emergence of new forms of diseases, such as chronic diseases (fibromyalgia, for example), autoimmune diseases and, more generally, all multifactorial diseases.[7] The effectiveness of the treatment for these new types of diseases is more difficult to demonstrate. 'Case by case' therapy is never conclusive, and therefore studies involving a large number of patients are needed to assess the comparative efficacy of drug treatment and placebo therapy. This is EBM's main area of expertise.

There is a second, more complex reason, which lies, on the one hand, in the specificity of training in the clinic of the caregiver/patient relationship and, on the other hand, in the obligation to go through EBM if one wishes to ensure one's professional promotion (be it through publications in international journals or to access positions of responsibility in the university–hospital system). It is well established that training in clinical relationships cannot do without personal experience of the practitioner's relationship to the disease and to the patient. Support systems for medical practice (in *Balint* groups, for example) are now familiar. Clinical training is long and requires personal involvement on the part of the practitioner, an inconvenience that the use of evidence-based medical practice would seem to circumvent. Correlatively, a treatment based on EBM 'recommendations' is very often drug-based. As it is limited to a prescription for a drug or to an intervention performed by auxiliary staff, it does not require listening to the patient. This type of treatment considerably reduces the time of consultation and therefore increases the profitability of medical procedures.

This is leading to a new configuration of the caregiver–patient relationship that will modify or even exclude many caregiving practices on the pretext that they do not lend themselves to the verification procedures promoted by EBM: using placebos and double-blind evaluations in the context of psychotherapies makes no sense. Therefore, these therapeutic modalities are discarded since they cannot be subject to the EBM standard. The ideal of scientific rigor promoted for the sake of improving treatments for better patient health is indeed a laudable ideal. However, it is becoming a war machine aimed at eliminating other ways of treating patients based on other rigorous criteria, involving subjectivity on the part of the patient and the therapist. The consequences for the patient – and more broadly for the society in which he must live – are nothing less than a reconfiguration of the relationship to the disease: the quality of life will no longer be taken into account in the choice of treatment, only the objectivity of measurable effectiveness.

In the end, it is the very notion of disease that becomes blurred. The calculation of the impact of a particular risk factor (the risk of hypercholesterolemia on the functioning of the heart, for example) changes the notion of disease by extending its scope to the risk and pathology it could cause. This produces an interpretation of life in terms of permanent pathology leading to generalized medicalization.

A new paradigm?

There are countless books and articles that salute the emergence of EBM as a new paradigm[8] in medical practice. Of course, the abundance of this research is not enough to legitimize its principles.[9]

Before engaging in a dialectical confrontation with what is commonly called the EBM paradigm, it seemed necessary to put into perspective the various meanings that emerge when we grasp the notion of paradigm through the prism of disciplines such as philosophy (logic and rhetoric), sociology and the epistemology of science.

In philosophy, the major reference is Aristotle and his treatise on *Rhetoric* (1989). It is in this book that the question of the respective status of proof and persuasion is raised, following Plato. That is why the reference to Aristotle is important to us. Does rhetoric belong to a science of logic or is it part of a manipulation technique? We can see the relevance of this issue in our time when there is a dominant movement to impose evidence-based medical practice and to ignore clinical intuition and the physician's strength of conviction. Aristotle opposes proof, the *tekmerion* (τεκμηριον), to the example (παραδειγμα) or paradigm. The example is used to generate an induction: it establishes a relationship between two entities on account of their similarity, it being understood that one entity is better known than the other. For Aristotle, achieving scientificity requires going beyond the register of rhetoric to 'go back to principles' (Aristotle, translated by N. Bonafous, 1856). However, Aristotle's position is more subtle than it seems, for he considers that rhetoric can very well use both the means of proof (logical and linguistic in nature) and those of persuasion (more psychological in nature). What is interesting about this perspective is that it allows us to grasp the double dimension of reason or, more exactly, a 'stratified rationality'. The first stratum is archaic; it calls for divinatory methods and interpretation based on clues. The second stratum uses 'modern' validity criteria such as argumentation and the need for convincing factual evidence. The use of the term 'stratum' implies that the first layer persists in interfering with the more recent layer, which results in persuasive effects that manifest themselves in the form of perceived evidence, exemplarity and the meaningful interpretation of representations constructed by the rational approach.

> In this historicized vision of human reason, rhetoric is neither a poor relation of logic nor an art of winning the cause through generalized nonsense. It is the art of providing evidence, arguments and justifications that are always subject to review, but whose criteria for persuasion

are not entirely arbitrary. They are rooted in an archaic reason that is still alive.

(Danblon, 2010, p. 213)

We must bear this vision of human reason in mind when we question EBM's claim to purge medical practice of any dimension other than that of so-called scientific evidence.

If we take the notion of paradigm from a sociological perspective, we will soon realize that it is closely linked to epistemology and the history of science. Most of the works that reflect scientific advances use the term 'paradigm' to salute the novelty of a configuration of knowledge which was born of a scientific revolution and which has attracted the support of a community of scholars. The support thus garnered is due to the relevance of the new solutions it offers in view of the impasses encountered in dealing with the reality of experience according to a model and methods that have become obsolete as a result. The term 'paradigm' is here referred to its promoter, Thomas Samuel Kuhn (1922–1996), who defined paradigm in these terms:

> [It is] the set of beliefs, recognized values and techniques that are common to the members of a given group. At the same time, it denotes an isolated element of this whole: concrete solutions to enigmas which, when used as models or examples, can replace explicit rules as the basis for solving the enigmas that subsist in normal science.

(Kuhn, 1983, p. 238)

This is the case with the law of universal gravitation in Newton's *Principia* (1833)[10] or the primacy of symbolism in early Lacan (Miller, 1999).

It is the conjunction of these two dimensions, that of the *episteme* and that of the adherence of a community, that according to Kuhn characterizes a paradigm. As Pierre Dumouchel says, a paradigm functions as a founding myth of a community of scientists who consider that such a theoretical *corpus*, together with application models and implementation procedures, is capable of producing novel but appropriate solutions to problems that have hitherto been without a valid solution (1990, p. 1847). It gives rise to a representation of reality nourished by values that guide the ethical choices of scientific research and its applications. This is the case for the side of objectivity vs. the side of subjectivity, the side of evaluation based on standards vs. the side of 'one by one' methods and of specificity based on principles.

Kuhn's originality lies in the assertion that these models are implicit. The researcher unconsciously puts them into play. They act through procedural memory. We could almost speak of the *habitus* of researchers working in a particular discipline (Bourdieu, 2018, p. 88).[11]

We could also compare the question of paradigm to that of ideology, the criticism of which was initiated by Marx and Engels. However, it is in Louis Althusser that we find a concept probably closer to that of paradigm: the spontaneous ideology of scientists (Althusser, 1974). In this sense, a paradigm is an interpreter of observation. Psychoanalysts would say that it works in the same way as the fantasy frame, although such a comparison is probably a little far-fetched.

This explains why paradigms die hard: they determine our relationship to the world while being lodged in our blind spot (*macula occulata*). And yet – and this is the whole point of the notion of paradigm – having encompassed and integrated a growing number of observations under the same principle of intelligibility, a paradigm ends up being like a straitjacket. In short, it is bursting at the seams. We have reached a crisis, and the need to move to a new paradigm can be felt at a time of instability, or even of war, in the interpretation patterns of reality (Crommelinck & Villers, 1993). We have seen that these models and examples were charged with beliefs and laden with values. This explains the often fierce conflicts between schools or laboratories.

While the reference to Kuhn is essential when it comes to unfolding the principles of this new discipline – that is, the social history of science – it should not make us forget the work of a pioneer in the field, namely Ludwik Fleck (1896–1961). Fleck was a renowned doctor and immunologist who in 1935 published *Genesis and Development of a Scientific Fact*, a work that truly inaugurated the social history of science with unprecedented vigor and relevance (Fleck, 2008). Fleck's theses interest us in more than one way. First, his criticism of science comes not from a philosopher or sociologist interested in the scientific approach, but from an authentic researcher, a biologist of genius, who developed vaccines under extremely difficult conditions, at a time when his Jewishness had kept him out of university circuits. It is in the Jewish ghetto of Lwow[12] in Poland that he set up his private laboratory. Deported to Auschwitz, he was assigned to the detection of syphilis and typhus. From December 1943 to the liberation of Poland on 11 April 1944, he was detained at the Buchenwald camp. At one point suspected of having used prisoners to experiment with his serological tests, he was eventually recognized as a resistance fighter, who on the contrary, along with other researchers, put up effective resistance by sabotaging their research.

Fleck goes against the commonly accepted doctrine that criticism of scientific theory essentially consists in 'examining the ability of concepts to form systems or the connections that these concepts create' (Fleck, 2008).

He demonstrates that human cognition is the activity 'most conditioned by the social world, and knowledge is just a social creation' (Fleck, 2008, p. 78). This is what leads the author to coin the phrase: 'collective of thought' (*Denkkollectiv*). From his experience as a researcher in serology and epidemiology, Fleck concludes that scientific knowledge is fundamentally marked by its socio-historical conditions of production. And this calls into question 'the sense of evidence that scientific truths spontaneously claim to have' (Macherey, 2008). Indeed, what *is* evidence? It is a conception in accordance with a 'collective of thought', expressed in a recognized 'style of thought' (*Denkstil*). Thought is not pure; it does not unfold in a neutral space. 'What is called clarity, rigor, is indeed nothing more than conformity to a style of thought that has succeeded in imposing itself and that, once established, tends to persist' (Macherey, 2008). The man who supports these positions that run counter to the prevailing ideas in the collective of thought that dominated the biology of his time is the same man who demonstrated the possibility of resisting the domination of the style of thought that ruled the community of scholars. Fleck is therefore a resistance fighter. He launches 'his own *aviso* for the resistance of thought'[13] (2008, p. 217). 'What a paradox to see the inventor of the notion of a "collective of thought" inflict such a denial on himself! His innovations provide ample evidence that it is possible to break, through one's own genius, the potentially harmful grip of a collective thinking framework' (Fleck, 2008, pp. 252–253). There is no discovery or advance in knowledge that occurs without the initiative of bold pioneers who take the risk of departing from the beaten track. Freud was one of them. Lacan too. Resistance to the 'collective thought' of evidence-based medicine is probably an urgent challenge if we do not want to see the life of thought die out.

Let us conclude this overview of the claims of EBM by recalling that medical practice, which claims to base its legitimacy on evidence acquired by the randomized controlled trials method, gets its status as a paradigm thanks to strategies aimed at obtaining the support of a scientific collective gathered around a collective thinking style. This was built on a limited number of standards such as the valuation of the objective fact established by experiment to the detriment of the clinician's subjective impression. The 'scientific' community gathered under such a paradigm is not aware of the irrational dimension of their adherence to the founding myth that evidence-based medicine has become.

The effects of EBM in the broad field of mental health

A 'collective of thought' such as the one established by evidence-based medicine is not just a doctrinal *corpus*. It is also and above all an ideological apparatus (Althusser, 2011) endowed with important powers, capable of producing norms for therapeutic action, accompanied with concrete provisions that reflect their obligatory nature, in other words, laws with their implementing decrees. In doing so, this apparatus becomes repressive.

We will pinpoint some manifestations of the functioning of what claims to be a method to improve medical therapeutics, when it is actually a seizure of power driven by the desire to transform the therapeutic landscape by imposing on it the 'mold' of evidence-based medicine. To this end, let us isolate some of the key events of this undertaking aimed at transforming therapeutic practices according to the EBM model. We limit our examination to what has happened in France and Belgium.

1. The first event happened in France 15 years ago. It was in February 2003 in Paris that the Ministry of Health, Family and Disabled Persons entrusted Dr. Philippe Cléry-Melin with a mission whose objective was to propose an action plan focusing on the reorganization of the supply of psychiatric and mental health care and to ensure its implementation.[14] The report, known as the Cléry-Melin report, was published in September 2003 under the title 'Action Plan for the Development of Psychiatry and the Promotion of Mental Health'.[15] This report proposed a remedicalization of all psychotherapies, extending psychotherapeutic intervention to all general practitioners, assisted by educational staff, social workers and therapists regarded as having the status of paramedical staff. It established a territorial division of the country and provided for a coordinating psychiatrist for each territory. This psychiatrist, a true 'prefect of souls', would have a list of all the approved professionals (psychiatrists and psychologists) to whom he would refer the patient as soon as he had made the decision at the end of his evaluation. On the other hand, the report recommended the evaluation of therapeutic practices in order to select only those that were considered to be the most effective. Finally, prevention and its early detection techniques were to be promoted in order to ensure mental health for all.[16]

2. In the wake of this report, a new public health law was drafted. Within the framework of this law, Bernard Accoyer, a UMP member of the National Assembly, proposed an amendment which he had championed for four years. The urgency of this amendment was motivated by the need to protect users against sectarian practices and self-proclaimed therapists. This amendment claimed to limit the use of the title of psychotherapist to psychiatrists and psychologists with a post-graduate degree (clinical specialization). The same logic as that of the Cléry-Melin report can be seen here. Psychoanalysis is implicitly excluded from the field of mental

health and treatment practices. Only training and practices defined by the State as 'good practices', that is, whose effectiveness had been scientifically proven, would be recognized and financed. The reference is not explicit, but it is evidence-based medicine that is referred to here. The consequences that such a legal system would have are as follows: the exclusion of psychoanalysis from university training institutions for psychiatrists and clinical psychologists; the exclusion of psychoanalysts from mental health care institutions (hospitals, psychological consultation centers, specialized institutions for children, adolescents and psychotic adults); and the suspicion of illegal practice of soul medicine.[17]

3. This crusade for the establishment of 'good practices' opened a third front, armed by the National Institute of Health and Medical Research (INSERM). Indeed, while the National Assembly and the French Senate were agitated by the debate on the Accoyer amendment, the General Directorate for Health (the administrative apparatus of the Minister of Health) commissioned INSERM to conduct a study on the effectiveness of psychotherapies. This comparative evaluation study of three psychotherapeutic approaches was published on 26 February 2004. The authors of the report argued that psychoanalysis was a psychotherapy like any other and as such could be compared with Cognitive Behavioral Therapy (CBT) and systemic therapy. Psychoanalysis was referred to as a 'psychodynamic approach'. In short, this study concluded that behavioral therapies were clearly superior in a large number of pathologies. This study was not an experimental study. It was not based on the analysis of observational data, but on the synthesis of about a thousand articles from international literature. The evaluation method used the nosographic categories of the *Diagnostic and Statistical Manual* of the American Psychiatric Association (DSM-IV).[18] Measuring the effectiveness of a therapy consists in matching a symptom or syndrome to a specific type of therapy and quantifying the outcome in terms of clinical improvement. This is done by using questionnaires to be filled out by patients. The second criterion of this so-called scientific evaluation is that of randomization, that is, as explained above, it is verified that the improvement obtained is due not to personal factors, but to the therapeutic method itself. To do this, patients are assigned to a particular therapist by drawing lots. Finally, control groups are used where patients are treated without a diagnosis or an *ad hoc* prescription for a type of treatment.

What can we say about this accumulation of epistemological and ethical, or simply deontological, biases? How can we accept a study in which the patient is treated as a guinea pig, is given random treatment without being heard and is misled about the therapeutic treatment proposed to him? How can we accept a study that is based on evaluation criteria specific to one approach, the so-called cognitive approach, and that extends these criteria to the other two approaches?

One of the authors of the report, psychiatrist and psychoanalyst Thurin, was in charge of the expertise of dynamic psychotherapies. He publicly expressed very clear reservations about the comparative evaluation method of the three types of therapeutic approaches considered.

To sum up, it should be noted that this study did not focus on the therapeutic process, but only on the relationship between the patient's condition before and after the intervention. This study only considers a literature focusing on application situations that do not take into account the reality of the clinical relationship. It is intended only for the treatment of simple – or, rather, simplified – symptoms or syndromes. It ignores the reality of pathological situations where the patient often presents a complex picture that combines, for example, anxiety, depression and personality disorder, to use the DSM-IV terminology.

For all these reasons, Thurin concludes that this INSERM study produces a 'methodological luring effect, which suggests the idea of a superiority of CBTs in the treatment of the most common mental disorders, but this has no scientific legitimacy' (Thurin, 2004). Need we point out that this opinion comes from one of the experts in charge of the evaluation report?

Thurin's position interests us in that it supports a middle way between the supporters of an evaluation conducted according to procedures that refer exclusively to EBM, such as randomized controlled trials, and the advocates of a radical rejection of any evaluation in the name of the absolute inadequacy of a clinical case-by-case method with standardized measurement procedures. That is the whole question. Some argue that evaluation methods have evolved, that they are closer to the complex reality of the relationship between therapist and patient, that the target of evaluation is no longer just the results obtained, but also – and equally – the various components of the therapeutic process. But such a position never questions the epistemic or even 'ontological' irrelevance of any form of evaluation of a process characterized by its evolving dynamics, as is the case with psychotherapies, particularly those oriented towards psychoanalysis. Eric Laurent reaches the same conclusions when he says that evaluation 'only takes into account the most superficial aspects of the processes involved' in order to homogenize them. And since misfortunes never come singly, the development of this evaluating imperative results in 'producing standardized therapies for formatted disorders' (Laurent, 2009, pp. 233–234).

It remains to be seen why, despite the serious shortcomings of the evidence-based medical approach, health authorities persist in their constant attempts to convince people of its virtues.

Evidence-based medicine and the impasses of evaluation

Far from being confined to the field of the medical clinic alone, the EBM model covers all sectors of human activity and especially the activities that fall within the scope of two other 'impossible' professions: teaching and governing (Freud, 1985, p. 263). In what way are these professions impossible? They are impossible in terms of their purpose: to bring about the desired transformation on the subject – health, education and living together. Each time, in each of these spheres, this intervention by the agent cannot produce its effects without going through the act of a subject. This act can only be performed in absolute solitude by the subject alone, not through any intervention on the part of a specialist, whether he is a medical worker, educator or ruler. However, what governs our time is what Baudelaire already denounced in 1852 in his tribute to the poet Edgar Allan Poe: 'the great poetic heresy of modern times', namely 'direct usefulness' (Baudelaire, 2011, p. 99). This is indeed the ultimate purpose of this all-round promotion of EBM: the evaluation of the direct usefulness of care practices. Only what is useful is worthwhile and usefulness is decreed by measuring the effectiveness of these practices, their effectiveness being itself defined by the instrument measuring it. We have come full circle. There is therefore a particular congruence between EBM and the numerical approach.[19] 'We are at a time when being is defined by and surrounded by number and quantity' (Miller, 2003, p. 323). To give a slightly caricatured image, let us admit that the evaluation of psychotherapies is similar to a control of the relationship between the number of sessions and the well-being obtained: if well-being is obtained after three sessions, will the patient feel three times better by tripling the dose? That is the situation now. The prescription of treatment is calibrated according to the type of disorder to be treated, and the duration of this treatment is determined on a flat-rate basis according to the severity of the disorder. It is obvious that the coupling of the evidence-based method and quantitative evaluation provides the State apparatus and its parastatal organizations (health and disability insurance funds) with all the means to control those social practices that are supposed to serve the well-being of citizens. The State requires counting and demands accounts.[20] This makes the DSM a key tool since it decides on a diagnosis based on a quantification of the occurrences of behaviors identified as belonging to a particular symptom or syndrome. The construction of a three-link chain is emerging and is no less than 'diabolical': diagnostic quantification, randomized clinical trials dear to EBM and statistical evaluation of practices in order to define the criteria for 'good practices' – at least those that will eventually be imposed because they are held to be the only ones that serve the patient's interests.

This chain linking the three modes of determining the practice of doctors, judges and teachers, for example, results in stripping practitioners of their activity in favor of a standardized protocol. For some, this de-subjectivation is experienced as a relief. Gathered around the 'EBM–DSM-Statistical Evaluation' paradigm, clinicians are 'relieved of the anxiety of their activity and its uniqueness. There is no longer any need to feel anxious about the decision in a context of uncertainty; it is enough to simply follow the protocol established for all cases and guaranteed by quantification' (Laurent, 2009, p. 235).

The ethics of psychoanalysis are poles apart from EBM

Faced with a clinic that ensures the certainty of scientific evidence and its normative protocols, psychoanalysis has only one medium: the words of the analysand, the time it takes to say them and, for the analyst, the time to hear them. Lacan states it very simply. 'What is psychoanalytical clinic? It's not complicated. It has a basis – it is what is said in psychoanalysis' (Lacan, 1977, p. 7).[21] At a time when clinical practice is relying on diagnostic assessment and treatment procedures using the DSM and EBM methods to decide on the prescription of a drug[22] whose effectiveness has been verified by randomized clinical trials, calling upon the subject's words in their dual *dit-mention* (note that, in French, *dimension* and *dit-mention* have the same pronunciation) – 'the act of saying' and 'what is said' – is evidence of another order than that which claims scientific knowledge (Villers, 2013).

Jacques Lacan was able to isolate the core of Freudian thought when he stated that 'what we say as fact remains forgotten behind what is said in what is heard' (Lacan, 1972, pp. 32–55). The subject of the act, the subject who says, and the fact that he is saying something, are forgotten in the staging of the utterance. And it is this fundamental disjunction that is mobilized in the relationship between the analysand and his psychoanalyst. By the mere fact that the analysand sends the analyst a message, a statement, which the analyst receives from the place of his address and returns it to him, there is an effect of significance of this message and an effect of production of the subject who utters it. The analyst attributes this subject to the message sent to him by the analysand. The paradoxical effect of this attribution is to separate the subject from his message in order to reach a 'beyond' that challenges the Other whom he is addressing and to ask him what he wants of him, to ask him to be recognized as a subject worthy of being loved. The silence of the analyst, who refrains from responding to this request for love that always underlies this call to the Other, will lead the analysand to produce a series of ideal figures of himself, which in turn reveal their function as a veil placed on what the said subject does not want to know about the pleasures of which he is the vessel. This pleasure unknown to him through the process of repression resurfaces in the subject's body. It constitutes a symptom. It is the whole purpose of the cure to bring to light this passion for ignorance and the horror of pleasure which the subject did not want to know anything about. An analysis comes to an end when the pleasure that causes the subject's desire is admitted. The subject can then give up the idealizing identifications and accept the fact that the Other, from whom he was asking for knowledge about the truth of his being, is an empty place, that middle empty space, a crucible from which a conscious desire for the inconsistency of the Other can spring. It is a desire that finds expression in a new utterance that is a little less dependent on the pleasure of the Other that had been embodied in the symptoms.

Such a course cannot be prescribed. It does not allow itself to be trapped in a protocol and does not lend itself to evaluation in the form of a term-to-term verification of the results obtained in comparison with the initial pathological state. However, there is a logic to the cure, and there are principles that guide its direction (Lacan, 1966, pp. 485–645). Thus, the International Psychoanalytical Association (IPA) adopted a 'Declaration of Principles', which was drafted and approved at its General Assembly on 16 July 2006 under the title 'Guiding Principles of the Psychoanalytical Act' (Laurent, 2006).

The practice of psychoanalysis does not take place unbridled. But these reins are not guided by a 'tutorial'; it does not work using skills assessment grids. It does not check the adequacy of the solution to the problem at hand. The control of analytical practice opens up a new space where the analyst reports on his practice based on what he hears from the analysand and on the divisive effect that these analyzing words produce at the heart of the analyst. The experience of an address from the analyst–subject to the controlling Other produces this 'third ear' (Reik, 1976) that the analyst makes present in the cure, a condition for the analysand to hear the 'beyond' of his request, the one that concerns the other Other, that of the transference. This method of control is not without anxiety because it does not produce any verdict with a guarantee stamped by some scholarly body. And it is from this very anxiety that the analyst must wrest the certainty of his act. Allowing for the absence of guarantee in the Other is the condition of the analytical act. 'Analytical ethics leaves no other recourse than to be able to wrest, through the act, certainty from anxiety' (Lacan, 2004, pp. 92–93). On the other hand, giving in to anxiety will lead the psychoanalyst to abandon psychoanalysis in favor of a psychotherapeutic practice that is protocolized for all cases and guaranteed by statistics. However, this choice will not allow the therapist to avoid the singularity of his act in the concrete exercise of the clinical relationship. In this case, he will again come face to face with the anxiety he thought he had avoided by absorbing his act into generalized compliance. Following this path would certainly lead psychoanalysis to its ruin (Laurent, 2009, p. 235).

Notes

1   Philippe Pinel (1745–1826). Among other things, he introduced the calculation of probabilities in medicine – Pinel (1808, pp. 169–205).
2   The French doctor Pierre-Charles-Alexandre Louis (1787–1872) was responsible for the introduction of the 'numerical method' in medicine.
3   It should be noted that these works predate Claude Bernard's (1813–1878) *L'Intro-duction à l'étude de la médecine*, which was published in 1865. *See* Cl. Bernard (1865). *Introduction à la médecine expérimentale*. Full text (fac-image): URL: www.irphe.fr/~-clanet/otherpaperfile/articles/Bernard/bernard_introduction_etude_medecine_experimentale.pdf
4   See also: ww.cochrane.org/docs/archieco.htm. Two of Cochrane's books are available for consultation. Archibald L. Cochrane, *Effectiveness and Efficiency*, Abingdon, UK, Burgess & Son, 1972; 2nd ed. *Effectiveness and Efficiency. Random Reflections on Health Services*, London, Nuffield Provincial Hospitals Trust, 1989. *L'Inflation médicale. Reflexions sur l'efficacité de la médecine*, the French adaptation by Drs A. Rougemont and E. Gubéran, Paris, Galileo, 1977.
5   A randomized controlled trial (RCT) is a type of scientific study used in medicine and more recently in the social sciences (more specifically, in economics). It is the scientific procedure *par excellence* for clinical trials. RCTs are often used to test the effectiveness of several therapeutic approaches in a patient population. They are therefore procedures for comparing different types of treatment. Subjects are randomly assigned to the groups corresponding to each therapeutic approach tested. Then, it is verified that the two populations are close by comparing basic characteristics including demographic characteristics. The advantage of randomization is that it limits selection bias and thus allows a homogeneous distribution of known and unknown prognostic factors among groups. It allows initial comparability. Then therapeutic intervention begins. Subjects, therapists and assessors are placed in a blind test situation, insofar as it is possible, that is, they do not know which group the patient is in. Therefore, the only variable that is different between the groups is the treatment. Blind testing is maintained through the use of *placebo* (drug treatment) or false procedure (non-drug treatment) techniques. This strategy allows comparability to be maintained.

6   The notion of evidence is hardly questioned by EBM supporters. Nor is the notion of fact. However, the history of science and of science philosophies shows that proof is not limited to the mere attestation of truth or to the evaluation procedures of a statement. Moreover, the methods of proof also have a subjective aspect such as belief or assent. The reader will benefit greatly from referring to F. Gil's entry 'preuve' in the *Dictionnaire d'histoire et de philosophie des sciences*, published under the direction of D. Lecourt, Paris, PUF, 1999, 755–759.

7   This is what Perino (2013) calls a 'progressive change in pathocenosis'.

8   The etymology of the word 'paradigm' is Greek. *Παράδειγμα (paradeïgma)* in ancient Greek is made up of 'para' (next to) and 'deigma' (model or example). This word itself comes from *παραδεικνύναι (paradeiknunai)* which means to show or compare, itself deriving from *δείκνυμι (deiknumi)*, meaning designate. Interestingly, the latter verb is constructed on the Indo-European radical *deik* or *dik*, which refers to the verb *say*. This would mean that, from the outset, the act of saying is recognized in its close proximity to reality: we can thus only *'say'* by referring to examples: *παρά –δειγμα*, 'next to' reality. Depending on the different disciplines in which the word 'paradigm' is used, its meaning varies. The category of disciplines that interests us here is that of language sciences, more specifically structural linguistics. In linguistics, Ferdinand de Saussure had already (between 1906 and 1911) identified the category of inflectional paradigms, a particular type of associative grouping that proceeds by grouping according to a common nominal topic, as *domin* generates the series *dominus, domini, domino* (Saussure, 1978, p. 175). It was Roman Jakobson who developed the notion of paradigm by speaking of 'paradigmatic class' to designate all the terms that can occupy the same place in the spoken word chain. The paradigmatic axis is therefore that of linguistic operations of a substitutive type: substitution of one signifier for another signifier within the same paradigmatic class. Thus, 'rag' can be substituted for 'newspaper', which has already substituted itself for 'gazette', etc. Each substitution adds a new meaning, which stands out against the background of the other signifiers and their own significant valence. The paradigmatic axis is thus the axis of resemblance, of similarity. The substitution operation from one term to another is located on the spoken chain, which organizes the utterance by combining the selected terms (Jakobson, 1963, pp. 43–67). Danish linguist Louis Hjelmslev later took up this principle by showing that language production links signs together according to rules that define the places they can occupy within the same chain. This is what constitutes the structure of a language (Hjelmslev, 1966, pp. 55–69).

9   Google produces hundreds of references on this subject. Propaganda for evidence-based medicine is well equipped. It has tutorials with well-constructed didactics. See for example the particularly well-documented tutorial published by the University of Paris Descartes:
    www.biusante.parisdescartes.fr/ressources/pdf/medecine-formation-ebm-tutoriel-biusante.pdf

10 The following is an electronic version of the French translation by Madame la Marquise du Chastellet of Isaac Newton's text *Philosophiae Naturalis Principia Mathematica*. The electronic version was produced by Jean-Marc Simonet, a retired professor of education at the University of Paris XI-Orsay: http://classiques.uqac.ca/classiques/newton_isaac/principes_math_philo_naturelle/principes_philo_naturelle_t1.html

11 P. Bourdieu (1930–2002): he defines *habitus* as 'a structured structure predisposed to function as a structuring structure'.

12 Today 'Lviv', in Ukraine, on the Polish border.

13 An *aviso* is a small, light, fast war-ship used to escort naval convoys, dispatch information, instructions or mail and reconnoiter the position of enemy ships. From the Spanish *avisar*, inform, order, warn, from the French *aviser*.

14 This report is signed by Philippe Cléry-Melin, a psychiatrist and clinical director, who was entrusted with an operational mission relating to psychiatry and mental health by M. Jean-François Mattei, Minister of Health; by psychiatrist and epidemiologist Dr Viviane Kovess-Masfety, President of APAQESM and Director of the MGEN Corporate Foundation for Public Health; and by psychiatrist Dr Jean-Charles Pascal, Vice-President of the French Psychiatric Federation and Sector Head at the Erasmus Hospital Centre in Antony.

15 http://www.ladocumentationfrancaise.fr/var/storage/rapports-publics/034000589.pdf

16 A six-page summary of the full 148-page report can be found at https://drees.solidarites-sante.gouv.fr/IMG/pdf/rfas200401art13.pdf

17 A vast movement of opposition to this amendment was launched by J-A. Miller through a 'Psy Manifesto' on 15 November 2003. The same J-A. Miller sent an open letter on 17 November 2003 to Bernard Accoyer and the informed public, denouncing point by point the threats that this amendment poses to mental health in France. Opposition to the Cléry-Melin report and the Accoyer amendment grew considerably, so that it was eventually abandoned.

18 *Diagnostic and Statistical Manual of Mental Disorders* is published by the *American* Psychiatric *Association* (APA). It describes and classifies mental disorders. Its fifth edition was published in 2013.

19 See Charles-Alexandre Louis' numerical method, cited above, note 2.

20 In Belgium, laws and their implementing decrees as well as reports from the High Council of Health (the scientific advisory body of the Federal Authorities) have multiplied the mechanisms for monitoring mental health practices, whether with regard to the treatment of 'autistic disorders', the granting of titles giving access to the practice of psychotherapy and the reimbursement of the fees of authorized practitioners, or the place of the psychiatrist in the mental health care system.

21 Psychoanalysis is therefore a 'method'; however, it is not based on evidence but on the subject's words.

22 Psychotherapy is regarded here as a particular category in the class of 'drugs'.

Bibliography

Althusser, L. (2011). *Idéologie et appareils idéologiques d'État*. Paris: PUF.

Althusser, L. (1974). *Philosophie et philosophie spontanée des savants*. Paris: Maspero.

Aristotle (1989). *Rhétorique*. Texte établi et traduit par Médéric Dufour et André Wartelle, annotated by André Wartelle. Paris: *Les Belles Lettres* (3).

Aristotle (1856). *Rhétorique*, Livre I, Chapitre 2, § 22. Trad. N. Bonafous. Paris: A. Durand. https://archive.org/stream/larhetoriquedar00arisgoog#page/n9/mode/2up

Baudelaire, C. (2011). *Baudelaire journaliste: articles et chroniques*. Paris: Flammarion.

Bourdieu, P. (2018). *Le sens pratique*. Paris: Éd. de Minuit.

Cochrane, A. L. (1972). *Effectiveness and efficiency: random reflections on health services* (Vol. 900574178). London: Nuffield Provincial Hospitals Trust.

Crommelinck, M., & Villers de, G. (1993). Formation scientifique et responsabilité du sujet politique. *Questions de formation*, vol. 10, Produire du savoir, Louvain-La-Neuve: FOPA.

Danblon, E. (2010). La rhétorique: art de la preuve ou art de la persuasion?. *Revue de métaphysique et de morale, 2*, 213–231.

Dumonchel, P. (1990). *Paradigme. Encyclopédie philosophique universelle. Notions philosophiques*, Vol. II. Paris: PUF.

Fagot-Largeault, A. (2018). *L'émergence de la médecine scientifique: Sciences et philosophie*. Paris: Éd. Matériologiques.

Fleck, L. (2008). *Genèse et développement d'un fait scientifique*. Paris: Champs Flammarion.

Freud, S. (1985). *Résultats, idées, problèmes*. Paris: PUF.

Hjelmslev, L. (1966). *Le langage*. Paris: Ed. de Minuit.

Jakobson, R. (1963). Deux aspects du langage et deux types d'aphasies. *Essais de linguistique générale*. Paris: Éd. de Minuit.

Kuhn, T. S. (1983). *La Structure des révolutions scientifiques*. Paris: Champs Flammarion.

Lacan, J. (1966). *Écrits*. Paris: Seuil.

Lacan J. (2004). *L'angoisse*, séminaire X. Paris: Seuil.

Lacan, J. (1977). Ouverture de la section clinique. *Ornicar, 9*, 7–14.

Laurent, E. (2009). Impasses de l'évaluation. In Fishmann, G. (Ed.), *L'évaluation des psycho-thérapies et de la psychanalyse. Fondements et enjeux*. Paris: Masson.

Laurent, E. (2006). Principes directeurs de l'acte psychanalytique. *Ecole de la Cause Freudienne*. www.causefreudienne.net/principes-directeurs-de-lacte-psychanalytique/

Gil, F. (1999). Preuve. In Lecourt, D. (Ed.), *Dictionnaire d'histoire et de philosophie des sciences* (pp. 755–759). Paris: PUF.

Macherey, P. (2008). A propos du livre L. Fleck, *Genèse et développement d'un fait scientifique*. Réflexions proposées au Groupe d'étude 'La philosophie au sens large' le 06-02-2008: https://f-origin.hypotheses.org/wp-content/blogs.dir/165/files/2017/09/06.-02-2008.pdf

Masson, A., De Nayer, A., Dubois, V., Pirson, O., Domken, M. A., Floris, M.,... & Detraux, J. (2008). Application de l'evidence based medicine (EBM) dans la schizophrénie. Supplément à *Neuron, 13*(9). http://webcache.googleusercontent.com/search?q=cache:HZ4RHOLc5fMJ:www.medtunes.org/documents/get/e6c45490e78e212b3e3e92c-d17eddc2a.pdf+&cd=2&hl=fr&ct=clnk&gl=fr

Miller, J-A. (2003). *Le neveu de Lacan: satire*. Paris: Éd. Verdier.

Miller, J-A. (1999). Les six paradigmes de la jouissance. *La Cause freudienne*, (43).

Morabia, A. (2006). Pierre-Charles-Alexandre Louis and the evaluation of bloodletting. *Journal of the Royal Society of Medicine, 99*(3), 158–160.

Newton, I. (1833). *Philosophiae naturalis principia mathematica* (Vol. 1). London: G. Brookman.

Perino, L. (2013). Evidence Based Medicine: critique raisonnée d'un monopole Première partie: aux sources de l'EBM. *Médecine, 9*(9), 416–419.

Pinel, P. (1808). Résultats d'observations et construction de tables pour servir à déterminer le degré de probabilité de la guérison des aliénés. *Lu à la classe des sciences mathématiques et physiques de l'Institut national de France le 9 juillet 1807*. Paris: Baudouin.

Reik, T. (1976). *Écouter avec la troisième oreille: l'expérience intérieure d'un psychanalyste*. Éditions Bibliothèque des Introuvables.

Saussure, F. de (1978). *Cours de linguistique générale*. Paris: Payot.

Schuster, M. A., McGlynn, E. A., & Brook, R. H. (1998). How good is the quality of health care in the United States?. *The Milbank Quarterly, 76*(4), 517–563.

Thurin, J-M. (2004). A propos de l'expertise collective INSERM. www.reseaupsychologues.
eu/Dr-THURIN-A-propos-de-l-expertise-collective-INSERM_a176.html

Villers, G. de (2013). Écouter le dire du sujet. In Niewiadomski, C. & Delory-Momberger,
C. (Eds.), *La mise en récit de soi, place de la recherche biographique dans les sciences humaines
et sociales*. Villeneuve d'Ascq: Septentrion.

Accompaniment in social work
A path of co-wandering

Jean-Bernard Paturet

Preamble

The medico-social and social fields have long used, and continue to use, the term 'care' to refer to the action taken to help the suffering people entrusted to them. Tinged with both benevolence and empathy, but most of the time with condescension or a desire to infantilize and dominate, the term 'care'[1] belongs to the semantic field of knowledge about the other person and about what is supposed to be right for him. Acting for the good of the other person is undoubtedly the principle that has governed the action of the social and medico-social world from its distant origins to the present day.

However, since a French law passed in 2002,[2] a new – and at the same time very old – issue has emerged: the rights of each person. Thus, in social, medico-social and health institutions, the law has recognized the need to reaffirm the place of the fundamental rights of each human being, probably drawing inspiration from John Rawls and his *Theory of Justice* published in 1990 in the United States (2009). This author makes a radical distinction between Just and Good. For him, a just institution[3] is defined first and foremost in its conformity with the law and democracy. It is thus primarily procedural, that is, it must clearly explain the modes of organization and functioning of the bodies

DOI: 10.4324/9781003296416-16

ordered by law in order to ensure that fundamental rights are respected. Institutions have often acted in the name of good but have sometimes neglected the law or even simply overlooked the rights of people by not always taking into account the individuals being cared for, hence the reintroduction of the rights of users or patients and the recognition of fundamental human rights: dignity, respect, integrity, privacy and security. Thus, no social action can make sense or be justified if the legislative framework is not respected and placed at the heart of the institutions.

Once we recognize the fundamental rights of each and every one of us, and once democratic rules are expressed in effective procedures and formalized institutional mechanisms, can we still maintain a firm stance with respect to the notion of care? Or is it not time to move forward on the concept of accompaniment in the field of social work? Accompaniment based on the respect of rights and the search for citizenship opens the way to a deepening of everyone's potential. The word 'capability' undoubtedly reflects the contemporary Anglo-Saxon notion of empowerment, [4] that is, the inner power (however limited) of each individual over himself and his environment.

In this context, this chapter aims to build and deepen a reflection on the concept of accompaniment so that law, ethics and institutions guarantee that the human subject can become not only a rational subject, but also a subject of desire and a subject of the unconscious, one following his own path without always knowing where it leads. But as the poet says, a path does not need a goal – a starting point is enough.

Introduction

What does it mean to accompany? From the Indo-European *pa*, to nourish, 'accompaniment' in its etymological sense refers first of all to the sharing of food and meals. The sharing relationship is neither symmetrical nor empathic; it is a relationship between people who are different from each other, located in distinct, sometimes divergent or even opposed places. Since the meal is a place to share, it immediately becomes a place to exchange words. Accompanying: sharing bread, talking, but also walking together part of the way. All of this is reminiscent of the famous evangelical account of the pilgrims from Emmaus, [5] a village two hours' walk from Jerusalem. Jesus' disciples meet a strange character. He approaches them and walks with them. During their discussion, he seems to know nothing about the recent events in Jerusalem on the previous Friday (later, Good Friday for Christians). But quickly, hearing the disciples' surprise, he begins to explain the Holy Scriptures to them. The disciples invite him to dine with them at Emmaus that evening, as the man makes out to continue on his way, and they invite him to sleep at their house. Now, when the time comes to share the bread (the time of 'accompaniment') the disciples finally recognize him: he is risen Christ. This is a demonstration of Jesus' tactfulness: he does not impose anything, but walks with the disoriented disciples (they have lost their way), who have been wandering, lost since the death of Jesus on the Cross on Good Friday. The disciples suddenly find comfort in this encounter. The journey from Jerusalem to Emmaus with this unknown character seems above all a journey of co-wandering: the disciples wander, at least in their hearts and minds. Jesus does not say where he is going and does not seem to have a precise goal, but he accompanies them. At the end of the road everything has changed because of this chance encounter[6] with the other, this surprising event. The disciples took the risk of meeting the other, the risk of a confrontation with somebody unknown, a stranger.

Accompaniment: a path of co-wandering

What does it mean, then, to follow a path? How can the path enlighten us in our reflection on accompaniment? Derived from *camminus*, which can be traced back to the 1080s, *chemin* (French for *path*) belongs to the popular Latin language that originated from the Gallic language and means the fireplace, the hearth. *Kaminos*: the oven and hearth where domestic – and therefore domesticated – fire burns, unlike uncontrolled wildfire. *Camminus* also means journey, that is, the idea of a more or less painful progress, a laborious approach, an uneasy walk, progress and regression but also discoveries, perhaps adventures and encounters. The French word *chemineau* (meaning 'vagrant') is the one who moves from one job to another, uncertain of the future. The vagrant's path can go towards the known or the unknown but always results in wandering between two fires, between two hearths, between two homes for life and work.

There are paths with landmarks, signposted paths (long-distance hiking trails for example) which necessarily lead somewhere; they indicate a way and tend towards a determined goal between two fixed positions; they sometimes specify, as happens in mountain areas, the time it takes to reach this goal. In this sense, the path belongs to the field of the control of space and time: a space that is representable and represented, mapped; a control of time and duration such that the walker is not overtaken by night or caught in the fog or does not get bogged in a marsh. Order and measure prevail and allow the vagrant to avoid the *distuché*, the bad encounter. The path is therefore safe since it keeps one from losing one's way, from getting lost in space and time.[7] Necessarily traced by other humans, who have previously taken and prepared this passage, the path is a proof of trust in other people; but even if it is marked out, it can still be dangerous because you do not know who might be waiting for you around the corner with hostile and malicious intentions: thugs, thieves, rogues and other bandits. The paths therefore indicate a link between men and women and a link between territories. They are links, facilitators of encounters, exchanges and communications.

However, there are also paths that do not lead anywhere: *Holzwege*, wooden paths to use Heidegger's expression, paths without maps where you get lost, [8] paths without signposts or where, sometimes, the signposts have been deliberately distorted. There are mazes in which you can go astray and from which you cannot get out. The maze, as we know, is this building built by Daedalus on the orders of King Minos in Crete to lock up the Minotaur, this hybrid monster with a bull's head on a man's body, the illegitimate fruit of the unnatural mating of Pasiphae, Minos' wife, and the wonderful white bull sent to him by Poseidon. King Minos, horrified by the fruit of the love between his wife and the wild animal, locks the Minotaur in the maze. Every year, the monster receives seven boys and seven girls as food, a human tribute imposed on the city of Athens, the vassal-city of Knossos, the capital of Crete. Theseus comes to fight and kill the Minotaur. Ariadne, Minos' daughter, instantly falls in love with Theseus and hands him a ball of yarn provided by Daedalus himself. Ariadne's thread will save Theseus from endless, deadly wandering. The undetermined maze, without a territory and without a path, is a space of illusion and death. Ariadne is the fixed point for the possible return of Theseus, who, upon entering the maze, immediately loses all his cardinal points: there is no longer any sense of geography here, only a dark, indefinite chaos where no landmarks are possible.[9]

In the relationship with the other person, accompaniment as co-wandering is the possibility of being 'held' by a thread that allows confidence, like the rope in mountain-climbing, while encouraging everyone to lead their own existence, to follow their own path with their advances, their discoveries or, on the contrary, to confront their regressions and myriad forms of danger.

What then does this brief etymological excursion tell us? Co-wandering is above all a journey from one place to another, on a marked or unmarked path. The guide walks beside the other person without always knowing where he is going or where the other is leading him. He remains what he is but takes the risk of the other person, that is, accepts to be possibly modified by his encounter with him. He is exposed to hesitations, to deadlocks and errors, but everyone knows that *errare humanum est*. He exposes himself because he is in what Arendt calls a *praxis* relationship.[10] He takes the risk of losing his own bearings, of making mistakes and of getting lost like Ariadne who falls in love with Theseus and whose adventure will end very badly. Every pedagogical act (the pedagogue is the one that accompanies the child – *pais*: the child, and *agogein*: leading) is therefore characterized by risk, uncertainty and fragility.

In *Télévision*, Lacan, playing a little tune of his own on 'Les non-dupes errent' and 'les noms du père' (both are pronounced in the same way in French), recalls, with reference to Freud, the meaning of *erre* (this French word refers both to wandering and to a ship's headway): 'You may know what *erre* means. It's something like momentum. The momentum of something when what has been propelling it stops. It continues its course' (2001). The term *erre* is used in the navy to refer to the speed acquired by a ship when the propellers have stopped working: the ship is said to continue its *erre*, its drift forward. In the human subject, it may be a family, parental or paternal propulsion that stops at a given moment and lets the subject continue on his way alone.

But drifting along can also mean resting on one's laurels, on one's achievements. Then comes the risk of a progressive loss and gradual reduction of the effects of propulsion, and thus the risk of remaining bound to the desire of the other – stifling parents, suffocating social structures or asphyxiating education.

> So, *les non-dupes errent* (those who are not fooled wander) and *les noms du père* (the names of the father), phrases that sound and rhyme so well together [...] In these two [...] terms, like that, put into words, the *noms du père* and the *non-dupes qui errent*, it is the same knowledge. In both. It is the same knowledge in the sense that the unconscious is knowledge whose subject can be deciphered. It is the definition of the subject that I give here, the subject as constituted by the unconscious. The one who speaks is in a position to decipher it, to carry out this operation; he is even, up to a certain point, forced to do it until he reaches a meaning. And that's where he stops, because [...] because you have to stop. [...] Do not be too surprised, after all, that here I leave the thing in the state of an enigma, since the enigma is the height of meaning.
>
> (Lacan, unpublished, 1973–1974)

Does accompanying, then, mean accepting not to be the propeller of others, so that they can discover their own propulsion, their specific momentum and their own desire, and pursue their own particular development? Does it consist in leaving the other person to the construction of a meaning that he elaborates for himself in the encounter with his own enigma and in letting him answer the old question that the Sphinge has been asking from the time of Oedipus until the present day, including the three Kantian questions that can be summarized in one: What is man?

Accompaniment: the art of knowing the right distance

A fascinating story told by Schopenhauer sheds light on the necessary recognition of the right distance in the accompaniment process:

> On a cold winter's day, a herd of porcupines had formed a tight group to protect each other from the frost by their own heat. But they immediately felt the pricking of their quills, which made them move away from each other. When the need to warm up brought them closer together again, the same inconvenience was repeated, so that they were hovering here and there between two pains until they finally found an average distance that made the situation bearable for them. Thus, the need for society, born of the emptiness and monotony of their inner life, pushes people towards each other, but their repulsive qualities and unbearable faults disperse them once again. The average distance they finally discover and by which living together becomes possible is politeness and good manners. In England, people shout *Keep your distance!* to the one who moves too close. In this way, the need to warm up is actually only half satisfied. But on the other hand, you do not feel the prick of the quills. However, if you have enough inner warmth, you prefer to stay out of society so that you do not experience or cause disturbances.
>
> (Schopenhauer, 2005, p. 938)

Not too close, not too far: such is Schopenhauer's lesson. In the accompaniment process, the right distance is necessary, but above all it is necessary to refrain from taking the place of the other person with a kind of empathy or compassionate[11] solidarity: as Lacan said humorously, 'If I put myself in the place of the other, where does *he* put himself?' This undermines the 'I understand you' statement that always risks putting an end to the discourse and the exchange with the other person. The right distance is determined by a relationship of singularity that fundamentally recognizes the autonomy of the other person. Accompanying inevitably requires the recognition of this autonomy.

What does this mean? The Greek root *nem* or *nom* from the verb *nemein* means to distribute equitably, to give everyone their due. The nomads who walked with their herds had to accept an equitable distribution of land so that everyone could feed themselves. *Nomos* first meant 'custom', 'unwritten rule' or 'habit', and the practice of fair distribution that kept the shepherds (nomads) from fighting and the herds of cattle from getting mixed up (Schmitt, Deroche-Gurcel & Haggenmacher, 2001, pp. 70–83). *Nomos* later became the law, the norm, when it was written. 'Autonomy' therefore first refers to the idea of a territory whose boundaries are never fixed, never limited by walls or fences. Autonomy invites us to build our own territories. It creates the conditions for sharing and separation without which only chaos, violence and non-differentiation prevail – in other words, the impossibility of any encounter or alliance. *Nemesis*, [12] goddess of righteous anger and redistribution, is often used as an antonomasia of justice and revenge.

The territory therefore is in essence moving in a permanent relationship with the territories of others; it moves forward and backward, and modifies and transforms itself unceasingly (Paturet, 2017). Human life is made up of many different territories: emotional, professional, financial, relational, physical, athletic, political and so on. It would therefore be an oversimplification to say that one is or is not autonomous. Rather, we have territories of autonomy that vary with time, age, physical and intellectual capacities, emotional, professional and sexual relationships, financial means and personal resources.

This is why autonomy does not mean giving oneself one's own laws, as it was sometimes interpreted in the reading of Kant's *Foundations of the Metaphysics of Morals* of 1785. When Kant defines autonomy in this way, he refers to a rational and reasonable being, whose reason precisely makes him a part of the universal sphere. Indeed, Kantian autonomy cannot be conceived without the categorical imperative: 'Always act in such a way that the maxim of your action can be established as a universal rule' (Kant, 1990). Let us imagine for a moment that autonomy consists in giving oneself one's own laws: the world would become even more of a merciless jungle, and the unconditional reign of small and big bosses, small and large feudalities of local powers and potentates would extend ever further. The autonomous subject is not one who makes his own laws – only a depraved mind could do so – because the law is always given. Autonomy is rather a conquest of new territories or, on the contrary, the preservation of what has been acquired. Constantly on the alert, it seeks to conquer, reclaim or even maintain its existing territories.

Therefore, accompanying means guaranteeing the territories of autonomy of each person and all people so that the social and symbolic link is possible. The social worker is a guarantor of the right distance, as illustrated by the fable of the porcupines. This right distance makes an alliance possible; it allows a link to be established between *aliens* (*alius*: the other who is radically other, which differs from the *alter* and therefore from the *alter ego*) in the radicality of their strangeness. However, as Freud showed, strangeness produces anxiety and great mistrust. The alliance therefore recognizes the difference between the *alter* as one's other self and the *alien* as strangeness. Thus, social partners are *aliens* who radically differ by their values and interests, and with whom it is necessary to build an alliance. The alliance, therefore, is built not only with *alter egos*, but above all with *aliens*. Any alliance results from overcoming mistrust.

Accompaniment: mediation through words

All accompaniment processes involve the mediation of speech. Speaking implies the Other as the one whom we are addressing and who calls, in a double movement of recognition. With speech, the human subject formulates a request: every word is thus addressed to someone. Socially, speech indicates the place that is given to each person and at the same time reflects the degree of their integration into the group as well as their power in the common space of a social structure. The question is therefore how the voice of suffering people, of people with disabilities, of women – but also of social workers – is recognized, for we have to admit that it is not equal for everyone (take, for example, the difference between psychiatric and educational speech). But how is this voice taken into account in the space of a service, and how does the institution go beyond the competition of vanities that constantly produces power-based relationships and endless games of domination? Does it guarantee the possibility of exercising the right to speak?

The place given to everyone's voice in the collective space leads Jacques Rancière to oppose policy and politics:

> Policy is thus first of all an order of bodies that defines the divisions between modes of doing, modes of being and modes of saying [...] It is an order of the visible and the expressible that makes one activity visible and another not, that some words are understood as speech and others as noise. Political activity is that which moves a body from its assigned place or changes the destination of that place; it shows what was not to be seen or makes a speech heard where only noise had its place.
>
> (Rancière, 1995, p. 53)

The accompaniment process could thus be understood as political in its purpose of moving the suffering people from their assigned places. First, it is a matter of acknowledging their words, which until then were not words because they were considered inaudible, barbaric, confused, assigned and regarded as noise that we did not listen to. The mainspring of the social and group link is above all language; it must be open to alienness, heterogeneity, dissimilarity and difference. This part of strangeness often remains untrans-latable and, in this sense, it forces politicians to create and to invent.

To un-assign, we must refer to another function of speech. Like the para-ble, speech (in French: *parole*) etymologically refers to what is thrown to the side and not directly in the face. *Para*, next to, near, unlike – and *bolé, bolis, bolidos*, what is thrown like a javelin, a stone, a racing car without any rule or law. The opposite is the symbolic, that is, the obligation to renounce being the whole and therefore accept symbolic castration, the limit, finiteness and the link with others. Speech is thus what is thrown aside, near.[13] Speech opens up other possibilities, other modalities of potential actions and thoughts. Like Pythia, speech indicates; it does not predict the future or say how to act, but rather it dis-places, un-settles and un-assigns the subject from the personal, social, physical, psychological or professional determinities in which he was in one way or another trapped.

Finally, with regard to accompaniment, we must never forget that social work-ers are above all professionals and that professionalism refers us back to speech – *profēmi*: to speak. The professional is not essentially an expert, which Latin rather considers to be on the side of skill – *Dux peritus belli*: a leader skilled in war –, but a creature of speech. Accompaniment will therefore be concerned with taking into account the words of each individual as required by the 2002 law.

Recognizing the ontological vulnerability of each individual

When we talk about vulnerability[14] in the social field, we immediately think of people suffering in various ways: lonely, elderly, disabled, homeless, unem-ployed people, with integration or inclusion difficulties and so on. Vulnera-bility is often linked to the register of pathos, compassion, victimization and even unbridled pity.

But we must undoubtedly consider vulnerability as belonging to the field of ontology, that is, the field of what defines a human being as a speaking, sexual and mortal being. Vulnerability in this sense would therefore funda-mentally have to do with the flaw, with the imperfection of the human being as incomplete, with the crack in the armor,[15] with the flaw under the mask[16] and under the social self, and with the failing of the divided being (as opposed to the undivided individual). Vulnerability brings to its peak the question of singularity. The human being is an irreplaceable singularity, Heidegger wrote, because only man dies whereas, according to him, the animal ceases to live. Each singularity feeds on uncertainty and weaves its threads with the prospect of death ever looming on the horizon.

Vulnerability forces the social worker to move beyond categories of suffering towards an encounter with the human being beyond any categorization. The social worker is confronted with the 'any', the 'quodlibet', to use Agamben's term. The Italian philosopher, reflecting on ethics, invites us to acknowledge the singularity of each person, which really finds its meaning and foundation in the 'any'.

> In the enumeration of transcendentals (*quolibet ens is unum, verum, bonum seu perfectum*, being any is one, true, good, or perfect), 'quodlibet' is the term, substrate, *chora, apeiron* that conditions the meaning of all other terms or attributes (age, profession, skin color, sex, types of disabilities, suffering, etc.). The common translation in the sense of 'any one', 'indifferently', is certainly correct, but in its form, it says exactly the opposite of Latin: 'quodlibet ens' is not 'being, no matter which one' but *'being such as it matters anyway'*. [According to this principle of an *any* singularity], the 'being such' is removed from his belonging to such and such property, which identifies him as a member of such and such a group, of such and such a class [...]. Thus the 'being such' that remains constantly hidden in the status of belonging which is in no way a real predicate, emerges of itself: the singularity exposed as such is 'any', in other words likeable.
>
> (Agamben, 1990)

Accompanying is therefore based on the idea that any action must go beyond all categories so that the person who is accompanied matters and therefore becomes likeable.

This vulnerability is sometimes changed into strength by inventiveness, flexibility or the spirit of finesse or cunning; it forces us to fight with other weapons, to think with other concepts, to transform our suffering. Of course, this reminds us of the story of David, the Hebrew shepherd, against the opposing champion Goliath, the Philistine, who represents brute force and omnipotence. Sure of himself and of his heavy weapons, helmet, shield, sword and spear, Goliath cannot imagine that it is possible to fight otherwise. If David had fought with the same weapons as Goliath, it is very likely that he would have been defeated. But his vulnerability makes him ingenious and skillful; it gives him capability, to use a term mentioned above. David surprises his enemy with the incongruity of his equipment: a sheepskin and a sling. At first Goliath considers himself insulted by the baubles of the young shepherd's equipment until a stone sent with strength and precision by David reaches Goliath in the forehead, throws him off balance and knocks him out. All that remains for the young shepherd to do is to cut off the giant's head with his own sword.

The Latins expressed this weak spot in the human being by *Tempus*, which means both time, as finiteness and death, and the temple, where the skull is most fragile (Goliath's forehead) and which must be aimed at if the goal is to kill. The Greeks translated it as *Kairos*, the art of opportunity. The essential idea is that of orifice, passage, penetration and fault. *Kairos* refers to the point where the penetration of a weapon could be lethal. In the famous contest imposed by Penelope in *The Odyssey*, the contenders for Ulysses' throne in Ithaca had to cross twelve axe-heads lined up at intervals with an arrow from Ulysses' bow. Only Ulysses was able to succeed. If he had missed his shot, the arrow would have spun off *para kairon*: it would have missed the opportunity by being shot off the mark (*para*). *Kairos* is also the art of threading the weft yarn through the warp of the loom. It was therefore necessary to be skillful to thread the weft yarn at the right time since the opening in the warp only lasts for a limited time.[17] We can therefore understand that *Kairos* is the moment when an opening is possible and presents itself to action. Acting, in this sense, would be seizing the more or less fleeting moment that passes by and reveals the fault in the other, which makes him fragile and vulnerable even if he still seems – like Goliath – protected by a shell of invincibility.[18]

What lesson can we find here for accompaniment in social work? On the one hand the social worker is not an all-powerful Goliath confident in his knowledge, missions, experiences or skills; on the other hand, he is often confronted with Goliaths who are paradoxically protected by their status as victims, their disability, their supposed knowledge, their opinions, their ideology and sometimes their all-powerful suffering. Accompaniment would then be an art of reversal, making weakness and vulnerability a force of invulnerability.

Social action therefore consists in the encounter between two vulnerabilities: that of people with disabilities or suffering, of course, but also that of social workers themselves, as a condition for the possibility of an encounter. The crack and flaw of the social worker are probably the best way to avoid a potential perversion made of deception, manipulation, psychological, physical and institutional violence, harassment, mistreatment, coercive persuasion or guilt towards the other person. This mutual vulnerability would lead to stopping thinking and acting for the sake of the other person's supposed Good. On the contrary, mutual vulnerability favors the implementation of a 'deliberative praxis' between social workers and suffering people, based on dialogue, humility, hesitation and wandering: these ethical values go against most of the practices of experts, including psychologists or doctors. The expert descends from heaven onto the stage of life like a *deus ex machina* with whom one does not argue and before whose knowledge one bows. Unfortunately, it is not uncommon for the suffering person to avoid taking his own responsibilities, lazily sheltered as he is behind the supposed skills of the expert. No doubt we find here the radical difference between social workers and experts because, confident in their competence in their own field, their scientific knowledge and their language, the experts know what is good for the other person or, in any case, are convinced that they know it.[19] Accompaniment leads to uncertainty about the future; the solution to a problem comes as a bonus, as in psychoanalysis, because if we insist on finding answers for other people, we inevitably come to submit the subject to the other's request. It cannot be said often enough: there is no other of the other (Lacan, 1966, pp. 824–825). This leads us to reflect on what an accompaniment clinic could be.

The clinic in question

Given these initial reflections, does an accompaniment clinic have anything to do with a clinic of not-knowing? The absolute master in this art was undoubtedly Socrates. An original, bizarre and eccentric character in his way of approaching his friends and particularly in his dialogue with them, Socrates never ceased to question, doubt and claim ignorance, as Plato described him in the *Republic*, refusing thus to be an 'intellectual guide' with a mission to undermine the specious, guiltily slanderous reasonings and the fallacious and seditious arguments of the Sophists. Socrates himself was accused of sophistry because he was not interested in any conclusion and gave the impression that he was trying to make sure that no dialogue really led anywhere, except to the experience of not-knowing.

Lacan takes up the Socratic practice of this not-knowing in his own way, while going infinitely far beyond it: it is not enough for the psychoanalyst to know that he knows nothing, because this position would be that of the sceptic, even if it is fair to say that the psychoanalyst must accept knowing nothing. Since Freud, this posture has constituted the ethics of analytical practice, that of equal suspension of attention.[20] Similarly, the title of the fourth part of the *Variantes de la cure-type* states 'what the psychoanalyst must know: ignore what he knows' (Lacan, 1966, p. 349). Lacan takes up the Freudian advice addressed to the psychoanalyst to take each case in the opposite way to the medical practice of diagnosis and to see each analysand as radically new, as original, as if his experience as an analyst were of no help to him, as if only his personal analysis could be of any use.

It is undoubtedly true that the experience would be more likely to hinder than to favor the direction of the cure. The analytical path is opposed to an accumulation of knowledge and experience, for clinical analytical experience is that of permanent novelty with a particular subject. Thus, analytical practice is poles apart from the meaning of the expression 'to have experience'. In his *Ecrits*, Lacan also indicated the specific affinities of psychoanalysis and ignorance.

Indeed, the analysand causes that subject 'who is supposed to know' (that is, the analyst) to fall off his mighty pedestal. The analysand in turn, losing his illusion of the alleged knowledge that the analyst had about him, discovers that this is not the case and that the analyst can in no way cure him. The analysand, then, can finally follow his own path to himself and to his own desire. That is why, whereas in philosophy there is a skeptical method (*épokhé*) or systematic doubt (Cartesianism), Lacan highlights on the contrary a methodical naivety specific to the analyst's position. The consequence is that the patient or the analysand interprets the analyst's ignorance as incompetence on his part, implying that the analyst, like a doctor, should know. Undoubtedly, the analysis at this moment is faced with the risk of being abandoned in the face of this supposed incompetence.

Could such an approach shed light on the field of social work and accompanying practice even if the social worker is not an analyst, and allow a person in difficulty to walk on his own path with a social worker who is also ignorant because he knows how to renounce his knowledge, does not fear wandering and does not care about any form of coherence?

Not-knowing as naivety invites us to be careful not to know in advance; perhaps this is what Lacan meant by 'the passion of ignorance', besides the other two passions of love and destruction. The expression 'passion of ignorance' is operative as methodical naivety, but this not-knowing, this methodical naivety, is not incompetence or passion for incompetence. Not-knowing is not nothingness but rather a void, because nothingness would refer to *nihil* while a void would refer to the vase whose hollow allows a space for possibilities.

Conclusion

According to Fichte's apt formulation, the human being is 'an unfinished being'[21] and at the same time a being of the always-possible. The human being can thus always surprise and amaze at every moment of his life. If, as Sartre

(2017) points out, 'hell is other people', is it not because these other people immobilize the human being in the determinisms of their indecent and petty glances, and thus deny him any prospect of hope and possibility of change? Man is a promise, Nietzsche said, because he carries within him 'the man to come' (1974). What a lesson this is in our understanding of accompaniment, for how can we conceive any action towards other people without placing ourselves in this perspective of hope and bet on the other person, capable of change in an ever-opening future?

Notes

1   This notion is also expressed in the political and economic field in particular, through the notion of a 'roadmap' which indicates to the other what he must do – a State for example, under drastic control of its actions, often against its will, in exchange for financial support most of the time. This willingness to impose itself on others from the outside is a denial of elementary freedom and democratic recognition.

2   In France, the law of 2 January 2002 renewing social and medico-social action sets new rules on support, individual rights and institutional arrangements (www.legifrance.fr). It is regularly the subject of controversy despite the stated intentions to promote rights (Ennuyer, 2005).

3   To use a well-known expression of Paul Ricoeur (2015), the ethical aim would be the realization of 'a good life, with and for others, in just institutions'.

4   Some people talk about *handicapowerment*, the ability to learn from one's disability and use it as a source of social connection.

5   *Gospel According to Luke*, 24: 13–31. Pilgrim, the one who travels. To walk is to be a *homo viator*. Meister Eckhart spoke of the peregrination of the soul on its path of spiritual search.

6   *Tuché* or *distuché* refer to those periods when a breach or a disruption forces one to change one's life, to review one's relationships, those moments when fortune, chance or luck lead one to modify one's own life or to support the direction taken by someone else's life. Lacan translated *tuché* by 'encounter'. *Tugchavô* means what is obtained by chance, what is there by chance at the right (or wrong) time –*distuché* (Paturet, 2018, p. 50, note 2).

7   In Borges' short story, *The Immortal* (short story 1), the hero has drunk from the river of immortality. He wanders like someone lost, outside of space and time since precisely he has become immortal, until, to his happiness and great relief, he finds his way and especially the river that will give him back his mortality and with it his place in temporality (Borges, 1967).

8   'Imitating in this the travelers who, being lost in some forest, should not wander about, now this way, now that way, still less stop in a place, but always walk as straight as they can in the same direction, and not deviate from it for no good reason, although it may have been only chance that determined them to choose it at the start: because, by this means, if they do not go where they want to, they will at least eventually get somewhere, where they will probably be better off than in the middle of a forest' (Descartes, 1987).

9   The tale of Little Thumb is also very instructive in this respect: having overheard his parents' intention to deliberately lose him and his brothers in the forest (another kind of maze), he collects stones to mark the path and return home. Is it difficult for Little Thumb to grow up? Undoubtedly, but he also shows finesse and intuition, a capacity for listening and adjusting to circumstances. The return path of Little Thumb is probably a regression unlike Ariadne's thread, which on the contrary allows Theseus to venture into the heart of the maze, on unmarked, confusing paths and to liberate the city of Athens from the formidable yoke of Minos and the Minotaur. Does growing up not mean setting off on paths of encounter with the risks inherent in adventure, wandering for what can be long periods of time until one finally finds a meaning to existence?

10 According to Hannah Arendt (Arendt, Fradier & Ricoeur, 1961), the *praxis* field is the place of human excellence because it is the very space of the political sphere. The field of activity (*homo laborans*) is that of biological life in which man seeks to satisfy his vital needs and seeks security. The field of *poiesis* is that of the instrumentality, existence and creation of a common world of objects. Hannah Arendt calls it biographical life (*bios*). The field of *praxis* is that of public life, where man has abandoned his private life, his private shelter (*zoé*), where he exposes himself. The field of *praxis* is that of *bios politikos*, which emphasizes courage and boldness. The hero's freedom consists in revealing and exposing himself.

11 'Consolation is not the same as compassion. To show compassion is to suffer with. It never comforted anyone. The absence or moderation of one's own suffering is thus, for those who wish to relieve the suffering of others, an almost necessary condition, or at least an advantage' (Comte-Sponville, 2018, pp. 13–18). Consoling is rather about not leaving the other person alone with his pathos, which should not necessarily be shared.

12 Nemesis restores balances, like the Roman goddess *Invidia*, indignation at an unfair advantage. These two divine figures could be likened to the notion of handicap, *hand in cap*, a term used in horse racing to ensure that jockeys compete with the same weight.

13 With *Logos*, the Greeks admired this other form of intelligence: cunning, or *Metis*. When we recall the famous episode of the Trojan War and the cunning of Ulysses, nicknamed the man with the *Metis*, hidden with his companions in the belly of the famous horse, we smile at the naivety of the Trojans refusing the prophetic warnings of Cassandra. They break down one of their walls, bring the horse into the heart of the city and thus open their city to the enemy. We admire the astuteness of Penelope, Ulysses' faithful wife, who weaves her father-in-law's shroud during the day before the pretenders to the throne of Ithaca and who during the night secretly undoes the work she has accomplished. And we laugh at the blindness of the pretenders who have become the victims of hallucinations. The goddess *Metis*, daughter of Tethys and Ocean, symbolizes the union of prudence and perfidy in primordial intelligence. The *Metis* is a kind of slyness which is flexible and devious enough to bend in all directions. It is the curved intelligence that adjusts to changing terrain and uncertain, ambiguous situations. By focusing on fluid, changing realities, the *Metis* remains changeable and polymorphic, quick to act in a flash. The word *techne* in Greek also refers to cunning, the manual and intellectual ability to circumvent obstacles; it is an art and a craft, it is synonymous with ingenuity. The *Metis* must undoubtedly be understood as subtlety,

as skillful diplomacy. To practice the art of the *Metis* is to be a fine player, a skillful negotiator and a subtle mediator, to have tact, a posture very different from that of contemporary technicians and experts of all kinds. The art of *Metis* requires a particular ability to listen. The hand and touch are then of the utmost importance and the subtlety of listening requires experience and above all a systematic and unconditional abandonment of the delusional desire to control. It is a paradoxical position if ever there was one, since our modern world dreams only of control and mastery, as evidenced nowadays by the impressive rise of evaluation agencies.

14 The term 'vulnerable' originates etymologically from *wel*, which refers to the semantic field of war: the Indo-European and Germanic *wel* means to wrest, to take by force, *wolna*, the scar, *vulnus* in Latin, the wound, *vulnerare*: to wound, *wall-statt*, the battlefield. The Valkyries in Nordic mythology were virgin warriors who served the god Odin, led battles, distributed death among the warriors and took their souls to the *Walhalla*. The term violence: *wi*, the vital force, *vayah*: force, *is* in Greek and *vis* in Latin, brutal male force, *vir* in Latin means the man that the woman, *mulier*, must channel and direct towards the processes of cultural sublimation. But this term also refers to the vulnerability of systems: information systems, banking systems, educational, political, economic and operating systems. It is the predisposition of a system to withstand a shock or stress – whether they are stresses or shocks external to the system (meteorological hazards, earthquakes, technological or socio-economic risks) or internal risks specific to the system itself. Vulnerability analysis includes the system's ability to respond. So to think of a system is to think of all its *stabilizing or destabilizing* feedback in the face of all external or internal impulses. Vulnerability would then be defined as a system's ability to withstand shocks.

15 Achilles' heel is the place in his body that his mother holds to plunge the hero into the fire and make him invincible; or the leaf of the tree that falls on Siegfried's back when, to become invulnerable, he bathes in the blood of the dragon he has just slain. The heel and the leaf on the back are the flaw, the rift through which death can enter.

16 *Prosopon* in Greek, the face, the mask of the actor, hence *prosopopeia*: personalization of an abstract thing.

17 Modern soldiers talk about a window of opportunity, the right time to act.

18 David appears *a contrario* in all his fragility, without any protection, in all his vulnerability. His very weakness is his strength. In his apostolic letters 2 Corinthians 12:10, Paul writes 'For when I am weak, then I am strong' since for David as for Paul, strength comes from God.

19 The expert, often an adept of 'scientism', cannot tolerate incoherence, wandering or a margin for interpretation that are forms of unbearable narcissistic violence.

20 Equal suspension of attention –*gleichschwebende Aufmerksamkeit*– first appeared in 1912 in *Recommendations to Physicians Practicing Psycho-analysis*. In *Analysis of a Phobia in a Five-Year-Old Boy*, 1909, Freud wrote: 'Let us temporarily leave our judgment pending (*in Schwebe*) and accept with equal attention (*mit gleicher Aufmerksamkeit*) everything that can be observed'. This idea was taken up again in 1923 in 'Psychoanalysis' and 'Libido Theory': 'Experience soon showed that the analyzing doctor behaves here in the most appropriate way if he abandons himself, in a state of equal suspension of attention, to his own unconscious mental activity, avoids reflection and the formation of conscious expectations as much as possible, does not want, from what he has heard, anything in particular fixed in his memory, and captures in this way the unconscious

of the patient with his own unconscious'. It is the opposite of *prosoche* or general-ized vigilant attention that is concerned with seeing and hearing everything without exception. The word originates from the verb *exo*, to stand, to be, *exis* refers to a way of being. *Prosoche* therefore consists in the action of applying oneself, of paying atten-tion to others. Undoubtedly close to that of the doctor, it is diagnostic listening built through a kind of nosographic grid that makes the patient enter the pre-established frameworks of any care.

21 Pico della Mirandola in his *Oratio de hominis dignitate, Discourse on Human Dignity* bases human dignity on the incompleteness of man. While all other creatures are contained by the barrier of instinct and natural laws, man is the one who invents his own nature. This makes him dignified and free. Pico della Mirandola imagines an encounter between God and Adam: 'O Adam, *we have given you neither a determined place, nor a proper physiognomy, nor any particular gift so that the place, the physiognomy, the gifts you would have wished for, you have them and possess them according to your wishes, according to your will*'.

References

Agamben, G. (1990). *La communauté qui vient, Théorie de la singularité quelconque.* Paris: Seuil.

Arendt, H., Fradier, G., & Ricoeur, P. (1961). *Condition de l'homme moderne* (Vol. 1983). Paris: Calmann-Lévy.

Borges, J-L. (1967). *L'aleph.* Paris: Gallimard.

Comte-Sponville, A. (2018). *L'inconsolable et autres impromptus.* Paris: PUF.

Descartes, R. (1987). *Discours de la méthode.* Paris: Vrin.

Ennuyer, B. (2005). Le droit des usagers. *Gérontologie et Société, 28/115*(4), 13–28.

Kant, E. (1990). *Fondements de la métaphysique des mœurs.* Paris: Delagrave.

Lacan, J. (2001). *Autres écrits.* Paris: Seuil.

Lacan, J. (1966) *Ecrits.* Paris: Seuil.

Lacan J. (1973–74). *Les non-dupes errent*, séminaire XXI, unpublished. Online: www.gaogoa. free.fr (consulted 10 January 2014).

Nietzsche, F. W. (1974). *La généalogie de la Morale.* Paris: Gallimard.

Paturet, J-B. (2018). *La passion aporétique de Sigmund Freud, followed by A propos d'un lapsus de Freud sur le Moïse de Michel-Ange.* Limoges: Lambert et Lucas.

Paturet, J-B. (2017). Le territoire et l'im-monde. In *Cave Califatvm! Le califat, un nouveau grand récit totalisant.* Paris: Lambert et Lucas.

Rancière, J. (1995). *La Mésentente.* Paris: Galilée.

Rawls, J. (2009). *A theory of justice.* Cambridge, MA: Harvard University Press.

Ricoeur, P. (2015). *Soi-même comme un autre.* Paris: Seuil.

Sartre, J. P. (2017). *Huis clos*, followed by *Les mouches.* Paris: Gallimard.

Schmitt, C., Deroche-Gurcel, L., & Haggenmacher, P. (2001). *Le nomos de la terre: dans le droit des gens du Jus publicum europaeum.* Paris: PUF.

Schopenhauer, A. (2005). *Parerga et Paralipomena*, Paris: Coda.

Conclusion

Christophe Niewiadomski and
Sébastien Ponnou

Having reached the end of the analyses and proposals developed in the preceding pages, we will avoid the conventional form of a thematic summary of the contributions. Instead, we will organize our concluding remarks around a few salient points which we feel characterize the epistemological, theoretical and clinical underpinnings shared by all of the authors who kindly agreed to contribute to this volume.

It is clear that this work is more than a questioning of the fundamentals of evidence-based practice in social work. Rather, it is intended to be a forum for academic *disputatio* around those representations that define the breadth of clinical practice in social work. The challenge here is therefore less to defend one single conception of the clinic than it is to show the degree to which the clinic is intimately connected to the socio-historical, political and ideological dimensions that determine its field of expertise. Our use of the term 'field' is, of course, deliberate and makes reference to the work of P. Bourdieu:

> When I speak of an intellectual field, I know very well that in this field I am going to find 'particles' (let us imagine for a moment that we are dealing with a physical field) which are under the influence of forces of attraction, repulsion, etc., as in a magnetic field. To speak of a field is

DOI: 10.4324/9781003296416-17

to give primacy to this system of objective relations over the particles themselves.

(Bourdieu & Vaillant, 1992, p. 82)

In other words, at a time when the figure of the specialized techno-scientific expert is gaining ground, it seems to us naïve to consider that the intellectual debate follows the dictates of purely scientific and objectifiable questions alone and at the same time avoids a set of influencing factors which determine the construction of knowledge in the spheres of social work. Indeed, the desire to orient professionals' activity on the basis of 'evidence' presupposes a supporting body of knowledge which, particularly in the field of the human sciences, is known to be built up in a system of relations established in differentiated spheres – spheres which themselves respond to specific rules and interests. Thus, as Bernard Charlot points out:

> Knowledge is built out of a collective history, that of the human spirit and human activities. It is subject to collective processes of validation, capitalization and transmission. As such, it is the product of epistemological relationships between people. However, people maintain with the world, and among themselves (including when they are 'men and women of science'), relationships which are not only epistemological. Therefore, knowledge relationships are, more broadly speaking, social relationships.
>
> (Charlot, 1997, p. 73)

Moreover, if the structure of the field we are dealing with organizes a struggle of intellectual competition around specific capital which determines differentiated non-substantialist positions, the relations between the actors in this field follow very different hermeneutic traditions whose evidential value is not exempt from issues that go beyond the scientific register alone.

Some fundamental epistemological differences

Let us attempt to briefly review the most striking epistemological differences between evidence-based practice and clinical-based practice. At one end of the spectrum of social intervention, there is a positivist conception of the clinic to which evidence-based practice can be easily linked. Evidence-based practice is based on an epistemology of the natural sciences wherein causal explanation tends to replace the significance of actual experience. In this perspective, and in support of the *law of the three states* formulated by Auguste Comte (1844), it is necessary to break with 'theological' and 'metaphysical' perspectives, which correspond respectively to the historical period of the Old Regime and to the Enlightenment, and to embrace the 'scientific' (or positivist) state, whose intention is to detach itself from the search for the 'primary causes of things' in order to focus on the formulation of invariable laws based on observation and reasoning. The aim here is to move from the fundamental uncertainty linked to the question of 'why?' to the rigorous and verifiable observation of 'how?', thus making it possible to explain the 'reality of the facts'. The concern surrounding objectification linked to the observation-based clinic is perfectly in line with this explanatory perspective, where it is a question of 'being scientific' by developing standardized protocols, randomized trials and, finally, evidence.

At the other end of the spectrum, we find a very different conception of the clinic based on the consideration of a *singular, willing subject*; this conception attaches importance to the processes of subjectivation that drive it. This orientation, which is more comprehensive than explanatory, focuses attention on the uses of language and its effects in an intersubjective relationship, one where the practitioner is considered to be fundamentally involved as a subject and not as a mere observer.

We find here the terms of a debate introduced at the end of the 14th century by Dilthey (1883), who wished to clearly distinguish between 'explanation' and 'understanding' in order to identify an epistemology of the human sciences to differentiate it from the natural sciences and scientific positivism. For Dilthey, the anthropo-social sciences aim above all to grasp the meaning of individual, actual experience, whereas the natural sciences tend to explain observed phenomena on the basis of causal determinism. For the cultural sciences, therefore, it is not only the observation of facts as they might be identified by an outside observer that makes it possible to understand the meaning of a behavior or situation, but also the analysis of the representation of these same facts by the people involved. And, therefore, if the object of anthropo-social sciences concerns the *Subject* in its multitudinous dimensions and in its interactions with itself, with others and with the historical–social world, it is postulated that this subject is no more reduced to the observation that can be made of it than to the apparent rationality of its discourse and actions because of the numerous determinations to which it is subject (De Gaulejac, 2009; Niewiadomski, 2012). For this reason, it is crucial to adjust the 'scientific tools' used for the study and support thereof. What is argued here is that methods of investigation concerning human beings cannot be limited to the sole perimeter of a supposedly axiologically neutral science, whereas the object of study considered is by nature essentially subjective. In this sense, therapeutic or educational orientations that are overly mechanistic or prescriptive fail to take into account and to ultimately understand the subjectivity inherent in all human conduct.

In contrast to explaining, the act of understanding aims to embrace a whole that should not be fragmented by favoring a purely analytical logic. The approach evokes the idea of *insight*, that is, the emergence of understanding. Humor, which is arguably more understandable than it is explainable, undoubtedly helps one to better grasp the work of understanding that we hope so fervently to promote:

> Traditional logic is linear and causal; this is what we call the principle of reason. To every cause there is an effect, to every effect there is a cause [...]. What was hidden must come to light and respond to reason. There is no place for that which is hidden and dark. [...] Humor goes the other way around and seeks the intimacy of shadow and the night. Humor does not say; it suggests, evokes, implies – the rustle of a border, the enigma of the visible / invisible that defines the world.
>
> (Ouaknin & Rotnemer, 1995, p. 10)

In the field at hand – that is, the collection of supposedly 'evidence-based' data in social work – the distinction between explanation and understanding leads to some essential epistemological implications. Michel Legrand insists on the importance of questions of meaning in human beings and stresses the need to distinguish between causes and reasons in order to understand more precisely the processes at play in any anthropological approach:

> Causes and reasons are opposed as two irreducible orders of explanation for human behavior. Cause looks backwards, as it were, designating an antecedent condition or event supposedly producing the behavior, whereas reason or motive is forward-looking, qualifying an end or project aimed at by the behavior. The distinction may seem subtle, but it is crucial: depending on whether one invokes causes or reasons, one will postulate either a man-object, subject to a game, albeit a complex one of determinations, or a man-subject, who gives meaning to his conduct.
>
> (Legrand, 1998, p. 111)

The comprehensive approach, comprehensive in the sense that it gives equal weight to uniqueness and to interpretative polysemy, thus makes it possible not to confine the subject to what is being stated, not to reduce the 'subject who says' to the 'subject of what is said'. It takes into account the fact that there is meaning in what the subject says and in the exchange that occurs concerning this, but that the utterer cannot be reduced to a simple system of causality. Very often, the meaning of the 'symptom', that is, the basis of the patient's request, needs to be questioned. One can listen to and understand the symptom as the literal translation of the request, but also sometimes as the substitutive expression of an unconscious conflict which calls for inter- pretation. In other words, the symptom (be it psychological or social) carries out an always unique compromise, translating the unconscious desire of the subject in a disguised fashion so as to respect his defensive demands. As an impulsive representation of that which cannot be said, the decoding of the symptom therefore requires the opening of a complex intersubjective space, which is precisely what is offered by a non-standardized educational accom- paniment open to the importance of understanding.

That being the case, this *clinic of listening* to the subjectivity of the sub- ject considers not only that the one who is trying to say something cannot be reduced to the content of the discourse and the factual information he conveys, but also that the listener finds himself caught up and engaged in a type of relationship where his psychological apparatus is solicited. Under these conditions, it becomes clear that the explanatory variables which form the basis of the scientific epistemology of the natural sciences are only very partially relevant to the work of intersubjective understanding.

Affinities and links between evidence-based practice in social work, social norms and managerial logic

However interesting it may be, the 'evidence-based practice in social work' model contributes in the end to putting the user's voice at a distance and to focusing on an objective orientation of situations, very much in line with man- agerial perspectives known to be reticent to the intersubjective meaning of the clinical relationship. The technocratic concern for the rationalization of procedures hinders the very possibility of hearing the subject; there is a pro- liferation of scoring and evaluation grids, which are held to reflect an objec- tive reality but which distance professionals from the people under their care. Moreover, the model for evidence-based practice in social work has a clear objective to adjust the user to the social norm. However, in a social context marked by difficulties in vocational insertion, rising unemployment and pre- carious employment, housing problems and lack of access to care, the subject nowadays is increasingly told to 'self-manage' and to take on more personal responsibility as regards the methods of his social integration and employability. At a time when an ever-increasing population of 'able-bodied indigents' (Castel, 1992) is confronted with a pace of daily existence where precariousness and its concomitant suffering are becoming commonplace, those who work must henceforth face the demands of a logic of competition with their fellow human beings; this results in their having to participate in a 'struggle for positions' (De Gaulejac & Taboada-Léonetti, 1994). Thus thrust into a universe that upsets old solidarities and existing values, and no longer able to find common means of defense in work collectives to resist increasing pressure, the subject today must deal with the fear of an ever possible social descent and the anguish that results from it. Confronted with a professional context that over-emphasizes personal evaluation and generates unbridled competition between individuals, the subject ends up exhausted and sometimes even experiences depression. Stress, musculoskeletal disorders, addictions, depression, burnout, even suicides in connection with work are steadily increasing: the so-called 'medicalization' of problems concerning suffering at work seems to have become a consensual response, and the questioning of the organization of work and its ideological underpinnings is thus conveniently avoided.

In a context of profound socio-historical changes and at a time when inequalities of all kinds are on the rise, the relation to the norm can be questioned in the light of the work of Canguilhem (1966). Canguilhem questions the experience of illness in terms of its relation to the norm and argues that the deep meaning of illness is essentially 'affective':

> We maintain that the life of a living being, even an amoeba, recognizes categories of health and disease only in terms of experience, which is first and foremost an emotional ordeal, and not in terms of science. Science explains experience, but it does not cancel it out.
>
> (Canguilhem, 1966, p. 131)

For Canguilhem, disease therefore cannot be reduced to an objectifying medical perspective or to a scientific orientation based solely on quantitative variation seen in relation to a norm:

> Human life can have a biological meaning, a social meaning, an existential meaning. All these meanings can be taken into account in the assessment of the modifications that disease inflicts on human life. A man does not live like a tree or a rabbit. [...] The obstacle to biology and experimental medicine lies in individuality.
>
> (Canguilhem, 1992, pp. 155–158)

Criticizing a 'mechanized' conception of the body and starting from a reflection on the terms 'normal' and 'pathological', Canguilhem shows that health does not respond to an objective standard but to a subjective one. On this basis, he suggests using the term *normativity* in reference to the effort that individuals make to adapt: in the end, these individuals judge the new standards of life that they will experience. Analogically speaking, evidence-based practice in social work can be compared to the reference to the norm whereas clinical-based practice and support is comparable to the work of normativity.

Potential compatibility between evidence-based practice and clinical-based practice

Norm and normativity, as well as explanation and understanding, should not in our view be opposed in an oversimplified way, be it in the health field or in social science research. As Kaufmann points out:

> If understanding and explanation may seem to be poles apart, sociology must rebel against the idea that they are two separate ways of thinking. The comprehensive approach is based on the conviction that people are not mere agents representing structures but active producers of the social sphere, and therefore custodians of important knowledge that must be grasped from the inside, through the value system of individuals; it therefore begins with intropathy. Sociological work is not, however, limited to this phase: on the contrary, it consists in the researcher's being able to interpret and explain on the basis of the data collected. The understanding of the person is only an instrument: the sociologist's aim is the comprehensive explanation of the social sphere.
>
> (Kaufmann, 1996, p. 23)

Therefore, despite the differences between evidence-based practice and clinical-based practice, how can we find a compromise between the two while at the same time giving each its due? For the former, as we have seen, it is important to base social work and social workers' interventions on evidence that is scientifically validated thanks to an epistemological approach to the natural sciences. For the latter, what matters is to recognize the importance of subjectivity, considered consubstantial with human nature, in order to understand and interpret by using the epistemology of the cultural sciences. While each of these approaches has its own logic and specific tools, practitioners do not necessarily pit one against the other as forcefully as in some academic debates. Moreover, recent research conducted in the field of statistical methods shows the benefits of combining clinical practice and the production of evidence.

However, the recent reactivation of research carried out in the field of applied statistical methods shows all the benefits of studying very small numbers, or even unique cases. The Single Case Experimental Designs (SCED) method aims to circumvent the methodological biases encountered in randomized, controlled studies in favor of a clinical reading of individual patients or users. In randomized controlled studies, the aim – which is very approximately summarized here – is to compare two groups. One receives an educative intervention or care and the other does not. The distribution of patients or users into the groups is randomly selected and the effects of the intervention in the group that receives it are measured as a statistical average. While this method is generally well suited to the study of large numbers and homogeneous groups, it is much less so when individual variables are involved. Such variables are difficult to control because they can vary greatly at the time of measurement (pain, psychological disorders, anxiety, etc.). Furthermore, the statistical average tends to reduce the differences between those who respond very favorably to a given treatment and those who benefit little or not at all, without these differences being clearly identified and explained. Rather than relying on groups, the SCED method proposes to take the individual as the unit of assessment, examining in detail the effects of a given intervention or treatment.

> The problem is that the patient can improve for many other reasons than the effectiveness of the rehabilitation or treatment: a developmental effect, spontaneous recovery, enthusiasm on the part of the patient [...], etc. We need a methodology that allows us to identify the specific effect of the intervention but which remains individualized to a single patient.
>
> (Krasny-Pacini, 2019, p. 24)

The SCED method therefore consists in carefully examining the effect specifically related to the intervention being tested. It does this by intensively multiplying the measures and introducing the intervention randomly to avoid bias. Without going into too much detail about the implementation of such clinical approaches, we must point out that the SCED method ultimately results in the production of data with a very high level of evidence.

> This methodology is recognized by the Oxford Center for evidence-based medicine, which places it at level 1 evidence, on the same level

as the metanalyses of randomized controlled trials. In this way, SCEDs make it possible to truly put the patient back at the center of the evaluation with his uniqueness, his associated deficits and his variability over time. The aim is to look at the personal benefit and not the general group effect by using a methodology that is rigorous, personalized and evidence-based.

(Krasny-Pacini, 2019, p. 24)

Consequently, although evidence-based practice and clinical-based practice each have their own logic and specific tools, future clinical and methodological bridges between the two are nevertheless possible. Moreover, it is not certain that practitioners make such a clear-cut difference between these two approaches as is observed in some academic debates. Indeed, practitioners very often operate by hybridizing knowledge in order to adjust the relevance of their interventions. It is thus not uncommon for a practitioner with a cognitive–behavioral approach to be attentive to the effects of unconscious phenomena in the people he helps, or to the transferential manifestations which never fail to appear in the intersubjective relationships encountered. In the same way, psychoanalysts have long been aware of the criticisms regularly aimed at the 'rigor' of the process of a typical treatment, and have accordingly adjusted it to the evolution of their patients.

However, in order to build a possible dialogue between evidence-based practice and clinical-based practice, it is necessary to promote their respective positions, as well as their approaches and practices. If the development of evidence-based practice today provides a broad echo to this approach, particularly in English-speaking countries, we deemed it necessary not only to question and discuss some of its characteristics, but also to give more insight into the alternative that, to our mind, clinical-based practice represents in the field of social work and social intervention. We hope that this volume will be an effective response to this project and that it will be, if not convincing, then at least challenging and thought-provoking for its readership.

References

Bourdieu, P., & Vaillant, L. (1992). *Réponses. Pour une anthropologie réflexive.* Paris: Seuil.

Canguilhem, G. (1965). *La connaissance de la vie.* Paris: Vrin (1992).

Canguilhem, G. (1966). *Le normal et le pathologique.* Paris: PUF.

Castel, R. (1992). Définir le social?. In Karsz, S. (Ed.), *Déconstruire le social. Séminaire 1.* Paris: L'Harmattan.

Charlot, B. (1997). *Du rapport au savoir. Éléments pour une théorie.* Paris: Anthropos.

Comte, A. (1844). *Discours sur l'esprit positif.* Paris: Vrin, 1995.

Dilthey, W. (1883). *Introduction aux sciences de l'esprit.* Translation and presentation by Sylvie Mesure. Paris: Éditions du Cerf (1992).

Gaulejac, V. de, & Taboada-Leonetti, I. (1994). *La lutte des places.* Paris: Desclée de Brouwer.

Gaulejac, V. de (2009). *Qui est 'je'? Sociologie clinique du sujet.* Paris: Seuil.

Kaufmann, J. C. (1996). *L'entretien compréhensif.* Paris: Nathan.

Krasny-Pacini, A. (2019). Le patient acteur de son évaluation. *Proceedings from the Colloquium Innover par le numérique pour l'autonomie* (pp. 23–25). Fondation Jacques Chirac, 15 February 2019, Paris.

Legrand, M. (1998). Les paradoxes de la liberté dans l'expérience alcoolique. *Revue Alcoologie, 20*(2), 109–115.

Niewiadomski, C. (2012). *Recherche biographique et clinique narrative.* Toulouse: Érès.

Ouaknin, M. A., & Rotnemer, D. (1995). *La bible de l'humour juif.* Paris: Ramsay.

Supplementary material
Two case studies
Sébastien Ponnou and Christophe Niewiadomski

Several chapters in this volume refer to clinical studies or field situations which will enlighten the reader on research and concepts related to clinically oriented social work.

With respect to clinical studies, see for example the following:

– p. 33–36: Jacqueline's story, presented by Vincent de Gaulejac, deals with the harmful effects of paradox-generating practices in social institutions;
– p. 91–93: Franck's story (as it relates to ADHD) presented by Sébastien Ponnou, addresses Lacanian practices with children diagnosed with hyperactivity;
– p. 97–99: the 'story of the thief', borrowed from August Aïchhorn and presented by Sébastien Ponnou, focuses on psychoanalytic practices in institutions;
– p. 127–128: Aminata's story, presented by Marie Rose Moro and Rameth Radjack, denounces the prejudices and risks of stigmatization involved in the reception of immigrant families in France.

For field situations, see the following relevant pages:

– p. 137–151: Pascal Fugier presents a series of field results dedicated to clinical practices used to support young people involved in drug trafficking and how these practices contribute to prevention;
– p. 152–171: Florence Giust-Desprairies decrypts a series of field results dedicated to clinical practices with multi-handicapped people in institutions.

Lost in sexuation[1]

Sébastien Ponnou

How can the question of gender and gender identities be apprehended within our model of the clinic? The perspective here is neither political nor social, although the question of gender can naturally take the form of a demand addressed to the Other. For our purposes, it is perhaps more essentially an opaque enigma, the condensation point of a *jouissance*[2] connected with the events and discourses that make up the history of an individual's life and that form the blueprint of that individual's psychoanalytic journey.

For a certain Suzon, the question of gender identity is irrevocably linked to having been the victim of sexual assault as an adolescent, an event which affected the most intimate part of her sexuation.

The goal of this clinical presentation is to demonstrate how analytical discourse can contribute to finding an 'elegant solution', one that allows the subject to seize upon her creative chance to become a part of some prototypical set of social relationships, but in her own, original way.[3]

Being a boy

Suzon was sixteen years old when we first met. Her clothes were dirty and shabby. Her eyes were hidden behind a long fringe of hair and her face was riddled with piercings, most of which she had given herself while she was hospitalized.

Suzon had taken refuge in my office and refused to meet with the girls in the group home, feeling persecuted by the gaze of the Other. Furthermore, she did not understand why she was assigned to the girls' section of the home rather than to the boys' section. This intrigued me. 'The boys' section?' 'Yes,' she answered with a broad, somewhat ironic smile. 'I want to become a boy'.

It is by way of this enigmatic formula that Suzon entered into this exchange with me. She then pointed to her androgynous look – her outfit, her haircut and her 'emo style'.[4] The reference to what are referred to as 'emos' (or 'emo kids') has a particular significance for Suzon. It is a signifier full of meaning, one which goes beyond the multiple imaginary identifications she has equipped herself with. It is a term that she has chosen, a replacement that allows her to assert her singularity vis-à-vis the Other and to society after the collapse of the symbolic, imaginary references within which she had previously taken shelter.

Sexual assault

Suzon was admitted to a specialized institution after a long stay in a psychiatric ward for adolescents. This had followed an incident of sexual assault committed by a young man whom Suzon had been seeing. 'I didn't know how to say "no"', Suzon explained with a shrug.

The incident was like a bombshell, the explosion of which affected Suzon's primordial identifications and the otherwise inexplicable decision concerning her sexuation. It also shook the foundations of her family. The girl's parents found the situation so unbearable that their reaction bordered on rejection: 'We realized that Suzon would do nothing with her life and that she would end up on the street'. Against the background of her parents' fantasy, the assault served as a condensation point for an insurmountable case of Lacanian *jouissance*. Suzon irremediably bore the mark of this to such an extent that her parents' words became for her a self-fulfilling prophesy.

Suzon's difficulties did not surface at the time of the attack. Rather, they resurfaced later by way of parental, and then social, discourse. Her illness began insidiously and was marked by a series of symptoms. She gradually withdrew from school and was later expelled. She experienced depression and her physical condition deteriorated considerably (she experienced homelessness and committed acts of self-mutilation). This ultimately led to hospitalization. The sexual assault was reported, but the sexual abuse charge was dismissed.

The question of sexuation: finding an 'elegant solution'

Forced to confront the sexual abuse she had suffered, and in view of her state of disarray as a subject in relation to the field occupied by the Other, the reference to emos and the change of gender identity emerged as solutions allowing Suzon to circumscribe the *jouissance*. Beyond the identifying functions of each change in her appearance (make-up, clothing, piercings, boyish haircuts), the signifier *emo* functioned as a naming device that made it possible to resolve, via the imaginary, the cracks which the sexual assault had opened in reality, and symbolically by the *mise en abîme* of the Other.

There is no doubt that this was a veritable 'find' for a psychoanalyst, given that the signifier *emo* is first taken from the Other. But both the inventiveness of this signifier and particularized use of it become even more obvious when we relate them to the question of sexuation and sexuality. Alongside the classic sexual difference between boy and girl, parallel to the hetero/homo dichotomy of the sexual object, Suzon invented yet another identity, that of *emo*. In other words, by pushing the boundaries of traditional categories, she created new divisions: hetero/homo/emo. She used irony with regard to the Other and demonstrated her ability to use language to deal with her trauma (Miller, 2004).

Wandering and the 'clinic of the borders'

In spite of these solutions, Suzon nonetheless continued to experience a number of difficulties. The relationship with her parents – ambivalent to say the least – became more complicated. And at school, the headmaster told her that she must choose between her education and her piercings. He expelled her rather than adopting a more individualized approach to the situation. At the group home where she was placed, Suzon risked compromising treatment as she left unauthorized every afternoon to join her emo friends.

Whereas the institution became more rigid in its positions here, the risk being that it would become yet another in a series of 'Villainous Others' (Miller, 2010), I opted to explore what has been called the *politique du symptôme* (Soler, 1998) with an eye to moving Suzon towards recovery. Indeed, invention implies that at least one other person notices it. Taking this perspective, I attempted to become a partner in Suzon's inventions by deploying a *clinique des bords* (or 'clinic of edges' (Stevens, 2018)). This approach recognizes that there is more to a painting than the frame that surrounds it and that the institution is a but a stage whose function is to place the subject on a podium. I thus allowed Suzon to use the office phone to contact her emo friends. Together, we mapped out her movements between different places in the housing estate. On two occasions, Suzon phoned me to ask for a counselor to come and pick her up.

Thus commenced a game of back-and-forth between the various places in the group home and a square in the estate where Suzon would meet her emo friends. She found herself repeatedly caught up in certain abusive situations. For instance, she would accept gifts of money, then refuse the concomitant sexual solicitations (by this time, Suzon had learned to say 'no'). This led to the young girl's incremental questioning of why she found herself in these places, and finally to her ceasing to go there: 'That's a place for people who have made a mess of their lives. I don't want to make a mess of mine'.

Turning boys' heads

Suzon gradually stopped running away, as she abandoned her references to emo culture. New requests were articulated: until then, Suzon had been educated in a specialized context, but now she wanted to go back to school, do work placements and find a job 'like young people her age'. What had previously been a chosen naming device and then the signifier of homelessness was now articulated in terms of 'scenarios'. She passionately tried out many new, more or less appropriate means of connecting. Suzon had had enough of feeling marginalized. She now wanted to be at the center. The imaginary part of her requests ('to be a high school student', 'to go to university', 'to be a stylist', 'to be a hairdresser' – in other words, her desire to make a name for herself out of the signifiers she borrowed from the Other) led the team to propose a customized schooling scheme in a private high school which was free of ordinary academic requirements and offered classes in the morning and pre-professional work-placements in the afternoon.

Suzon began to take care of herself, her body and her clothes. One by one, she removed her piercings and allowed the holes she had created in her body – especially on her face – to close. She re-established a healthier relationship with her parents and began spending weekends at home.

At school, she met new people and returned to the institution 'with stories about girls and boys'. The question of gender identity was still prevalent, and Suzon found a new way of resolving it: she now wanted to be 'the girl who turns boys' heads'. Suzon adopted a posture bent on seduction: she wore more feminine clothing, tried to catch peoples' eye and sought to position herself as an object of desire. As such, she found intense pleasure in evading the advances made to her: she played with the Other, evading the advances. She made use of the role of decoy and the art of semblance.

The incident of sexual assault had turned Suzon's sexual identity upside-down. And it is by means of semblances (both emo culture and games of seduction) – that is to say, substitutes for fundamentally impossible sexual relations – that she would manage to find her way through the confused entanglement of sexuation.

Metamorphosis and structure

One of the main criticisms leveled at psychoanalysts is that they tend to view transgender identities as pathological. But that is not what is happening here. Nor is there any question of gender norms. 'Turning boys' heads' does not necessarily make Suzon female or straight any more than the signifier 'emo' makes her trans.

The analyst does not proceed in terms of categories but rather with the singularity of a subject's 'text', the reality that emerges via language and of which the analyst becomes the depositary.

For all that, the diversions via structure, defense mechanisms, and even nosographic discussions must not become taboo or be excluded from the analytical field on the pretext of progressivism. It is indeed this reference to structure that leads the analyst to carefully handle the signifier 'emo', whose value as a substitute is reflected in flesh itself: Suzon's self-made piercings and acts of self-harm are iterations of the traumatic assault upon her body. It is not (or not only) a '*trans*-formation', but also the revival of the trauma encapsulated in the signifier, the irruption of the real into the snares of the symbolic, which reveal the limits of Suzon's solutions.

This structural modality also opens up for discussion Suzon's quasi-systematic adjustment to malleable imaginary identifications, with the consequence of being stuck on the 'a–a' axis (Lacan, 1966), that is, a form of indeterminacy and precariousness of identification modeled on the partner's traits and, consequently, a renovation of the 'desiring dialectic'. This perspective has two major clinical effects. On the one hand, it makes Suzon particularly vulnerable to the Other's desire for pleasure (by way of, for example, compliance, suggestibility and repetition of abusive situations). On the other hand, this identity-forming plasticity opens up the possibility of inventing a series of solutions which allow her to deal with the delicate question of *jouissance*, the enigma of the Other's desire and the trauma of the sexual attack. Suzon, in the end, will have mastered the art of metamorphosis.

References

Evans, D. (1996). *An introductory dictionary of Lacanian psychoanalysis*. London: Routledge.

Lacan, J. (1966). *Écrits*. Paris: Seuil.

Miller, J.-A. (2010). *L'Autre méchant: six cas cliniques commentés*. Paris: Navarin.

Miller, J. A. (2004). The psychotic invention. *Quarto, 80*, 6–13.

Soler, C. (1998). La politique du symptôme. *Quarto, 65*, 71–76.

Stevens, A. (2018). Devant l'enfant violent, un cadre ou un bord. Extrait de l'intervention du 29.09.2018 au groupe CEREDA de La-Roche-sur-Yon, http://institut-enfant.fr/zappeur-ji5/devant-lenfant-violent-un-cadre-ou-un-bord/

The temperature curve in the analysis of educational work

Christophe Niewiadomski

In this contribution, I outline a method of narrative description and an analysis of what one might call educational 'problem situations' using a specific tool, the 'temperature curve'.[5] Based on a brief description of a situation of violence in the field of educational work in schools, I will show how this seemingly simple analytical tool can nevertheless contribute to understanding much of the complexity of the phenomena as they occur in educational situations. We will first see that this approach makes it possible to identify thresholds of intensity, chronological branching points, hitherto hidden interactions and elusive data. We will also see how it contributes to making sense of the situations encountered and thus opens up the possibility of developing new hypotheses. These hypotheses will shed light on the links between individual, collective and institutional phenomena that are closely intertwined in educational work.

The use of this approach also constitutes a powerful training lever for educational teams. Indeed, the educational situations and the development of the temperature curve can, with the help of a trainer, be carried out in small groups before giving rise to broader exchanges. For the sake of brevity, I will not deal with this question here, as it has more than adequately been addressed by others (Casanova, Cellier, Robbes & Bagur, 2005). Rather, I will focus on the in-depth analysis of a specific educational situation to demonstrate the heuristic potential this model has.

The situation described in the following pages, which might be entitled 'Strangulation in a bridging class', involves a conflict between two young adolescents we will call Gaël and Yann. Having been verbally attacked, Gaël physically assaults Yann, attempting to strangle him in class and thus forcing the educational team to separate and contain them and then dissipate what will ultimately be described as a severe emotional episode.

The situation within the educational context

The situation takes place in a French *classe relais* (or 'bridging class')[6] located in a large provincial secondary school with more than a thousand students. The educational counselors are highly motivated and have a good relationship with the teachers at the school. Most of these teachers welcome the students to the bridging class scheme without any major difficulties and allow them to be partially integrated into their classes.

One of the young people in the class, Gaël (aged fourteen), was referred to this structure after dropping out of school and repeatedly running away. He had been the victim of racketeering in the school he had previously attended. At the time the incident occurred, he was living in a group home far from his family. He had witnessed abuse and violence between his parents and no longer saw them, although it is not clear whether this was due to a judge's decision or to his parents' having rejected him. At school, Gaël gradually regained his self-confidence and progressively reintegrated. One of his classmates, fifteen-year-old Yann, had a completely different profile and was antagonistic and defiant with the teaching staff. Yann's orientation was more vocational (he was currently doing a course in plumbing). His aim was not reintegration into a school system with which he had a difficult relationship. Let us now look at the sequence of events.

It is nine o'clock at the school, and the young people are welcomed by two members of the educational team (a teacher and a counselor) for a 'What's new?' session, regularly used in institutional pedagogy. The device is intended to regulate the group by tapping into the 'existential weather' of the small group before beginning the pedagogical activities. Yann makes the following remark: *'Nice to have jerks in this class who will kiss up in the other classes'.*

'What do you mean by that?' asks one of the adults.
'You know, that jerk here (pointing to Gaël) is gonna show off to us again because he's off to do math with the other jerks in the school.'
'You can't say that,' replies the other adult. 'We're in this bridging class to get back on track. That's what Gaël is doing. He's an example for everyone. You can do it too, here at school or in the plumbing business.'
'Yeah, right,' replies Yann, mockingly.

The next part of the 'What's new?' session deals with various topics raised by the teenagers in the class before one of the adults suggests that they talk about the day's activities. In turn, each person explains what they are going to do and how they have prepared for it. When Gaël's turn comes, he says that *'It's easy today. It's math.'*

The young people then leave for their various activities. As he has done every Thursday for the previous four weeks, Gaël goes to the math class. However, when the teacher asks him a question, he cannot answer. The teacher asks him to define a concept. Panic-stricken, Gaël cannot remember, stammers and loses his nerve completely.

'But you knew the other day. It's not so difficult, if you just look here ...'

The teacher explains to him while some of the other students begin making fun of him:

'No wonder, he's a loser.' 'He's a loser.' 'You're just a loser.'

The teacher intervenes and defends Gaël:

'No, he's not a loser, he's just experiencing difficulties. It can happen to anyone; in fact
   some people here are not much better!'
'Ha! He's a loser, we do it on purpose, we're not jerks! Only jerks work hard.'

Gaël bows his head, wipes away a few tears and looks at his notebook while
the teacher addresses the class. 'That's enough, get back to work!'. This calms
everyone down and restores order. Gently approaching him, the teacher whis-
pers to Gaël. 'I know this isn't easy, but it's normal that it takes you more time.
Don't worry, it will get easier.'

   The class ends. Gaël leaves the classroom, crosses the courtyard and meets
an educational counselor whom he sees regularly and whom he likes. The
counselor greets him warmly:

   'Everything still going okay? We're counting on you, right?'

Gaël does not answer, shrugs and enters the classroom. He then runs into the
teacher.

   'How did it go? Everything okay?'

Again, Gaël does not answer. He goes to the computer room, where he finds
Yann. Yann immediately sees that Gaël is upset and, smiling sarcastically, calls
out to him:

'So you've been showing off again? You've been a clown in math again.'

Yann does not have time to continue his mockery. Gaël jumps at his throat
and attempts to strangle him. The teacher and the counselor in the room
run over to deal with this severe emotional episode. They are insulted by and
receive blows from Gaël but eventually manage to calm him down.

Analysis

A superficial reading of this episode might lead one to suppose that the situation stems from a lack of emotional control in a teenager 'experiencing
difficulty' and who is also suffering from an emotional 'deficit' due to a family
history marked by violence and unstable family ties. Indeed, we know that
the adolescent has a complex family history and is currently separated from

parents, who are known to have been abusive. From this perspective, Gaël's behavior can be seen as a classic case of an expression of that which cannot be put into words. Gaël's inability to bear the insult can be seen as referring him to some other situation, which we can assume was traumatic enough to lead to violent behavior towards a third party. In other words, the impulsiveness shown here by Gaël can be understood as the result of an unconscious displacement between two situations with only contingent associative links. Seen in this light, Gaël is no longer able to take not being accepted and conflates Yann's verbal aggression and the violence and rejection that mark his family history.

This hypothesis is no doubt partially relevant. However, the links of meaning between the observed situation and its possible unconscious roots remain imprecise. In addition to the fact that we do not have enough elements to support this interpretation, it also evokes a meaning that grants too much importance to a somewhat risky intrapsychic understanding of the phenomenon observed. In adopting this traditional approach, we run the risk of enlisting the young man to 'work on himself', assuming that this will encourage him to put his act into words and make sense of it. Another unfortunate but frequent solution is even easier to implement: the prescription of a psychotropic drug to regulate aggressiveness that has become too difficult for the group to manage. While it is important not to exclude any hypotheses linked to Gaël's 'psychic economy', I will now attempt to formulate other paths to account for the relational complexity of the phenomenon we have observed above.

I will first argue that Gaël's behavior is probably more akin to 'acting out' than to the what we will call 'acting upon'. Second, I will attempt to show how what is seen can also be understood on a register where phenomena of resonance and assemblage testify to the complexity of these agonistic behaviors. Finally, we will try to identify some of the educational issues suggested by the facts reported here by proposing a cross-reading of the individual, collective and institutional registers that are interconnected in this situation.

Before going into the details of the analysis, however, let us first try to illustrate the situation with the help of a temperature curve along two axes, where the y-axis indicates the level of intensity of the situation and the x-axis represents its chronology.

We immediately notice that the culminating point of the situation occurs at point 7, that is, the point at which Gaël has an irrepressible, violent expression of emotion. Although point 5 is obviously a turning point which opens onto the violence shown in point 6, it is at point 7 that Gaël seems to lose control of himself. What has occurred here?

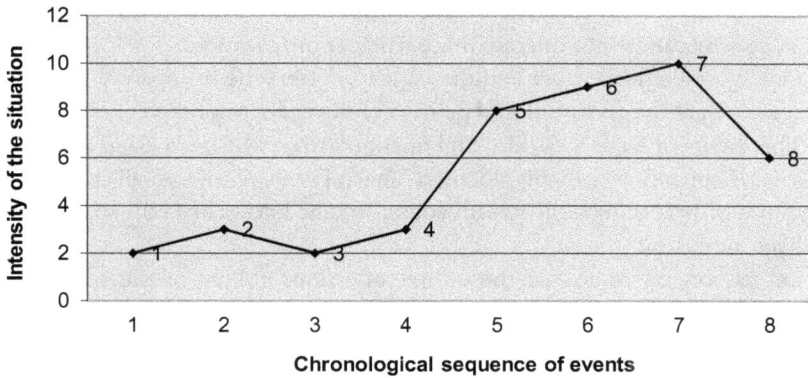

Temperature curve of the situation

Legend

1 Meeting with the educational counselor: 'We're counting on you, right?'
2 Shrug of the shoulders.
3 Meeting with the teacher: 'How did it go? Everything okay?'
4 No answer. Gaël goes to computer room.
5 Turning point: Yann's provocative remarks: 'So you've been showing off again? You've been a jerk in math again'.
6 Gaël's acts violently towards Yann.
7 Climax of the episode: Gaël's emotional crisis.
8 The educational counseling team manages to calm Gaël down.

Three decisive clinical questions

In formal terms, it seems that the sequence of events is as follows: Gaël, on his return from school, meets the educational counselor who greets him with a few words of encouragement. 'Inexplicably', Gaël responds with a mere shrug of the shoulders. This nevertheless suggests the depth of the anxiety he is experiencing. The second meeting, with his teacher, is not much more successful than the previous one: Gaël, without answering, leaves for the computer room. A first question thus arises: why is it that, although Gaël knows and appreciates the counselor, he cannot speak of the problem with this adult or with his teacher, both of whom seem to offer themselves as potentially attentive and understanding listeners?

While Gaël is in the computer room, Yann picks up on Gaël's anxiety and, as usual, verbally provokes him. It is the proverbial straw that breaks the camel's back. Gaël jumps at Yann's throat[7] and tries to strangle him.

A second question thus arises: Gaël is obviously used to Yann's provocations, so why can he not tolerate this particular provocation?

Finally, while the teacher and the educator intervene to separate the protagonists, Gaël shouts insults and delivers blows indiscriminately.

This behavior leads to a third and final question: why does Gaël, involved in what is apparently a highly 'focused' quarrel with Yann, lose all control to the point of becoming violent with adults who he knows like him and whom he likes in return?

Let us now try to answer these three questions in light of the additional information available to us and with the help of a few addition concepts.

Acting *upon* or acting *out*? A subtle distinction that opens up key interpretative possibilities

Often used synonymously, the two expressions designate an impulsive act of unconscious origin in which the subject[8] acts rather than puts into words. In the context of psychoanalytic transference, such an 'act' can be seen as the re-actualization of a previous situation that is now repressed. Nevertheless, 'acting *upon*' and 'acting *out*' should not be confused. To characterize what happens when one 'acts upon',[9] one might consider that there is a lack of symbolization leading to impulsive action. It takes place against a background of radical despair and is ultimately addressed to no one in particular. 'Acting out', however, is a mode of behavior held by one subject and ultimately given to another to decipher. In acting out, one means to avoid overly violent despair; acting out might thus be seen as

> a staging of both the rejection of what the distressing words of the other could be, and the unveiling of what the other does not hear [...]. Acting out serves to bring hearing and understanding back to one who has become deaf. It is a demand for symbolization, an unbridled transference.
>
> (Chemama, 1995, p. 5)

The distinction between the two expressions (acting *upon* and acting *out*) is thus vital in understanding and interpreting the situation in question here.

If we hypothesize that the event is a case of 'acting upon', we presuppose that Gaël's gesture towards Yann largely escapes an intersubjective interpretation of the situation. It is a 'short circuit' in the psychological functioning and leads to the very negation of a subject who is capable of exchange and introspection, at least in the short term. In this perspective, how can we expect the subject to make sense of an act that escapes all symbolization? However, if we adopt the 'acting out' hypothesis, attentively listening to what was not able to be said or heard can enable the subject and the protagonists involved to move beyond the act itself and to once again become part of the usual order of discourse and of mutual exchange. In other words, I consider that viewing the situation in terms of 'acting upon' conceals possible signifying associations that would allow a plural reading of the situation. A more careful deciphering of the notion of 'acting out', however, opens up the possibility of identifying a 'shared latent meaning' that goes beyond the apparent meaninglessness of Gaël's behavior.

What, then, is the nature of what Gaël is 'staging' here that could not be said or heard in the end?

Paradox and conflicting loyalties

At this point, let us take a careful look at the additional information available to us with the help of a second temperature curve. This will illustrate the sequence of events that precede the situation in which Gaël physically assaults Yann.

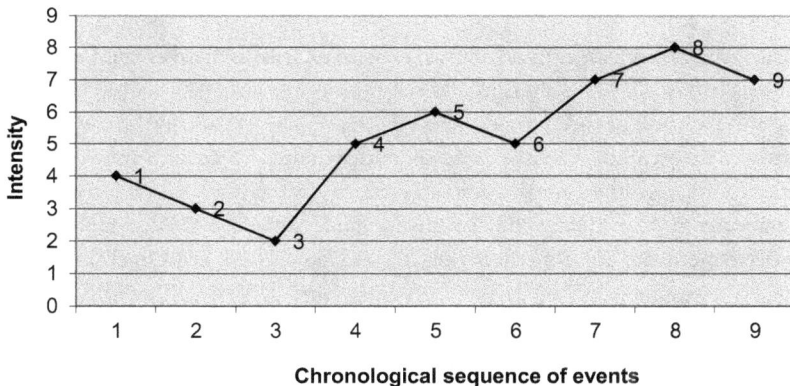

Temperature curve of the events preceding the violent assault

Legend

1 Welcome meeting and public questioning of Gaël by Yann.
2 Position of the educational team: *'Gaël is an example for the group'*.
3 Gaël's response to the team's offer of help: *'It's easy today. It's math'*.
4 Math lesson: Gaël cannot answer the teacher's questions.
5 The other students mock Gaël: *'He's a loser'*.
6 The teacher tries to restore order.
7 More gibes: .
8 Gaël cries.
9 The teacher attempts to comfort Gaël.

The curve here exhibits a sawtooth pattern which nevertheless follows an overall progression of increasing intensity. The first three points of the curve refer to what occurs during the initial meeting. Indeed, we know that that very morning, Yann publicly challenged Gaël by calling him a jerk during the session organized by the educational team: *'You know, that jerk here is gonna show off to us again because he's off to do math with the other jerks in the school'* (Point 1). We also know that the members of the team clearly took Gaël's side by indicating how much they thought he was an example for all the members of the bridging class: *'You can't say that. We're in this bridging class to get back on track. That's what Gaël is doing. He's an example for everyone. You can do it too'* (Point 2). Nevertheless, during this same meeting, the members of the educational team offered to help Gaël with his math homework when planning the day's activities. Gaël declined the offer, saying *'It's easy today. It's math'* (Point 3). The intensity, which was relatively high at the beginning due to the comments made by Yann, decreased as the educational team regulated the situation. It was as if Gaël had accepted the role that the adults had assigned to him: 'You are the one who succeeds.' His reference to an *'easy'* day seems to sum up Gaël's desire to conform to the image of himself that is suggested to him.

But in the math lesson that follows, Gaël is unable to answer the teacher's questions (point 4). He is then mocked by the other students (point 5). Even though these students are reprimanded by the teacher, who minimizes Gaël's difficulties by recalling the low level of performance of certain members of the class (point 6), they mark their 'difference' by saying: *'He's a loser, we do it on purpose, we're not jerks! Only jerks work hard'* (point 7). Gaël's anxiety and disappointment are then at their height, and he cannot hold back his tears (point 8). The teacher then tries to reassure him by saying that she understands that he is having difficulties in math (point 9). However, nothing is said about the relationship difficulties that Gaël is obviously facing.

But is Gaël really experiencing cognitive difficulties in math? It is impossible to answer this question clearly here, but we can assume that the relational difficulties he encounters do not make his task any easier and that they may 'occupy his mind' to the point of significantly limiting his cognitive performance. In my opinion, Gaël is caught up in a paradox whose terms can be summarized as follows:

- If I succeed, I meet the expectations of the educational team (success is rewarding here) but I stand out and become a 'jerk', both in the eyes of certain members of the bridging class and in the eyes of the members of the class I wish to join (success is stigmatizing here).

- If I don't succeed, I am close to my friends in the bridging class (not succeeding means having a position and not being stigmatized) but I don't
meet the expectations that caring adults have placed on me and I am also
considered a 'loser' by the members of the 'ordinary' class (not succeeding is therefore stigmatizing).

In short, whichever position Gaël occupies, he is inevitably put in a difficult
situation.

Furthermore, it can be assumed that Gaël is struggling with a conflict
of loyalties which will contribute to increasing his difficulties even further.
Indeed, like any group, the bridging class implies a number of injunctions
internalized by its members and which contribute to the homeostasis of the
system. Now, apart from the fact that we notice a split between the injunctions of the educational team[10] and the injunctions suggested by Yann[11] (who
we can also assume occupies an important place in the bridging class), we
immediately perceive here the classic opposition between 'in group' and 'out
group' described by psychosociologists concerning the normative function
which affects membership and non-membership groups.[12]

Indeed, when members of a group are confronted with another group,
they will tend to increase the differences between the groups and minimize
the differences within their own group. Within his group, a subject usually
uses the group's mark to assert his specificity, thus making his group a
place of differentiation (Gaël in the bridging class when he is perceived as
'the successful one'). However, when confronted with another group, that
same subject will tend to minimize these differences and be faithful to the
norms of his own group (Gaël in the math class). So, which norms should
Gaël follow in the end? What identity risks does he expose himself to when
he tries to 'distinguish' himself by joining a class composed of students
who are supposedly more 'successful'? In short, to which 'world' does he
belong?[13]

We have seen that, within his membership group (the bridging class), succeeding means both responding to the request of the educational team and
showing that he is different by distancing himself from his peers. Within the
bridging class, however, 'to succeed is to betray' and ultimately to feel guilty
about it. We have also seen how the terms of the paradox mentioned earlier
testify to the complexity of his situation in the non-membership group: Gaël's
math class.

However, we have so far attempted to decode Gaël's situation on a relatively individual level. Let us now move on to a more collective level of understanding of the situation observed by reading the facts more systemically.

The intersection of the implicit and explicit representations of the different protagonists

Let us agree, on the basis of the work carried out by systemicists, that this situation can be read through the study of the relational and interactional processes that take place. From this perspective, it is not so much the individuals that are important here as the relationships that are established between these same individuals. We will therefore postulate that the sequence of facts gives rise to phenomena of *assemblage*[14] and resonance[15] that can favor an understanding that goes beyond a level of linear causality and views Gaël's act as a message and a solution within and for the observed system. We will base ourselves here on the work of Mony Elkaïm (1989) who distinguishes, in interaction situations observed in family therapy, the notions of 'official program'[16] and 'world map'.[17] The 'official program' refers to the explicit demand of each member of the system, whereas the 'world map' refers to a system of representation created from previous experiences and which sometimes clashes with the explicitly stated official program. Let us examine the interplay between the official programs (OP) and the world maps (WM) of the main people or groups of people involved in the situation:

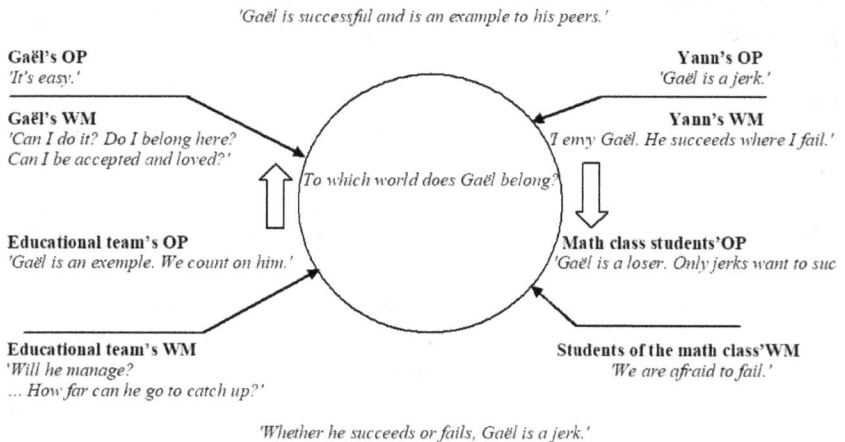

'Gaël is successful and is an example to his peers.'

Gaël's OP
'It's easy.'

Gaël's WM
'Can I do it? Do I belong here? Can I be accepted and loved?'

Yann's OP
'Gaël is a jerk.'

Yann's WM
'I envy Gaël. He succeeds where I fail.'

To which world does Gaël belong?

Educational team's OP
'Gaël is an exemple. We count on him.'

Math class students'OP
'Gaël is a loser. Only jerks want to suc

Educational team's WM
'Will he manage? ... How far can he go to catch up?'

Students of the math class'WM
'We are afraid to fail.'

'Whether he succeeds or fails, Gaël is a jerk.'

We can see here that the intertwining of the official programs and world maps of the various protagonists involved in the situation determine various assemblages and resonances, thus leading to a particularly complex situation. Let us cross-reference these different elements and analyze their effects:

	Gaël's OP	*Gaël's WM*
Yann's OP	Strengthening of both postures in the 'high' position	Strengthening of Yann's OP in the 'high' position and strengthening of Gaël's WM in the 'low' position
Yann's WM	Strengthening of Gaël's OP in the 'high' position and strengthening of Yann's WM in the 'low' position	Strengthening of both representations in the 'low' position

Concerning the two official programs, Gaël is all the more justified in ensuring his 'easy-going' posture as he is 'provoked' by Yann. At the same time, echoing this position, Yann can only reinforce his own posture: the escalation is symmetrical. For both protagonists adopting another position would mean not only surrendering to their opponent's explicit arguments but, above all, finding themselves confronted with the hardly acceptable representation of their world map. Thus, for Gaël, 'letting his guard down' implies confronting doubt and a particularly distressing image of himself that has probably been built up through a family history that we know was traumatic for him. For Yann, there is no information here that allows us to understand why Gaël's success is so unbearable for him. Nevertheless, it is reasonable to assume that Gaël's position brings about a resonance effect in him that is difficult to bear, as it undoubtedly arouses more or less conscious feelings of envy and jealousy. Furthermore, we can assume that each of the protagonists, even beyond the explicit discourse of his 'opponent', intuitively senses what preoccupations this discourse implies, thus reinforcing each one's explicit posture.

	Gaël's OP	*Gaël's WM*
Educational team's OP	Strengthening of both postures in the 'high' position	Strengthening of the educational team's OP in the 'high' position and strengthening of Gaël's WM in the 'low' position
Educational team's WM	Strengthening of Gaël's OP in the 'high' position and strengthening of the educational team's WM in the 'low' position	Strengthening of both representations in the 'low' position

In terms of Gaël's and the educational team's official programs, each is bound by the other's supposed expectations. In fact, by succeeding, Gaël responds to the explicit request of the educational team, plays the role of 'model' for the group and finds himself accepted and valued by adults. The stakes are all the higher for Gaël when we know that some adults, including his parents, have probably not always played this role in his life. The educational team, on the other hand, finds in Gaël's success a legitimization of their pedagogical activity, which one can imagine may sometimes prove thankless in terms of results, given the difficulties of the students they are usually faced with. Nevertheless, for each of the parties involved, holding this high position is not without its worries. Indeed, although success is clearly desired by everyone, it is never guaranteed. Doubt is therefore ever present and generates an apprehension whose effects can easily be guessed. For Gaël, the prospect of not succeeding in meeting the expectations of the adults who trust him triggers the repetition of a scenario that is difficult to bear: *'If I don't succeed, it's because, as I have always been shown, I am not worthy of attention'*. For the educational team Gaël's failure would mean questioning their pedagogical activity in an institutional context where the status of the bridging class is fragile.

	Gaël's OP	*Gaël's WM*
Math class students' OP	Collapse of Gaël's OP and strengthening of the math class' OP	Strengthening of the math class' OP in the 'high' position and strengthening Gaël's WM in the 'low' position
Math class students' WM	Collapse of Gaël's OP and denial of the math class students' WM	Strengthening of the two representations

Here, Gaël's official program is doubly challenged by the official program of the students in the math class. Gaël is confronted with a particularly painful situation of failure: not only do the students who attend the class he would like to join tell him that he is a 'loser' (thus generating the anxiety linked to the representations that form the basis of his world map), but they also say that 'succeeding is something only jerks want', thus echoing the position of Yann, Gaël's 'opponent' in the bridging class. One can well imagine Gaël's state of confusion. Furthermore, the teacher, trying to reassure Gaël, only deals with Gaël's supposed cognitive difficulties and cannot grasp all the implications of the situation for him. For the students in the math class, the distress that Gaël shows will allow them to rid themselves of their fear of failure in math in a denial of their difficulties in which Gaël acts as a scapegoat. Gaël here is the object of a concentration of negative vectors whose origin is rooted in mechanisms of projective identification:[18] *'We're not bad at math, he is, insofar as he represents what we are not, that is, a "jerk". Moreover, if we are bad at it, unlike Gaël, it is because we have chosen to be'*.

	Yann's OP	*Yann's WM*
Educational team's OP	Strengthening of both postures in the 'high' position	Strengthening of the educational team's OP in the 'high' position and strengthening of Yann's WM in the 'low' position
Educational team's WM	Strengthening of Yann's OP in the 'high' position and strengthening of the educational team's WM in the 'low' position	Strengthening of both representations in the 'low' position

It is easy to understand here the cross-reinforcing effects of Yann's and the educational team's implicit and explicit positions. For Yann, stating that Gaël is a 'jerk' invalidates the educational team's pedagogical effort, which is unacceptable to them insofar as Yann's position reactivates the anxieties generated by their world map: 'Failure is always possible with our students'. Correlatively, the educational team's official program painfully reactivates Yann's world map: he clearly finds it hard to accept Gaël's possible success.

	Math class students' OP	*Math class students' WM*
Educational team's OP	Collapse of the educational team's OP and strengthening of the math class students' OP in the 'high' position	Collapse of the educational team's OP and denial of the math class students' WM
Educational team's WM	Strengthening of the math class students' OP in the 'high' position and strengthening of the educational team's WM in the 'low' position	Denial of the math class students' WM and reinforcement of the educational team's WM in the 'low' position

Clearly, the educational team's official program[19] is being put to the test here. Gaël's obvious difficulties, and above all the explicit reaction of the other students, ruin, at least momentarily, a generous pedagogical intention which aims to make room for the students considered to have the greatest difficulties. In this configuration, the only one to encounter difficulties is Gaël, a student considered by the others to be intrinsically a 'loser' or a 'jerk', whatever his level of performance. Indeed, according to the math class students' official program, if one of them performs less well than Gaël, it is ultimately because he 'does it on purpose', the explicit norm being 'if you want to fit in, don't succeed'. Of course, it is likely that this explicit norm is counterbalanced by a system of implicit norms that allow these students to continue to work and succeed while explicitly showing contempt for these implicit norms.

Nevertheless, Gaël is unaware of these 'hidden' norms which allow each of them to situate themselves in relation to others by taking into account the demands of the reality principle. Finally, we have seen how this situation puts the educational team in a very difficult position, since Gaël's underachievement casts doubt on the relevance of receiving students from the bridging class.

Message and 'solution'

In conclusion, and on the basis of the elements we now have, it is possible to formulate a few working hypotheses in response to the three questions identified in the first part of our paper. We can then attempt to summarize the individual, collective and institutional implications of this situation.

The first question we asked dealt with Gaël's attitude regarding his refusal to respond to the two adults who questioned him after the math class: why, even though he appreciates the educational counselor, could Gaël not open up about his problem to this adult or to his teacher, both of whom seem to be attentive and understanding potential listeners?

We have seen that Gaël has abruptly experienced the effects of a trans-contextual communicative paradox[20] based on a conflict of loyalties and taking the form of a double bind that can be summarized as follows: 'Succeed' vs. 'To be accepted, you must not succeed'. To Gaël's confusion was added the experience of not having been understood and protected by one of the members of the educational team. In fact, despite the benevolence shown by the math teacher who tried to console him, Gaël was all the less aware of the paradox he was caught up in since he was involved in it. Therefore, in addition to the feeling of humiliation experienced by Gaël, there are the effects of the reactivation of the representations associated with his world map, which can be assumed to lead to a scenario of the type: 'So, I cannot trust any adult'.

The second question raised the issue of the 'saturation' point that Gaël has suddenly reached with regard to Yann: Gaël is obviously used to Yann's provocations, so why can he not tolerate it this time?

This question is all the more interesting when we know that in most social groups, and perhaps even more so among adolescents, the systematic use of insults[21] contributes to the definition of the places and roles of each person in relation to the others, in a casual exchange based on rules that feed a system of power and hierarchy in peer groups. Nevertheless, it is up to the 'insulter' to know how far he can go. It can be assumed that the system of communication that had been established between Yann and Gaël up to that point was based on an implicit negotiation that allowed both of them to deal with their respective official programs and world maps. However, in this particular situation, the insult uttered by Yann takes on a completely different dimension, since the implicit 'rules of the game' are here distorted by the situation that Gaël has just experienced in the math class. We can therefore assume the following: by violently attacking Yann, the act Gaël is committing cannot be reduced to a form of 'acting *upon*' that expresses the cognitive and affective overflow he is experiencing. In my opinion, Gaël's act here has the value of a message and a solution within and for the system under observation.

The third question, relating to the 'targeting' of Gaël's violence, will enable us to shed light on this precise point: why does Gaël, involved in an apparently very 'targeted' quarrel with Yann, lose control to the point of being violent with adults who he knows like him and whom he likes in return?

We have seen that Gaël's violent attitude can be linked to the hypothesis of an acting out, that is, the formulation of a message to 'others who have become deaf'. Indeed, although his act is primarily aimed at Yann, Gaël necessarily knows that members of the educational team will inevitably come along to separate them. However, when the adults arrive, their intervention does not succeed in putting an end to Gaël's violence, which is indiscriminate and involves blows and insults. Let us therefore assume that Gaël's reaction here is aimed not only at the instigator of the insult, but also at all the people involved in the system.

Although the information available to us does not allow us to grasp all the nuances of the message addressed to those involved, decoding it does suggest two intertwined levels. We have pointed out the heuristic limits of an interpretation wherein Gaël's attitude can be likened to the expression of a feeling of being 'fed up' signifying an 'overflow' that has become psychologically unmanageable for him. This is the explicit message addressed to others. But, on another level, Gaël's attitude expresses his revolt against the double constraint with which he is confronted and which goes beyond his personal involvement. The message here is all the more implicit because its roots remain invisible.

Therefore, what becomes visible constitutes both a message and a solution within and for the system observed: the violence and gravity of the act signifies what can no longer be tolerated, but which, by its very expression, protects the implicit rules of the system that cannot be revealed. In this way, Gaël's attitude can be read as a message that allows the system to 'change without changing', since the implicit foundations of the interactional situation are not questioned.

In the end, there are individual, collective and institutional issues at stake. This presupposes the setting up of a regulatory body, the form of which remains to be defined with the people concerned, and which could enable them to meta-communicate[22] about the links between the explicit and implicit rules that govern the system.

At the individual level, it is important for Gaël not to remain stuck in a reading of his act that would be reduced to a supposed shunting[23] of his affective–cognitive functioning. At the collective level, the balance between implicit and explicit rules, now undermined by Gaël's acting out, should be clarified in order to avoid the crystallization of behaviors and attitudes that are clearly problematic for everyone. Finally, at the institutional level, it seems essential that work questioning these aspects be carried out insofar as an institution always determines, in a performative perspective, [24] a set of processes for structuring the relationships between its members.

The importance of this issue can be appreciated when we know that the pedagogical project of this work group is inspired by institutional pedagogy. I have no doubt that the educational team, strengthened by this theoretical foundation, can finally take up, in a way that is truly relevant, the challenges it faces for the benefit of all the people involved in the situation.

Conclusion

I have favored an analysis of the situation presented using a few conceptual keys borrowed from the field of the clinic as addressed in this volume, a field of research and intervention that I have been exploring for some years (Niewiadomski, 2012). These notions, which are basic enough, should not, however, be considered hegemonic. There is no doubt that other theoretical notions could have been mobilized to enrich the analysis proposed here.

Recall that our objective was to show how a relatively simple narrative description method can be used to develop an analysis that can quickly bring out added value in terms of understanding certain educational situations. This demonstration did not allow for the collective use of this approach, but it should be emphasized that such a method benefits from being enriched by exchanges in small working groups made up of professionals from multidisciplinary educational teams. Indeed, far from reinforcing disciplinary compartmentalization, such arrangements – provided they can be managed with sensitivity – could deconstruct the educational presuppositions of each party to the benefit of an opening up of unexplored possibilities. This approach would further enrich the partnership strategies that are indispensable to educational work worthy of this name.

Notes

1 According to Lacan, *'sexuation*, as distinct from biological sexuality, designates the way in which the subject is inscribed in the difference between the sexes, specifically in terms of the unconscious and castration, that is, as "inhabiting language" (Lacan, 1998, p. 80). [...] Lacan's choice of the term sexuation, and not sexuality, indicates that being recognized as a man or woman is a matter of the signifier'. www.encyclopedia.com/psychology/dictionaries-thesauruses-pictures-and-press-releases/sexuation-formulas

2 In English-language Lacanian literature, the term *jouissance* is often left untranslated in order to highlight its specialized usage (see, for example, Evans, 1996).

3 This text is taken from a lecture given during the event 'What does it mean to be a girl or a boy today?' organized in Verneuil-sur-Avre on 3 October 2020 as part of the preparatory workshops for the *Institut de l'Enfant*'s one-day symposium on the theme of the sexuation of children. The work that came out of this event was also published in *Letterina*, the journal of the *Association de la Cause Freudienne de Normandie*.

4 It is then that I learned that emo is a style of music and punk culture, somewhere between soft gothic and a manga universe.

5 I am particularly indebted to our colleague and friend Rémi Casanova, lecturer at the University of Lille, for drawing our attention to this approach.

6 French *classes relais* – or 'bridging classes' – were first created in 1998. They are part of a partnership between the French National Education system and the judicial protection of youth. Bridging classes aim to fight against school dropout and the social exclusion of young people who, though required to attend school, usually reject learning and, more generally, the institution of education itself. The idea is to reintegrate young people into the mainstream school system after a period of attendance in the bridging class, which is limited to one school year.

7 There is certainly a risk here of suggesting a convenient, overly facile interpretation. And yet it is hardly surprising that the aggression takes the form of an attempt at strangulation rather than a punch, for example. The throat – the anatomical and physiological site of speech *par excellence* – is clearly a significant location for Gaël.

8 Etymologically, the 'subject', from the Latin *subjectus* ('put under'), is one who is 'subjected', submitted to a necessity, to a law – in short, one who is dependent on a superior authority. Within this perspective, psychoanalysis evokes the notion of the 'barred subject', that is, a subject caught in the clutches of language and who cannot be reduced to the 'biological individual' or to the 'rational subject' due to the very existence of an unconscious from which it is separated. The psychoanalytic 'subject', then, differs significantly from the Cartesian subject in that the subject is caught both in language and in his relationship to others in a structural manner.

9 'The *passage à l'acte* (here, acting *upon*) is irrecoverable and irreversible. It is always a crossing of the stage, into reality; it is an impulsive act, the most typical of which is defenestration. It is a blind game and a negation of the self; it constitutes the only time-bound possibility for a subject to find his place, symbolically, in a dehumanizing reality [...]. It is also the price always paid too dearly to unconsciously claim a position of mastery, in the most radical alienation, since the subject is even ready to pay for it with his own life' (Chemama, 1995, p. 7).

10 *'We're in this bridging class to get back on track.'* So you have to work to be able to 'get back on track' and ultimately leave the bridging class.

11 Working hard ultimately means being like the 'others', that is, being a 'jerk'.

12 The process whereby the individual adheres to the norms, models and values of the group to which he refers. In order to be accepted by this group, the subject will try to regulate his behavior, his norms and his values on what he perceives to be the values and norms of the group.

13 Let us admit here the possible analogy of this situation with the phenomenon of 'class neurosis' described by Vincent de Gaulejac. The author shows how changes in social position can lead to major identity conflicts. These are rooted in the reinforcement effects between intrapsychic conflicts and tensions generated by the internalization of new habits that contradict those previously acquired (Gaulejac, 1997).

14 An *assemblage* can be defined as a set created by different elements interacting in a particular situation. The set defines a system, one of whose intrinsic properties is that it cannot be reduced to the sum of its parts.

15 Phenomena of resonance refer to situations of coupling between verbal or non-verbal communicative modalities that are generally unconscious (for example, modes of thinking, speaking, feeling, or the phenomena of punctuating communication with gestures, which can give rise to the repetition of events that define and regulate the nature of the exchanges).

16 The 'official program' can be defined as a discourse explicitly held by a subject in a given situation, and in which the subject believes deeply and authentically.

17 The notion of 'world map', which has only a partial relationship with the territory to which it refers, is 'quite similar to that of representation in psychoanalysis. It corresponds to the system of location that the person has within himself to orient himself in time and space, and is an asymptotic simulation of the territory from which it is fundamentally different' (Miermont, 1987, p. 89).

18 This is a defense mechanism consisting in attributing to another person certain traits of oneself that cannot be accepted, which allows the subject to ignore them in himself.

19 For the sake of brevity, no distinction will be made here within the educational team. Nevertheless, we can assume that there are differences between the representations of the members of the educational team who work in the bridging class and those of the math teacher.

20 The communication unfolds in at least two different contexts (the bridging class and the math class) and involves different people. In addition to this register, there are several latent contexts which are partly reflected in the world maps of the various protagonists.

21 The term 'insult' refers here to 'all kinds of virulent remarks, derogatory jokes and mockery exchanged in a humorous tone between people who know each other or at least show a certain complicity. The principle of the insult is essentially based on the symbolic distance that allows the interlocutors to mock or even insult each other without negative consequences' (Lepoutre, 1997, p. 173).

22 That is, to 'communicate about communication'.

23 The term *shunting* is to be understood here as a lack of symbolization leading to 'acting upon'.

24 Acts, behaviors or statements can have a performative impact when they establish a modification of reality for one or more individuals. For example, in an institution, declaring that 'the meeting is open' refers to a reality that the statement will itself bring about.

References

Casanova, R., Cellier, H., Robbes, B., & Bagur, J-P. (Eds.) (2005). *Situations violentes à l'école: comprendre et agir*. Paris: Hachette.

Chemama, R. (Ed.) (1995). *Dictionary of psychoanalysis*. Paris: Larousse.

Gaulejac, V. de (1997). *La névrose de classe*. Paris: Hommes et groupes.

Elkaïm, M. (1989). *If you love me don't love me. Approche systémique et psychothérapie*. Paris: Seuil.

Lepoutre, D. (1997). *Cœur de banlieue. Codes, rites and languages*. Paris: Odile Jacob.

Miermont, J. (Ed.) (1987). *Dictionary of family therapies. Théories et pratiques*. Paris: Payot.

Niewiadomski, C. (2012). *Biographical research and clinical narrative*. Toulouse: Érès.

Summary

Based on a critical reading of evidence-based practice in social work, this book aims to denounce the growing risk of commercialization, technocratization and standardization of relational practices in the various fields of care, education and social intervention.

It brings together specialists in the main components of research and clinical practice in human sciences (psychoanalysis, educational clinic, narrative clinic, institutional clinic, clinical sociology, clinical psychology, ethno-psychiatry, philosophy) to discuss their effects and issues in the field of social work. These contributions will make it possible to capture the theoretical, practical, ethical and methodological coordinates of a clinical-based practice in social work as an alternative to technocratic, neo-positivist and liberal conceptions of helping relationships.

Presentation of the authors

Michel Chauvière is Director of Research Emeritus at the CNRS, CERSA, at the University of Paris 2. His main work focuses on the history and ongoing transformations of social action and social work (what he calls the 'social *réalisé'*) with equal attention to social policies, institutions, associations and other supports necessary for action, key players (especially those doing social fieldwork) and rights holders or users, as well as the exchanges that take place between them. He is the author of many books and contributions on these various subjects.

Mireille Cifali is a Historian and Psychoanalyst. She was a Professor in the Department of Education Sciences at the University of Geneva until 2010. The purpose underpinning her teaching and research is to enable those who work in relationship professions, or who are preparing for them, to understand the relational and emotional dimensions of their actions and words so as to construct a daily ethic. She has published several books and coordinates collective works for a clinical approach to professional practices.

Pascal Fugier is a Lecturer in Education Sciences at the ESPE of the Académie de Versailles, within the University of Cergy-Pontoise (UCP). He is a member of the EMA laboratory and is in charge of the EPDIS Master's course (Supervision, Piloting and Development in Social Intervention). His research focuses on the professions and different publics in the social, health and educational sectors. Favoring a clinical psycho-sociological approach in participatory research, he focuses more specifically on the effects that the institutional and organizational changes implemented in these relationship professions have on professional practices and cultures as well as on professionals' liberty of action and that of the people they accompany.

Vincent de Gaulejac is a Sociologist and Professor Emeritus of Sociology at the Department of Social Sciences of the University Paris Diderot. He is the author of some twenty books and is in charge of the clinical sociology collection at ÉRÈS. He was Director of the Laboratory for Social Change from 1981 to 2014. A founding member of the international network of clinical sociology, he is one of the main initiators of this scientific orientation, which focuses on the relationship between the human being and the social being and on the existential dimension of social relations. He has developed involvement and research groups in more than fifteen countries in Europe, North America and South America. His research has led him to explore class neurosis, the sources of shame, the struggle for positions, the cost of excellence, a society driven to sickness by excessive management and the causes of malaise at the workplace.

Florence Giust-Desprairies is a Clinical Psycho-Sociologist and Professor Emeritus of Clinical Social Psychology at the University Paris Diderot. She is a founding member of the International Center for Research, Training and Intervention in Psychosociology (CIRFIP). Her work focuses on the evolutions and transformations of social imaginations and their consequences on modes of subjectivation and socialization as they can be observed in clinical intervention and research practice. Contemporary malaise is captured through subjective and intersubjective turbulence related to the social and cultural issues of the development of an interiority.

Philippe Lyet holds a doctorate in Sociology and a French *habilitation à diriger des recherches* (accreditation to supervise research) in education sciences. For the past twenty-five years, he has been conducting research on collaborations between social action players and on the dynamics of 'hybridization' at work in social policies.

Marie Rose Moro is Professor of Child and Adolescent Psychiatry at the University of Paris. She is department head at the Maison de Solenn, AP-HP (www.maisondesolenn.fr). She heads the INSERM Team 'Methods and Cultures' U 1178. Her research focuses on the clinic for babies, children, adolescents and migrant families. She is the editor of the transcultural journal *L'autre*, the main reference in the transcultural field in France. She is the current leader of the transcultural clinic in France and Europe. She is President of the International Association of Ethno-psychoanalysis (AIEP, www.clinique-transculturelle.org). She is a consultant for Médecins Sans Frontières (Doctors Without Borders) for mental health missions for children and adolescents around the world. Email: marie-rose.moro@aphp.fr

Christophe Niewiadomski is a Professor of Education at the University of Lille. A member of the CIREL laboratory (Lille Inter-university Center for Research in Education), he is also a founding member of RISC (International Network of Clinical Sociology) and CIRBE (International College of Biographical Research in Education). His work aims to lay the foundations for a narrative and educational clinic in the human and social sciences by examining the specificity of biographical research in the fields of adult education, socio-educational environment and health.

Jean-Bernard Paturet is Professor Emeritus at the University Paul-Valéry Montpellier III. He was director of the psychoanalysis department and a member of the CRISES research team. His latest works are: *Faut-il brûler les institutions*, EHEPS Press and *La passion aporétique de Sigmund Freud suivi de A propos d'un lapsus de Freud sur le Moïse de Michel-Ange*, Lambert et Lucas Publishers.

Sébastien Ponnou is a Psychoanalyst, Doctor in Psychoanalysis (Paris 8) and Lecturer in Education Sciences at the University of Rouen Normandie (IUT d'Evreux – Social Careers Department, Interdisciplinary Center for Education and Training Research in Normandy – CIRNEF, EA 7454). His work focuses on clinical and psychoanalytic studies, mental health issues, clinical practices and the training of social workers (http://cirnef.normandie-univ. fr/?page_id=1440).

Rahmet Radjack is a Psychiatrist and hospital practitioner in charge of consultations at the Cochin Hospital home for teenagers, as well as Head of Liaison Child Psychiatry at the Port Royal maternity ward (Perinatal Team, *Bébémat*, Paris). She was trained in the transcultural approach with Marie Rose Moro and for several years has been leading a weekly transcultural consultation at the home for teenagers. As a researcher, she coordinated an action research project (CESP-INSERM, Centre Babel) on the adaptation of the transcultural system to the support of unaccompanied minors. She is completing her doctoral thesis on this subject at the University Paris 13. She is a trainer in a transcultural clinic at the Centre Babel (resource center for transcultural clinics, www.transculturel.eu). She coordinates a research group (INSERM-Paris 5) on the theme of involvement among young people.

Bertrand Ravon is Professor of Sociology at the University Lumière Lyon 2 (bertrand.ravon@univ-lyon2.fr), where he directs the ANACIS Master's course – Analysis and Design of Social Intervention (http://assp.univ-lyon2. fr). His research within the 'Knowledge Policies' team at the Max Weber Center focuses on the reconfiguration of support for people in vulnerable situations (www.centre-max-weber.fr/Bertrand-Ravon).

Guy de Villers is a doctor of philosophy and Professor Emeritus at Louvain Catholic University (UCL) in Louvain-La-Neuve (Belgium). He is a member of the IACCHOS Institute of Analysis of Change in Contemporary and Historical Societies (UCL). He is also a member of the Association Internationale des Histoires de Vie en formation et de Recherche Biographique en Education (ASIHVIF-RBE) (France). A psychoanalyst, he is a member of the École de la Cause Freudienne (ECF) in Paris, the Association de la Cause Freudienne in Belgium (ACF-Belgium) and the International Association of Psychoanalysis (IAP). His publications and works concern the philosophy of education and the family. As a teacher, practitioner and researcher in life history, he has developed a reflection on the anthropological, epistemological and ethical foundations of the autobiographical approach. His latest work focuses on the tension between the dimension of identity and that of subjectivity.

Stephen A. Webb is Professor of Social Work at Glasgow Caledonian University, Scotland. In 2018 he was awarded the prestigious Fellowship of the Academy of Social Sciences (FAcSS). He is author of *Social Work in a Risk Society* (2006, Palgrave), and co-author/editor of *The New Politics of Social Work*, (2013); *Evidence-based Social Work: A Critical Stance* (2009); *Ethics and Value Perspectives in Social Work* (2010); *Social Work Theories and Methods* (2012);

The SAGE Handbook of Social Work (2012) and the major international reference work *International Social Work* (2010, 4 Volumes). He has recently edited the *Routledge Handbook of Critical Social Work*, a major international reference work.

Presentation of the translators

Chad Langford is an independent translator based in the north of France. He is head of Foreign Language Teaching for Continuing Studies at the Center for Languages (CLIL DELANG) at the University of Lille. He is the co-author of *Advanced English Grammar: a linguistic approach* published by Bloomsbury and now in its second edition.

Judith Van Heerswynghels taught translation at the University of Lille, where she was in charge of the Masters in subtitling. Her translation of a collection of short stories and poetry by Rudyard Kipling appears in La Pléiade collection (Gallimard).

Langford and Van Heerswynghels are frequent collaborators.

Acknowledgments

We would like to express our sincere thanks to Fabien Clouse for his careful review of the manuscript.

Funding partners

UNIVERSITÉ DE ROUEN NORMANDIE

Université de Lille

IRIHS Institut de Recherche Inter-disciplinaire Homme Société

CIRNEF Normandie Université · EA 7454

CIREL

Groupement d'intérêt scientifique HYBRIDA-IS

les deux séquoias

EoViMcd fondation

FONDATION DE L'AVENIR Accélérateur de progrès médical

Index

Note: Page numbers followed by "n" denote endnotes.

For Product Safety Concerns and Information please contact our EU
representative GPSR@taylorandfrancis.com
Taylor & Francis Verlag GmbH, Kaufingerstraße 24, 80331 München, Germany

9 781032 283463